Lord Mahavira

Series Editor

Dr. M.H. Syed

Editors

R.K. Singh **P.K. Choudhry**

Himalaya Books Pvt. Ltd.

Kundanlal Chandak Industrial Estate, Ghat Road, Nagpur - 440 018.
Mobile: 09325409992, 09325908881
E-mail: himpub@bharatmail.co.in

Edition : 2026

Publishedby : **H.B.P.L.**
KundanlalChandakIndustrialEstate,GhatRoad,
Nagpur-440018.**Mobile:**09325409992,09325908881
E-mail:himpub@bharatmail.co.in

SoleDistributers : **HIMALAYAPUBLISHINGHOUSEPVT.LTD.**

BranchOffices :

NewDelhi : "PoojaApartments",4-B,MurariLalStreet,AnsariRoad,
DaryaGanj,NewDelhi-110002.
Phone:011-23270392,23278631;Fax:011-23256286

Nagpur : KundanlalChandakIndustrialEstate,GhatRoad,
Nagpur-440018.Mobile:09325409992,09325908881

Bengaluru : PlotNo.91-33,2ndMainRoad,Seshadripuram,Behind
NatarajaTheatre,Bengaluru-560020.
Phone:080-41138821;Mobile:09379847017,09379847005

Hyderabad : No.3-4-184,Lingampally,BesidesRaghavendraSwamy
Matham, Kachiguda,Hyderabad-500027.
Phone:040-27560041,27550139

Chennai : No.34/44,MotilalStreet,T.Nagar,Chennai-600017.
Mobile:09380460419

Pune : "Laksha"Apartment,FirstFloor,No.527,Mehunpura,
Shaniwarpeth(NearPrabhatTheatre),Pune-411030.
Phone:020-24496323,24496333;Mobile:09370579333

Cuttack : PlotNo.5F-755/4,Sector-9,CDAMarketNagar,
Cuttack-753014,Odisha.Mobile:09338746007

Kolkata : 3,S.M.BoseRoad,NearGateNo.5,AgarparaRailwayStation,
North24Parganas, WestBengal-700109.
Mobile:09674536325

Printedat : InfinityImagingSystem,NewDelhi.OnbehalfofHPH.

Preface

Biography, is now a form of literature, very much in vogue. In fact, biography is a description or account of someone's life and the times, which is usually published in the form of a book. A biography is more than a mention of personal facts (life, education, work, relationships and death), it also portrays the subject's experience of events. Technically speaking, a work is biographical, if it covers, all of a person's life. Biography writing has a long history. A biography is real. Ancient Greeks developed the biographical tradition, which we have inherited, although until the 5th century AD, when the word 'biographia' first appeared, in Damascius' "Life of Isodorus," biographical pieces were called simply "lives". It is quite likely that the Greeks were drawing on a pre-existing eastern tradition. Certainly Herodotus' "Histories" contains more detailed biographical information on Persian kings and subjects. The earliest surviving pieces, which we would identify as biographical are Isocrates' "Life of Evagoras" and Xenophon's "Life of Agesilaos," both from the fifth century BC. "Parallel Lives" by Plutarch, a Greek writing under the Roman empire, is a series of short biographies of eminent men.

The Golden Age of English biography emerged in late eighteenth century, the century in which the terms "biography" and "autobiography" entered English lexicon. The classic works of the period were Samuel Johnson's "Critical Lives of the Poets" and James Boswell's "Massive Life of Johnson". Generally American biography followed English model. By World War I, cheap hardcover reprints had become popular. The decade of the 1920s witnessed a biographical 'boom'. Later, biographical writings developed a lot and today biographies are written and compiled in the finest form of the genre. In India too, biography, as a form of literature has been evolved, cultivated and polished over the years. Here is an effort to promote this tradition further.

This series of biographies of great men, great women and celebrities in all walks of life is an adventurous academic endeavour, in its own right. A team of researchers and compilers has worked for a good period of time to accomplish the project. For this purpose, hundreds of books by eminent authors and editors have been consulted and referred to. We have benefited from various works, liberally, in order to illustrate and enrich this effort of ours. Present book is devoted to the great personality of Lord Mahavira.

Mahavira is the name, most commonly used to refer to the great sage Vardhamana, who established, what are today considered to be the central tenets of Jainism. According to Jain tradition, he was the 24th and the last Tirthankara. His courage and bravery earned him the name Mahavira. Mahavira's preaching and efforts to spread Jain philosophy are considered the real catalyst to the spread of this ancient religion, throughout India and into the mainstream. Vardhaman's birthday is celebrated as Mahavir Jayanti, the most important religious holiday of Jains, around the world.

This is a compact and comprehensive account of the above mentioned great life, which is bound to attract the attention of scholars, researchers, students and the general readers alike. Let's hope this humble effort would receive a warm welcome and due applause.

— ***Editors***

Contents

1

Age of Mahavira

Sixth century BC, the age in which Mahavira was born, was a period of great intellectual stir practically all over the world. Greece, Egypt, Persia and China as well as India- all centres of important civilisations experienced ferment in the realm of thought. The advent of Socrates and his distinguished pupils and contemporaries in Greece, of Zoroaster in Persia, and of Lao Tse and Confucius in China marked a revolution in the thought of those countries in just the same way as the coming of Mahavira and the Buddha meant the advent of philosophical rationalism in our own country.

Conditions in India

In Indian society this age was in many ways a period of transition and uncertainty. The state of society which is revealed in the religious literature of the Jainas and the Buddhists is quite different from that which is depicted in the Epics of the later Vedic literature and is, of course, fundamentally different from that depicted in the Vedas. From the simple and on the whole republican social organisation of the Vedic times the country and been passing through a process of gradual stratification until by the time of the birth of Mahavira caste distinctions and priestly oligarchy had become a source of enormous social irritation and a means of popular exploitation. The simple religion of nature worship implied in the hymns of the Rigveda had similarly been developing into a curious combination of theoretical monotheism and practical worship of a multiplicity of gods and divine satellites with an admixture of elaborate rituals and superstition.

This development was disturbing to the equanimity of the thinking part of the population, and already there had grown up a school of mediators who discarded the rituals and pantheistic worship under priestly auspices and retired to forests for meditation and contemplation of the truth, thus giving rise to a form of philosophical pantheism. In economic life agriculture was still the main occupation of the people and the village (*gram*) the unit of administration and the centre of all activities, but the period was marked by a transition to cottage industrialism and a remarkable growth of trade and commerce. Politically, a new type of republican and tribal kingdom was arising, which was rapidly assuming a monarchical form of government and imperialistic designs in the sense of territorial conquests. The whole life of the community was in short undergoing fundamental transformation.

The geographical outlook of Indo-Aryans, limited for a long time to the *Gangetic* valley, had extended to the eastern and southern regions. The art of writing had got diffused among men and women, and because of the development of commercial contacts with foreign lands the mental horizon of the people had greatly broadened. These changes had their impact on the social, religious, economic and political conditions of the country, and this needs to be examined in some detail.

Philosophy and Religion

In the domain of religion and philosophy, 7th and 6th centuries BC were a period of great confusion and doubt. The period was marked by growing orthodoxy on one side and extensive revolt against it on the other. The Buddhist literature mentions as many as sixty-three different philosophical schools, all presumably non-Brahmin, existing at the time of the Buddha; Jaina literature, which is more analytical in its approach, mentions an even larger number of such heretical doctrines.

The religion of the early Aryans had been simple nature-worship. Its simplicity stands in striking contrast to the later elaboration of the religious side of life by the priests. The objects of worship were the great phenomena of nature, conceived as alive and usually represented in anthropomorphic shape like *dyo*: (the Heaven), *Prithvee* (the Earth), *Surya* (the Sun), *Usha* (the dawn), *Agnee* (the Fire) and *Som* (the well-known sacrificial drought). In the late tenth book of the *Rgveda*, beginning of philosophy made its appearance; the multiplicity of Gods was questioned and the unity of the universe asserted. As the centre of culture shifted from the west to east, new gods- originally perhaps of the aborigine-like Brahma, Vishnu and Shiva, came to be included in the Hindu pantheon, the original Vedic gods were thrust into the background, and as a result a change occurred in the spirit of religion and in the spirit of worship.

The borrowed gods belonged to a system which was nurtured under a different conception of godhead from that underlying the Aryans nature-gods; they had to be dreaded and appeased by the performance of sacrifices and not approached in confidence, but once propitiated they were supposed to help their worshippers against their enemies, open or hidden. Their gods were terrific, and so the propitiatory ritual became weird and mystic. Originally the post-priest of the Rgveda was content to invite the gods, in the fullness of his heart, to partake of his offerings; now the priest becomes more anxious to secure a monopoly of the God to himself and to his patrons and to avert him and his grace from his rival worshippers. So the technique of sacrifice became enormously elaborated and obscured, religion became formalised and completely divorced from ethics.

This development was a particular characteristic of the age which marked the composition of the Brahminas. The growth of ritualism led to the increase of the priestly class, and since the priestly class was the beneficiary of the performance of these rituals and sacrifices it was in its interest to develop ritualism still further. It became a vicious circle. The earlier sacrifices used to occupy one day, now they began to last for weeks, months and even years. The earlier sacrifices used to require as the most seven priests, *hotri, potri, naishtri, Anidhr, Prshastri, Advaryu and brhamn*;

now the sacrifices required seventeen. 1. *Hotri* with *maitravarunr, achhavak,* and *gravrutut* 2. *Udgatri with prstot, pratihartri, subrhanyi* 3. *Adhvryu* with *pratiprasthapu, naishtri and unaitri* 4. *Brahmin with brahminrhachhansin, agneedhr* and *potri.*

On its part, the priestly class directed all its energies to the further development of ceremonial side, which they worked out in endless detail and to which they attached the most fanciful and mystic significance. The elaboration of the technical part of the sacrifice and the growth of a special class of experts who make a monopoly often art became so marked that intellectualism of this kind began to be confused with morality, and virtue became a byword for fineness and fussiness over little things.

This state of things was very disconcerting to the serious-minded section of society, and many people took recourse to meditation and contemplation of the truth. They discarded the rituals and the pantheistic worship of the priests, and developed what is known as the way of knowledge (gyanmarg) distinguished from the way of ritualism (*karmmarg*) of the Brahmin. From out of their philosophical and metaphysical speculation there developed the six famous schools of Indian philosophy-the *Samkhya* school of a Kapila, the *Yoga* school of Patanjali, the *Nyaya* school of Kapila, the *Yoga* school of Patanjali, the *Nyaya* school of Gautama, the Vaisesika school of Kanada, the *purva-Mimamsa* of Jaimini, and the *Uttara*-Mimamsa or *Vedanta* of Vyasa. These *Upanisadic* philosophers concerned themselves with the problems of the origin of the world, the nature of godhood and the creative process in general; and in seeking to solve these problems they expounded in fact a new religion which aimed at the achievement of deliverance from mundane existence by the absorption of the individual soul (*atma*) in the world-soul (*Brahma*) by virtue of correct knowledge.

The underlying principles of this new religion upon which all philosophers were agreed were, first, that all reality in the ultimate issue must be reduced to one, called variously the holy power or the soul; and secondly, that a man may die repeated deaths in the next world, the doctrine, that is to say, of transmigration of soul, first mentioned in an outline form in the Chhandogya *Upanisad* and then involved in the form of the gospel of *karma* or action which determines on a man's death the nature of his next birth in the *Vrihdaranryak Upanishad.* But these philosophers disagreed on many other points. Pantheistic ritualism was producing its parallel in the world of thought, a philosophical pantheism. The excessive devotion of the priest to the ritual had thus produced a reaction, but the reaction was proving as confused as the stimulus itself. Neither ritualism nor philosophy really succeeded in restoring to religion that element of ethical values which it had possessed in an eminent degree in the early Vedic period but which had inevitably got eroded from it during its progress from Kuru-Panchala country to Kosala-Videha and the country to the further east. The prevailing religion in 6th century BC, therefore, when Mahavira was born, was significantly unsatisfying and in a chaotic state.

Society of the Time

Society in 6th century BC had definitely come to be organised on the basis of caste. Historians are not always agreed on the origin of the caste system in India. When the Aryans came to India, it seems quite certain that they were a homogenous mass of people and were not divided into distinct castes or even classes. The formation of classes did not occur until after their settlement over extensive territories in the *Gangetic* plains, and it took place in the age of the later *samhitas,* but not in the form of a rigid caste system at first. There are passages in *Sruti* literature which indicate quite clearly that the knowledge of Vedic texts and ceremonies rather than the fact of birth in a Brahmin family, qualified a person to be a *Brahmin.*

The development of caste rigidly can be traced through the period of latter *samhitas,* the *Vajasaneya Samhita* for instance prefers a *Brahmin* for priestly duties descended from three generations of *Rsis.* Such rules are evidence of a deliberate attempt to make caste system more and more static. But as yet those essential features, the prohibition of inter dining and intermarriage, which are the special characteristics of caste system today, had not developed in their fullness, nor had the *Brahmin* yet attained and unquestioned position of supremacy, the *Ksatriya* being able to contest it with him at every step. In establishing the supremacy of the Brahminas the most important part was played by the sacrifice (*yagya*), the ritual.

The early Vedic age was one of creative impulses. It was marked by "charming appreciation of all that is good and sublime in nature, leading to outburst of individual enthusiasm in inspiring stanza addressed to various divinities". The theology of the later Vedic literature did not much differ from the theology of the hymns, but the religious spirit had undergone a change. The creative age had changed into an age of criticism, and inspiration naturally yielded place to formalism. Of this formalism the priestly class now devoted its whole attention to find out the hidden and mystic meaning of the rites and ceremonies.

The ceremonies were multiplied until they comprehended both domestic and other great sacrifices. The domestic ceremonies embraced the whole course of a man's life, right from the conception in the mother's womb up to death, or rather beyond it, for several ceremonies refer to the departed souls. The well known forty *samskaras* or sacraments, although finally drawn up at a later period, reflected the conditions of the age before the birth of Mahavira. These sacraments included twenty-six *Grhya*-rituals (1) Garbhadhan, the rite to cause conception; (2) *Punsvan*, the rite to secure the birth of a male child; (3) *Simnthotryan*, the parting of the pregnant wife's hair by the husband; (4) *Jatkarm*, the rite for the newborn child; (5) *Namkaranr*, the ceremony of naming the child; (6) *Atrprashan*, the first feeding of the child with solid food; (7) *Choodakarm*, the tonsure of the child's head; (8) *Upnyan*, initiation ceremony; (9) to (12) the four vows undertaken for studying the different Vedas; (13) *Smavartan*, the completion of studentship; (14) *Sehdharmcharinreesanyog*, marriage; (15) to (19) five great daily sacrifices to the Gods, manes, men, goblins and Brahmin; (20) to (26) the seven *Pakyagya* small sacrifices-which had to be performed mostly by the householder himself, and fourteen major rituals-the seven kinds of *Haviryagya* and seven kinds of *somyagya* in which three sacred fires were kindled, to which offerings of cake, grain, milk, honey, etc. were made. In the *Samayajnas* even animals were killed. To this list could be added numerous other sacrifices, like the *vratya-stoma*, the *Rajasuya*, the *Asvamedha*, and the *Purusamedha*. Some of these sacrifices were informed by a new spirit of symbolism and spirituality, evident for instance in the building of the altar, and lasted from twelve days to a year or years.

The elaboration of these rituals led to the growth of Brahminism, or the hierarchy of Brahminas; and with Brhmanism came the rigidity of the caste system. Under rigid caste system, in which a man's caste was determined by the fact of birth, the Brahminas became parasites living on the resources of the industrial classes without doing anything worthwhile to compensate the other classes. The *Ksatriya* class which had always been active evolving philosophical system and which had stood for experience as against the Brahminic emphasis on intellect, felt the inequity and injustice of this position and revolted against it. Mahavira and the Buddha freely denounced the arbitrary distinctions of caste and proclaimed the equality of all human beings, and in doing so they were giving an effective expression to the innermost feeling of the masses.

With the growing rigidity of the caste system, the position of women had also deteriorated. During even the later Vedic age there were exceptional cases of women attaining a high position in society and in the learned world. The stories of *Gargi* and *Maritreyi* mentioned in *Brihdaranryak Upanisad* are remarkable examples of this. But by the 6th century BC the position had become deteriorated. With the increase in royal power, Indo Aryan chiefs had become polygamous. Women were denied the right of inheriting property, and a father had the right to divide his property among his sons according to his will. On the death of her husband, a widow passed on to his family like his property.

The prevailing attitude towards women is apparent in the initial reluctance of the Buddha to admit them into his religious order. A little later, Megtasthenes also said that "the Brahmins do not communicate a knowledge of philosophy to their wives". But Mahavira and the Buddha took a highly rational attitude in this matter; both permitted the inclusion of women into their *sanghas*, and this step marked a revolutionary improvement of their status in society.

Economy of the Time

From the point of view of economic structure, Indian society in 6th century BC was passing through a transition from a cultivating and handicraft to a cottage industry stage. Early Aryans were a pastoral people, their chief occupations being cultivation and cattle -rearing. The land was ploughed, the plough was drawn by oxen. Cattle consisted of kine and sheep. Weaving in cotton and wool was done but of industries very little was known. As the Aryans spread towards the east and the south and occupied the fertile plains of the Ganges and the Yamuna, their material prosperity considerably increased.

The plough gradually assumed a large and heavy form; there is mention at one place of twenty-four oxen being harnessed to one plough. Irrigation also improved, and along with it the quality and variety of grains raised from the ground. At this time the society got divided into a number of classes and castes; and among the servile castes we find mention of such as fishermen, shepherds, fire-rangers, charioteers, workers in jewellery, basket-makers, washer-men, rope-makers, dyers, chariot-makers, weavers, slaughters, cooks, professional acrobats, musicians, etc. In the literature collectively known as the later Samhitas there is frequent mention of merchant and also users. The knowledge and use of metals had become quite extensive; besides gold, we find mention of tin, lead and silver, and possibly copper and iron. But during this period Indian economy remained on the whole a purely rural economy, with arts and crafts only incidentally developed.

In the 6th century BC, however, and about this period our information is both large and accurate, the structure of economy began to get fundamentally transformed.

- The *gram* was still the unit of administration and the centre of all activities; but the grama was apparently a generic term, meaning almost anything from a group of two or three houses to an indefinite number. In the Buddhist texts there is also an occasional mention of cities in northern India, about twenty such having been recounted, six of which are reckoned as sufficiently important ones.
- Further, rural economy was based upon a system of village communities of land-owners and marked by instances of collectivist initiative. The peasant proprietors had a nominal head in the *bhojak* (or headman) who, as their representative at political headquarters and municipal head, was paid by certain dues and fines.

- Above all in the arts and crafts considerable proficiency and specialisation of industry had been reached. "A list of callings given in the *Milindapanho* reveals three separate industries in the manufacture of bows and arrows, apart from any ornamental work on the same. In the same work, the allusion to a professional winnower of grain indicates a similar division of labour to our own threshing-machinists and steam plough-owners who tour in rural districts". Important handicrafts were organised into guilds, and at the head of each guild as a president (*prmukh*) or elder man (*jaithak*), and these leaders were often important ministers in attendance upon and in favour with the King. There is evidence that regulation of industrial life was on a corporate basis; not only individual but families were often referred to in terms of traditional calling.

- The age was marked by freedom of initiative and a high degree of mobility in labour. This finds exemplification in stories like those of enterprising woodworkers who, failing to carry out the orders for which prepayment had been made, were summoned to fulfill their contract and, instead of abiding in their lot, secretly made a mighty ship and emigrated with their families shipping down the Ganges by night and so out to sea till they reached a fertile island.

- Trade and commerce was fast developing. Partnership in commerce either permanent or on specified occasions only, are frequently mentioned in Buddhist and Jaina texts. The overland caravans are sometimes represented as going "east and west" and across deserts that took days and nights to cross. They may have gone from Benares, the chief commercial and industrial centre in early Buddhist and Jaina age, across the deserts of Rajputana to the seaport of modern Broach or the seaboard of Sovira and its capital Roruka. Westward of these ports there was traffic with Babylon. The nature of exports and imports is not always specified, but they would seem to include such articles as "silks, muslin, the finer sorts of cloth, cutlery and armor, brocades, embroideries and rugs, perfumes and drugs, ivory and ivory work, jewelry and gold". It appears that trade was free, in the sense that it was determined solely by supply and demand and unhampered by any system of statutory fixed prices. The use of standard currency and of substitutes for money, like instruments of credit, also appear to have become common. The taking of interest was considered legitimate and the payment of debts an honourable obligation.

Of this developing capitalist economy the natural need was that there should be a theory of economic individualism to support it. This found its echo in spiritual doctrines like Jainism and Buddhism, which placed their emphasis upon the individual rather than upon a World-Soul. The prevailing Brahamnic religion with its traditional restrictions, its caste system, and its expensive sacrifices had begun to collide at an ever-increasing number of points with the existing economic ethics, and this made the growth of "heretical" sects inevitable which, originating outside hieratic circles, would offer a philosophic justification for a concept of individualism and a development of individual personality.

Polity of the Time

The economic changes leading to the growth of capitalism in society caused corresponding changes in the political Constitution of the country. The power of the tribal chieftain of old increased and he became more or less a real King, with power to deprive any commoner of his private property. The nobbles obtained the position of landlords or intermediaries between the cultivators and the King. Slaves and serfs also increased in number. Within the framework of autocracy, there were still operative certain democratic elements, e.g.:

- the people's voice in choosing the King;
- the promises made by the King at his coronation;
- the King's dependence on the ministry;
- the popular assemblies the *Sabha* and the Samiti; but these democratic limitations upon the powers of the King were becoming increasingly obsolete.

The territorial concept of the state was becoming more pronounced.

In the 6th century BC northern India seems to have been divided into the following sixteen states:

- *Anga,* covering possibly the Patna and Monghyr districts,
- *Magadha,* covering the Patna and Gaya,
- *Kasi,* covering Benares, Ghazipur and Mirzapur districts,
- *Vajji,* covering Muzaffarpur, Saran and Champaran districts of north Bihar,
- *Kosala,* possibly covering the Gorakhpur district,
- *Vamsa,* covering the modern Allahabad and Banda districts,
- *Cheti,* possibly the present Kanpur and Unnao districts,
- *Panchala,* which may by identified with modern Rohilkhand,
- *Kuru,* covering the Aligarh, Meerut, Delhi and Karnal districts,
- *Matsya,* possibly covering the present Gurgaon district along with portions of Alwar and Jaipur states,
- *Surasena,* possibly covering the Muttra district and portions of Bharatpore and Jaipur states,
- *Asuraka,* on the Godavari,
- *Avanti,* which seems to be just another name for Malwa,
- *Gandhara,* presumably covering the northwest districts of the Punjab as far as Peshawar and adjoining districts, and
- *Kamboja,* which may possibly be identified with the modern districts of Kabul and Jalalabad.

These names are given in several places in the Buddhist text, *Anguttara-Nikaya* and partially repeated in the Sanskrit work *Mahavastu*. The Jaina text *Bhagavati,* which also enumerates sixteen names, described the delimitation of states at a somewhat later period; the geographical margins of states mentioned there is much wider.

Among these states four seem to have been particularly powerful Kosala with its capital at Sravasti, Avanti with its capital at Ujjaini, Vamsa (or Vatsa) with its capital at Kausambi, and Magadha with its capital at Fajgriha; and the period was marked by perpetual military contests between them. Ultimately Magadha, under its King Bimbisara (or Srenika), rose to the position of paramountcy. It is possible that the big states included certain more or less autonomous clan or tribal areas, which enjoyed a form of home rule. The Sakyas, for instance, were a tribe of the Kosalas, but held an autonomous tenure.

Besides kingdoms, republic states also existed. Among the republics the following names were prominent: The Sakyas, with their capital at Kapilvastu; The Bulis, with their capital at Amalkappa; The Kalamas, with their capital Kesaputta; The Bhaggas, with their capital at Sumsumara; The Koliyas, with their capital at Ramagama; The Mallas, with their capital at Pava; The Mallas, with their capital at Kusinara; The Moriyas, with their capital at Pipphalivana; The Videhas, with their capital at Mithila; and the Licchavis, with their capital at Vaisali.

These tribal republics seem to have occupied in 6th century BC the whole country east of Kosala between the mountains and the Ganges. Each one of them included several big towns besides the capital. In the territory of the Sakyas, which covered the lower slopes of the Himalayas, there is mention of a number of towns like Catuma, Samagama, Khomadussa, Silavati, Medalumpa, Negaraka, Ulumpa, Devadaha, and Sakkara. The administrative business of these tribal republics and the more important judicial work was carried out in public assembly at which the young and old were alike present. The meetings were held in motehalls, i.e. roofy structure supported by pillars without walls, and the procedure adopted in these meetings seems to have been as in modern Parliaments. A single chief was elected as office-holder; he bore the title of *raja*, although the term did not mean King. He was something like the Roman consul. There were tribal confederacies also, a classical example of which was the Vijjian confederacy, comprising the Licchavis, the Videhas and other clans.

2

The Holy Life

The Backdrop

India in the 6th Century B. C. was not under the political control of one single power. There was no Empire at that time which could bring all regions of the country under one administration. Instead India was divided and sub-divided into a number of large and small Kingdoms and principalities. Among such major Kingdoms those of Magadha, Anga, Kashi, Kosala, Vatsa, Panchala, Kalinga, Avanti, Gandhara, and Kamboja were more prominent in the northern and eastern regions of India. Even among these Kingdoms, the Kingdom of Magadha in the east corresponding to the modern Bihar, enjoyed a very pre-eminent position and hence it was often described as the Empire of Magadha. This Empire was ruled by the monarchs belonging to the Shishunaga Dynasty and its capital Rajagraha was the most leading city of the times. Naturally Magadha exerted much influence over the lives of the people in eastern India.

His Father

Siddhartha, the father of Mahavira, also known as Sreyamsa and Jasamsa in the Shvetambara Granthas, was a Kshatriya ruler of a place called Kundalpura situated in that part of Northern

India which was called Pavan in very ancient times and Videha or Magadha in later times. He belonged to the clan of Gnatrikas who are also known as Natikas in the Buddhist works, and who were a powerful clan in ancient times. Many of the ruling dynasties of later times are said to have sprung from this clan, and even the ruling chiefs of those times, who were also related to him through his wife, belonged to this clan. It is why Mahavira has been very often called Gnatriputra or Nataputta in the Buddhist works.

The Digambaras also call him a Haribansi and even a Nathbansi. As to his gotra it is asserted on both hands that he was a Kashyapa. In Buddhist works his gotra is confounded with that of his pupil Sudharmacharya and is, therefore, said to be Agnivaishayana. The description of the magnificence of his palace, the ceremonious rejoicings with which the birth of Mahavira was celebrated and the grandeur and pomp of his court, make us believe that Siddhartha was a powerful monarch of his time and his metropolis, Kundalpura, a big populous city.

His Mother

Trisala or Priyakarini, the mother of Mahavira, was a beautiful, meritorious, a loving and a virtuous lady, who is said to have possessed all the good qualities of the head and the heart. In the Shvetambara shastras she is spoken of as sister to Ketaka (Ohetaka) the powerful ruler of Videha who belonged to the Vashistha gotra. For this also she is called Videhadatta. In the Digambara Shastras she is called as daughter of Chetaka, the King of Siddhadesha. It is not known whether these two Chetakas are the same or different persons. She was an affectionate mother and would not allow her son to become a Sanyasi, when he was a boy.

Elder Brother

The Shvetambara Granthas also say that Mahavira had an elder brother, Nandivardhana, with whom Mahavira is said to have lived in his boyhood. They also assert that he had one elder sister known by the name of Sadarsana. On the other Jiand we find no mention of them in the Digambara shastras. Mahavira's parents were both fortunate men, inasmuch as they lived to see their son a grown up man of thirty-two. The Mahavira Purana says nothing in connection with this.

Sixteen Dreams

When Siddhartha and Trishala were passing their days in happiness, a pleasant and unusual event occurred in the life of Trishala. It so happened that on the last part of the night of the sixth day of the bright half of the month of Ashadha when Moon was in Hasta Nakshatra; Queen Trishala in her sound and calm sleep saw sixteen beautiful dreams. In these 16 auspicious dreams she witnessed the following 16 objects in succession. • Gaja, i.e. an elephant, • Vrishabha, i.e. a bull, • Simha, i.e. a lion, • Lakshmi, i.e. goddess Lakshmi, • Mala-Yugma, i.e. pair of garlands, • Shashi, i.e. the Moon, • Surya, i.e. the Sun, • Jhasha-yugala, i.e. a pair of fishes. • Kalasha-Yugala, i.e. a pair of pitchers, • Sarovara, i.e. a lake. • Samudra, i.e. an ocean, • Simhasana, i.e. a throne, • Deva-Vimana, i.e. a divine aerial car, • Nagendra-bhavana, i.e. a house of Nagendra, • Ratna-rashi, i.e. a heap of jewels, and • Nirdhuma-agni, i.e. a smokeless fire.

Queen Trishala got up immediately after witnessing these dreams and began to contemplate over them. Indeed she was extremely eager to know the meaning and indication of the succession of the special objects seen in these sixteen dreams. Soon after finishing her bath and worship, she hurriedly went with high expectations to meet King Siddhartha in the Palace. It was really a pleasant surprise for King Siddhartha to find Queen Trishla entering the Palace in great eagerness at an early hour of the day. King Siddhartha received her with great love, made her to seat near him on the left side of his throne and anxiously enquired the reason of her morning visit. Queen Trishala communicated to, him the succession of sixteen dreams seen by her in the very early hours of the morning and respectfully asked the purport of these dreams. The King was extremely happy to know about these dreams as he was an expert in the art of interpretation of dreams. The King predicted that the Queen would give birth to an illustrious son destined to be a Tirthankara in this very life and while explaining in detail the meanings of these dreams, he narrated the good things and qualities suggested by them.

Realising the special significance attached to these dreams that only the mothers of would-be Tirthankaras get such a succession of sixteen dreams, both King Siddhartha and Queen

Trishala felt extreme happiness and eagerly awaited to see the auspicious face of their son. They had not to wait for long. On the conclusion of nine months, seven days and twelve hours of the period of pregnancy after the day of conception when she saw those sixteen dreams. Queen Trishala gave birth to a son at Kunda pura (Vaishali) during the last hours of the night on the thirteenth day of the bright half of the month Chaitra. Thus Mahavira saw the light of the day on Monday, the, 27th March 598 BC. At the time of his birth the Nakshatra (i.e. constellation) was Phalguni, the Rashi (i.e. a sign of the Zodiac) was Kanya, the Samvatsara (i.e. the name of the year) was Siddhartha, the Chinha (i.e. the emblem) was Lion, and the Varna (i.e. the colour was Svarnabha (i.e. golden).

His Birth

The happy tidings of the birth of the Prince to King Siddhartha and Queen Trishala was received with great joy by all residents of Vaishali (Kundalapur) city and the Videha republic and the entire region wore a festive appearance. King Siddhartha and his relatives celebrated the occasion with royal pomp and glory. Common people also participated in the celebrations with great enthusiasm and love. They bedecked their houses with lamps, flowers, buntings, and flags, adorned their bodies with new garments and ornaments, decorated the streets with arches and auspicious symbols, performed worships in the temples, sang eulogistic songs, staged dance and drama performances and thus gave expression to their joy and mirth in innumerable ways. In memory of this great event King Siddhartha made special arrangements to give presents of different kinds to the needy and poor people of his republic. These festivities continued unabated for ten days and on the twelfth day the auspicious naming ceremony of the Prince was accomplished in the presence of the persons specially assembled for the purpose. While addressing the gathering King Siddhartha declared that "Since the conception of their child nine months ago we have witnessed every prosperity in Vidaha republic, in Vaishali capital, in Kundaipur suburb and in our family, we have decided to name the Prince as `Vardhamana' (i.e. the Prosperous One): The declaration was highly appreciated by the public with great applause.

Different Views on Birth

The first difference between the Svetambara and Digambara version relates to the fact of Mahavira's birth. Both versions agree that Mahavira was the son of Siddharatha and Trisala, that he belonged to a clan of the Ksatriyas called Jnatrkas (known as Natikas in the Buddhist works), and that he was a Kasyapa by *gotra*. But the Svetambara version speaks of a transfer of embryo; the *Acaranga* says:

> "Here, forsooth, in the continent of Jambudvipa in Bharatavarsa, in the southern part of it, in the Brahamanical part of the place Kundapura, he took the form of an embryo in the womb of Devananda, of the Jalandhrayana gotra, wife of the Brahmin Ṛsabhadatta, of the gotra of Kodala......". "Then in the third month of the rainy season, the fifth fortnight, the dark (fortnight) of Asvina, on its thirteenth day, while the moon was in conjunction with Uttaraphalguni, after the laps of eighty-two days, on the eighty-third day current, the compassionate god (Indra) reflecting on what was the established custom (with regard to the birth of the Tirthankaras), removed the embryo from the southern Brahminical part of the place Kundapura to the northern Ksatriya part of the same place, rejecting the unclean matter, lodged the fetus in the womb of Trisala of the Vasistha gotra, wife of the Ksatriya Siddhartha, of the Kasyapa gotra, of the clan of Jnatrs, and lodged the fetus of the Ksatriyani Trisala in the womb of Devananda, of the Jalandhrayana gotra.......".

The *Digambara* account rejects this legend as 'absurd', but the *Svetambaras* strongly uphold its truth. As the legend is found in the *Acaranga*, the *Kalpasutra*, and many other books it cannot be doubted that it is very old; but it is not at all clear why it was invented and given such currency. There are, however, in the *Bhagavati*-another *sutra* in the *Svetambara* canon, two references that would throw further light on the question and would possibly help us in finding a solution. In Sataka V Updesa IV, in reply to a question regarding the possibility and the procedure of the change of embryo, Mahavira declared that a change of embryo was quite possible and stated his position regarding the procedure by which the change might take place, but significantly omitted to mention- although it would have been quite proper for him in that context to do so- the change of his own embryo. Again, in Sataka IX, Updesa XXXIII, there is reference to the visit to Mahavira's camp of the Brhmana Rsabhadatta and his wife Devananda. On the sight of Mahavira, Devananda had a sudden maternal emotion and milk started coming out of her breast. Asked by his chief disciple Gautama to explain the reason of this unusual occurrence, Mahavira plainly stated that Devananda was his mother. He made no mention whatever of Trisala or of the episode of the change of embryo.

These two references are pointer to the fact that actually there was no change of Mahavira's embryo. The Bhagavati, which makes a record of the actual conversations and sayings of Mahavira, is certainly more trustworthy as a source of information than the *Kalpasutra*. Which after all is the work of an *acarya,* however learned. It is not impossible that the story was invented by the author of the *Kalpasutra* as an occasion to express the prevailing sentiment of contempt for the Brahmins, and that it was later on embodied in the second book of the *Acaranga*. But that alone does not solve the problem.

In the *Bhagavati Mahavira* says that Devananda is his mother and in the *Acaranga* and the *Kalpasutra* the name of Mahavira's mother is given as Ksatriyani Trisala. Of this Professor Jacobi offered a some what fanciful solution. "I assume", he said "that Siddhartha had two wives, the Brahmini Devananda, the real mother of Mahavira, and he Ksatriyani Trisala; for the name of the alleged husband of the former, viz. Rsabhadatta, cannot be very old, because its Prakrit form would in that case probably be Usabhadinna instead of Usabhadatta. Besides, the name is such as could be given to a Jaina only, on to a Brahmin. I, therefore, make no doubt that Rsabhadatta has been invented by the Jainas in a order to provide Devananda with another husband. Now Siddhartha was connected with persons of high rank and great influence through his marriage with Trisala. It was, therefore, probably thought more profitable to give out that Mahavira was the son, and not merely the stepson, of Trisala, for this reason that he should be entitled to the patronage of her relations". This is obviously far-fetched and also incorrect, for it is certain that in the days of Mahavira the marriage of a Brahmin girl with a Ksatriya was not at all an easy adventure and that anyhow the offspring of such a marriage would not be considered very respectable. What seems more likely is that Devananda was Mahavira's foster-mother. This likelihood finds substantial support in the text of the *Acaranga* (second book) which specifically speaks of Mahavira as having been attended by five nurses, one of them being a wet-nurse.

Birth Place

As to the birth place of Mahavira, it is probable but not certain, however, the Jaina traditions represent Kundalpura as a large town, inasmuch as Kundalpura is taken as equivalent to Vesali (Sanskrit Vaishali). There is no mention of this place in either of the authorities. Had it been the actual birth place of Mahavira, the Jainas, careful writers as they were, would have never left it unmentioned. There does not seem to be any good reason to prefer the unauthentic traditionary evidence of the Buddhists to that of the Jainas themselves. His second supposition though based on traditionary evidence, seems, in all probability, a reasonable one; and we may rest assured that Kundalpura, a suburb of Vesali, as really it was the birth place of Mahavira.

Date of Birth

Mahavira was born on the thirteenth day of the latter half of Chaitra about 72 years before the end of the fourth Kal in the Dushama-sushama period. On this occasion great performances and rejoicings took place in the King's palace which lasted for ten days. Streets were illuminated, charitable deeds were performed, and prisoners were liberated. It was in such circumstances that Lord Mahavira was born.

Generous and Kind Parents

King Siddhartha and Queen Trishaladevi were leading a religious and peaceful life in the seven storeyed Palace, known as Nandyvarta Rajaprasada situated in Kundalapur, the suburb of Vaishali which was the capital city of Videha republic. As Trishaladevi belonged to Videha republic, she was termed as Videhi (i.e. of Videha) or Videhadatta (i.e. given by Videha). Due to her amiable and kind acts towards others, Trishala was: popularly known as Priyakarini, i.e. the doer of good acts. Trishala was also famous as an ideal lady and Queen since she possessed in a great measure all the essential attributes of a faithful wife and a devoted Queen. Naturally Trishala was very dear to King Siddhartha and was immensely loved and respected by her subjects.

His Childhood

The child-prince Vardhamana was not only extremely beautiful but also possessed various physical traits of an unusual nature: His limbs were greatly proportionate and without defects of any kind. His body-structure was strong and his body-odour was pleasant. His speech was soft and melodious. His body possessed 1008 auspicious physical attributes like Shankha (Conch), Chakra (circle), Kamala (lotus), Dhanusha (bow), etc. He also showed superb intelligence and developed grasping capacity.

The Boyhood

As Prince Vardhamana entered boyhood, people soon realised that he possessed in great measure the rare qualities like bravery, self-control, fearlessness, helping-nature, courage, etc. Many events gave eloquent testimony of the attributes of his gifted personality. Once while Prince Vardhamana was engrossed in play with his friends in the courtyard of his Palace, he was suddenly disturbed to hear a loud noise of screams in fear and helplessness from the streets of Kundalapura. Instantly, he came out of the Palace and ran towards the site of the noise. There he saw that one royal elephant had gone amok and that the citizens were running frightfully in different directions in a frantic bid to escape from the onslaught of the mad elephant. This dangerous sight did not create any fear in his mind. On the contrary he immediately showed his presence of mind and staring straight at the elephant he loudly ordered the elephant to remain calm. To the great surprise of the frightened persons the elephant instantly became peaceful. After pacifying the elephant, Prince Vardhamana personally mounted the elephant and in a cool manner directed the elephant towards its resting place. People were tremendously impressed by this rare feat of courage and bravery and from that time began to address him by the name "Vira" i.e. the Hero.

The Youth

Gradually Prince Mahavira passed the stage of adolescene and entered adulthood. The advent of youth bestowed additional charm and dignity on his natural beautiful personality His physical strength increased to a great extent and his knowledge developed beyond measure. His elligence became more acute and his beauty surpassed the usual limits. Thus different facets of his personality sufficiently bloomed as he be came a young man. Further, being a Prince, all comforts and luxuries of the royal life were at his disposal. He was very well connected to several important royal families of the time through his father and especially through his mother.

A Selfless Youngman

In this way young Prince Mahavira possessed various accomplishments and developed a handsome personality. He had all opportunities and different facilities to build a political career for himself. But he never showed any inclination towards harbouring political ambitions and securing more and more wordly pleasure. In fact, he never aspired for acquisition of material wealth and political power. On the contrary Mahavira never took any interest in family affair and in political matters. He did not indulge in extravagance of any kind. Instead he always valued the virtue of self-control and invariably attached great importance to the actual practise of giving help to others. He firmly believed in the principles of right conduct and of equality towards all living beings. That is why it is stated that right from his eighth-year Mahavira used to observe five Anu-Vratas (i.e. small views) prescribed by Jaina religion. These facts clearly reveal that aspirations of young Prince Mahavira were not towards leading a life of worldly pleasants but were in the directions to lead a life of self-control and to help others in securing ultimate happiness.

Holy Visitors

The news about the most beautiful and talented child-prince Vardhamana did spread far and wide and many persons of authority were eager to see the child-prince. Once a couple of sages, named Sanjaya (or Sanjayanta) and Vijaya (or Vijayanta), who had heard about the greatness of this baby-prince, came to see him. At his very glance they felt so much exhilarated that they exclaimed: "How beautiful he looks!" Not only this much; they also felt that their philosophical doubts, which were troubling their mind since long, had disappeared. They went their way duly satisfied after bestowing the name of `Sanmati' (i.e. Good Intellect), and proclaimed a great future for him.

Anecdotes about Early Life

The facts of the early life of Mahavira given in the several biographies whose names we have recounted above are very few indeed. The later accounts have connected him with certain anecdotes, myths and miracles; but they appear to have been allied from the other traditional sources and cannot, therefore, be justifiably recounted as the facts of Mahavira's life. There is, for instance, an anecdote in one of the *Digambara* books, illustrative of Mahavira's supreme valour, which runs thus: "One day, while playing with his friends in the garden of his father, Mahavira saw an elephant, which was mad with fury with juice flowing from his temples, rushing towards him. His companions, all boys, shocked and frightened on the sight of the impending danger, deserted their comrade and ran away. Without losing a moment, Mahavira made up his mind to face the danger squarely, went towards the elephant, caught hold of his trunk with his strong hands and mounted his back at once".

It is nevertheless a fact that the Jainas never attempted to give a connected account of the life of his great Master as the Buddhists gave a life of the Buddha in the *Mahavagga*, from the obtainment of the Enlightenment to the admission of Sariputta and Moggallana into the order and in the Mahaparinibbana sutta, which recounts the events of Buddha's last days. The *Kalpasutra* used a somewhat conventional style while writing about the great rejoicing that took pace in the family and the town on the birth of Mahavira, about illumination of the streets, about he liberation of prisoners, and about the performance of numerous other charitable deeds. At the core of much that is conventional, however, a few facts would seem to clearly emerge. In person Mahavira seems to have been handsome and impressive; all descriptions agree on that point. The several names by which he is called in the Jaina books-Vira, Ativira, Mahavira, etc. all clearly indicate that the chief quality of his character was courage and valour. Being the scion of a Ksatriya chieftain and brought up in the free atmosphere of a republican society, he must have right from his childhood taken the most vigorous interest in the outdoor games and material exercises. He was naturally intelligent and possessed of a very keen intellect.

The Kalapasutra mentions that from his very birth he possessed "supreme, unlimited and unimpeded knowledge and intuition" and that he had the aspirations of a man of knowledge. That his education was carefully looked after may be safely presumed: the Jaina scriptures speak again and again of princes who were trained in "the seventy-two arts," the list including dancing, music gambling, rules of society, fighting, archery, knowledge of birds, animals and trees, etc. besides purely literary and philosophical attainments.

The Svetambara books say that Mahavira had an elder brother, whose name was Nandivardhana, with whom he lived in his boyhood. This fact is omitted, but not positively denied, by *Digambara* books. Both books, however, agree that Mahavira was very well- connected. By birth he was a member of at least the ruling class in a republican democracy. The description of his father's palace and the dimensions of rejoicing made there on the birth of Mahavira, who according to the Svetambara version was only a second son, would lead one to the conclusion that Siddhartha was a ruling Prince. Jacobi, however, does not feel inclined to that view. According to him, Kundagrama (or Kundalapura) was "a halting place of caravans, an insignificant place and an outlying village and a suburb of Vaisali, the capital of Videha", so that Siddhartha was only "a petty chief, a baron, no King, nor even the head of his clan, but only a landowner, and exercised only the degree of authority which in the East usually falls to the share of one belonging to the recognised aristocracy of the country". Such description is belied by later historical research. Historians are now prepared to accept that Kundagrama was the headquarters of the Jnatrka Ksatriya, "who were already known for their piety and non-violence, and abstention from sin and meat-eating," and that the republic was governed by an assembly of elders, one of whom assumed the position of the president. It is presumable that Siddhartha occupied the position of the president of this republic; for otherwise it might be somewhat difficult to explain his marriage with the sister of Cetaka, whom even Jacobi recognises as "the powerful King of Videha," belonging to the Licchavi sect of the Ksatriya. Through his wife, Siddhartha-and following him, Mahavira-was related tot he ruling dynasty of Magadha and the dynasties of Sauvira, Anga, Vatsa (Vamsa) and Avanti. Cetaka had seven daughters, one of whom became a nun, but the other six were married in one or the other royal family of Eastern India. The youngest Celana became the wife of Srenika (Bimbisara), King of Magadha: one Prabhavati was married to King Udayana of Vitabhya, which has been identified at various places in Jaina literature with a town in Sindhu-Sauvira country; another Padmavati was married to King Dadhivahana of Campa, the capital of Anga; Mirgavati was married to King Satanika of Kausambi, the capital of Vatsa; and Shiva was married to Canda Pradyota of Ujjani, which was the capital of Avanti.

That the tie of these relationships was real and strong, may be judged from the fact that the books are always very particular in stating the names and *Gotra* of all relations of Mahavira, although they have recorded little further information about them.

From the above it is clear that the environment in which Mahavira grew up was necessarily royal atmosphere tempered with healthy influenced of a republican character. His maternal relatives were practically all of them ruling Princes, but his father was a republican chief and even his maternal uncle was a territorial ruler under the auspices of a republican confederacy- the famous Vajji confederacy of which eight republics, Vajji, were constituent units. The real strength of the republic in Mahavira's time as, to a large extent, today lay not so much in its government as in the character of its people. The Buddha mentioned in one of his discourses that republican population was free from luxury and sloth, "sleeping on logs of wood as pillows and not on cushions of the finest cotton, active in archery, and not delicate, tender and soft in their arms and legs".

The youths were rowdy, but by no means devoid of honour or lacking in moral courage; they frankly admitted their mistakes, and were inspired by a fundamental sense of respect for elders and women, and their national institutions. It was in this atmosphere that Mahavira's early life was spent. His upbringing must have been quite exceptionally balanced and his development proportionate, for his life was a life of comfort but not luxury and his ambition was an ambition to conquer but not with view to mastery over others. He was deeply influenced by the democratic ethos of the society in which he lived. He was impressed by the inadequate application of this ethos in the political, economic and social life of the community without its being based upon a really democratic religious system; and he took it upon himself to workout and propagate a system of complete spiritual democracy in the form of Jainism.

A Brave Act

On another occasion when Prince Vardhamana was out in the royal gardens playing with his companions the game of hide and seek, he and his playmates were surprised to hear clearly a hissing sound. When the sound came quite close, they found a large poisonous cobra coming towards them. The boys immediately scattered away in all directions, screaming with fear, but the Prince did not budge an inch and stood calm and quiet at his place. When the cobra came almost near him hissing out poisonous sparks vehemently and tried to attack him, the Prince caught hold of its tail, lifted it and threw it away easily.

The playmates witnessed this unusual feat of great courage with awe and surprise. But their curiosity became highly increased when they saw the transformation of the cobra into a semi-god of the heavens. The real fact was that the cobra was the form assumed by one good named 'Sangama' to test the power and fearlessness of Prince Vardhamana. After realising the strength and courage of Prince Vardhamana, Sangama-deva revealed his real identity and in praise said to him that he is indeed a Mahavira, i.e. a Great Hero. Sangama-deva was so much overjoyed that he placed the boy-prince on his shoulder and began to dance along with Chaladhara, Kakadhara and Pakshadhara, the three close companions of Prince Vardhamana.

Title of Mahavira

After this incident Prince Vardhamana was known as Prince Mahavira and eventually 'Mahavira' became his popular name so much that later on Vardhamana was always referred to as Mahavira. Other synonymous terms like 'Ativira', "Viranatha" and "Mahativira" were also commonly used to denote him. Because of his intimate connections with Vaishali city and Videha republic, the names like "Vaishalika', "Vaishaliya (i.e. belonging to Vaishali), "Videhadatta" (i.e. given by Videha) and Videhasukumara' (i.e. tender prince of Videha) are freely assigned to him. Since Vardhamana hailed from the Jnatr or Jnatrika clan of the Kshtriyas, he was also referred to as "Jnataputra", or Jnatrpufra". As the terms "Nata" or "Natha" are derived from the word "Jnatr" many a time Vardhamana was mentioned as "Nataputta" (i.e. the son of the Jnatr clan) in Pali literature and "Natha-kulanandana" or "Nathanvaya" (i.e. hailing from the Jnatr clan or family) in Sanskrit literature.

Early Education

Prince Mahavira's regular education started at the age of eight. Soon his teachers realised the extraordinary talents possessed by him. He rapidly began to imbibe knowledge imparted to him and even to show proficiency in the acquired knowledge. He had the rare capacity to grasp easily any new subject and to express effectively the learned subjects. His teachers always used to appreciate the learned way in which he usually gave answers to various questions.

Spiritual Inclinations

King Sidhartha and Queen Trishala had an idea about these spiritual and religious inclinations of their son, Mahavira. They were aware that he did not belong to the category of ordinary Princess who are deeply interested in building their political careers: They were equally conscious of Mahavira's aversion to increase worldly attachments and his intense desire to concentrate on thinking and self-contemplation. They were also sure that Mahavira would eventually follow the path of asceticism prescribed by Jaina religion and would achieve the highest - position as the promulgator of Jaina religion.

Marriage Declined

Even though these facts were weighing very heavily on the minds of King Siddhartha and Queen Trishala, their parental affection goaded them to see that Mahavira leads a married life before he embark on his path of spiritual progress. They did not feel anything wrong in planning this householder's stage, in the religion-oriented career of Mahavira because they knew that Lord Rishabhadeva, the first Tirthankara entered the ascetic order after leading a contented married life. They really thought that in deference to their ardent desires Mahavira would adopt this course of life.

Accordingly King Siddhartha and Queen Trishala gave to their relatives the indication of their mind to arrange soon the marriage ceremony of their son, Mahavira. As many Kings of the time became aware of this intention to get Mahavira married, they hastened to make their proposals. Naturally different Kings vied with each other to have a matrimonial alliance with this scion of the Jnatrka clan. Among these marriage proposals King Siddhartha and Queen Trishala finally gave approval to the proposal of Princess asllasla, the daughter of King Jitashatru and Queen Yashodaya of Kalinga State. This proposal was given highest preference because Princess Yashoda was most superb in beauty and other accomplishments among-the Princesses of the time. There was another consideration also in the proposal of Princess Yashoda and that was she happened to be the daughter of Yashodaya, who was younger sister of King Siddhartha. Hence King Siddhartha and Queen Trishala finally decided to get Prince Mahavira 'married to Princess Yashoda.

When Prince Mahavira came to know of the negotiations going on about his marriage, he felt extreme grief about these developments. He never harboured any idea to indulge in sensual pleasure and did not even think of the gratification of sex-desire. In fact he had already made up his mind not to get himself entangled in any 'kind of worldly activity which would detract him from his path of spiritual progress. That is, why Mahavira outright rejected the marriage proposal and in a polite manner conveyed to his parents his firm resolve to observe strict celibacy throughout his life and to devote his energies in future to conquer the worldly desires and passions. He further made clear that he aspired to emulate the examples of four earlier Tirthankaras, viz. Vasupujya, Mallinatha, Neminatha and Parshvanath, who remained celibate and revealed the path of liberation to the people.

This well thought out and planned decision of Prince Mahavira made King Siddhartha and Queen Trishala to reconsider their proposal of Mahavira's marriage with Yashoda. The parents were completely convinced of his firm resolve and hence did not wish to come in his way of realising his goal of life. The parents, therefore, did not press the matter further and accordingly communicated their decision, to allow Mahavira to lead a celibate life, to King Jitashatru of Kalinga. Thus Prince Mahavira was free to realise his aspirations in life. Naturally Mahavir felt a great relief and began to plan to take definite step in the desired direction.

The Republics

Along with the major Kingdoms there flourished a number of Ganarajyas or republics formed by different Kshatriya clans. The Ganarajyas were established mainly for securing protection against external attacks from the adjoining Kingdoms. These Ganarajyas were based on democratic traditions and were governed by the representatives of Kshatriya Clans. Such a representative was given the appellation of 'Raja', i.e. the King. Among the Ganarajyas of the time, the Ganarajya of Videha was very famous. Videha corresponds to mostly with the modern Tirhut Division of Bihar State. In ancient times the region from the bank of the river Gandaka to the forest of Champaranya was called Videha or Tirabhukti. It was bounded on the East, West and South by three big rivers, the Kosi, the Gandaka and the Ganga, while the Nepal Tarai regions formed its northern boundary. This area comprises the present Districts of Muzaffarpur, Darbhanga,

Champaran, Munger and Purnia of Bihar State. The capital of Videha was Vaishali, the modern Basadh in Hajipur Sub-Division of Muzaffarpur District. This Videha Ganarajya was constituted by eight Rajas representing eight major Kshatriya clans, viz. • Lichchhavi. • Vrji. • Jnatrika. • Videhi. • Ugra. • Bhoga. • Ikshvaku, and • Kaurava.

Among these eight Kshatriya clans, the Lichchhavi clan was very powerful and enjoyed the most respectable position. The Lichchhavis were known for their bravery, wealth, education, beauty and other accomplishments. They always valued freedom and self-respect. They consistently opposed the attacks on their territory and preferred to lead an independent life. They were religious-minded parsons and for a long time they were the devout followers of Jainism. In view of this dominent position wielded by the Lichchhavis in the Videha Ganarajya, the latter was often referred to as the Lichchhavi Ganarajya. Similarly, Chetaka, the Raja or the representative of the Lichchhavi clan on the Videha Ganarajya or republic, was known as Ganarajya-pramukha, i.e. the main Raja of Videha Ganrajya.

The Capital

Vaishali" the capital of Videha and of the Lichchhavis was a very prosperous, beautiful and rich city. Hiuen-tsang, the famous chinese pilgrim, has described Vaishali as a great, extensive city abounding in palaces, temples, parks and lakes. It is stated that the population of Vaishali at that time was 1,68,000 and that there were about 8,000 big houses in the city. These big houses were just like palaces and to each such house was invariably attached a garden and a lake. It is, further mentioned that the city was divided into three district areas such as the Rich class areas, the Middle Class area and the Low Glass area. These areas could, be easily identified from the metal used in the construction of Domes in the area. It is also reported that in Vaishali city there were 7,000 Gold Domes, 14,000 Silver Domes and 21,000 Copper Domes. The city was always busy in varied political, religious, educational and cultural activities carried out through the agencies of Parishads or Councils. It is mentioned that eight such Parishads, viz. • Kshatriya Parishad, • Shramana Parishad, • Brahmin Parishad (or Vidvat Parishad), • Grihapati Parishad • Chaturmaharajika Parishad • Trayamtrimsa Parishad, • Mara Parishad and • Brahma Parishad were usually working in the city.

Vaishali city was surrounded by 'Upanagaras' i.e. suburbs like Kundalpura, Vaniyagrama, etc. Among these suburbs, Kundalapura was very adjacent to Vaishali and was known as an important centre of the Jnatrika Kshatriya. Kundalapura is now known as Vasukunda or Vasukunda. Kundalapura has been referred to in Prakrit and Sanskrit books by different names like Kundaggama, Kundagrama, Kshatriya Kundagrama, Kundalipura, Kundapura, Sirikundagama, Kundala and Kundanagara. Vaishali and Kundalapura had not only close geographical ties but had very intimate political, social and religious ties. This intimacy could be gauged by the family and clan relationships between Chetaka, the Ganaraja Pramukha of Vaishali and Siddhartha, the Ganaraja of Kundalapura (Vaishali).

Significant Ruler

Chetaka, the Ganaraja-Pramukha of Videha republic was renowned as the great Lichchhavi King of Vaishali. In Jaina books he is referred to as the Kshatriya Prince belonging to Ikshvaku Vansha and Vasishtha Gotra. Chetaka was married to Bhadra or Subhadra. Both Chetaka and Subhadra were great devotees of Parshvanatha, the 23rd Tirthankar as the Lichchhavis were the devout followers of Jainism. They had ten Princes and seven princesses. The names of ten Princes were as follows: • Simha or Simhabhadra, • Dhana, • Dantabhadra, • Upendra, • Sudatta, • Sukumbhoja, • Akampana • Supatanga, • Prabhanjana and • Prabhasa.

All these Princes were valiant and helped their father, King Chetaka in the defence of their territory. In fact, the eldest Prince Simhabhadra was the Senapati, i.e. the Chief of the Army of Videha republic.

King Hetaka and Queen Subhadra were blessed with seven daughters, viz. (1) Trishala, (2) Mrugavati or Priyavati, (3) Suprabha, (4) Prabhavati, (5) Chelana or Chelani, (6) Jyeshtha (7) Chandana. The second Princess Mrugavati was married to King Shataniki of Kaushambi. The famous King Vatsarja Udayana was their son. The third Princess Suprabha was given in marriage to King Dasharatha of Dasharna State The fourth Princess Prabhavati became the Queen of King Udayana of Sindha-Sauvira or Cutch in Gujarat.

The fifth Princess Chelana was given in marriage to the Emperor Bimbisara of Magadha and became his senior queer. Both Emperor Shrenika and Queen Chelana were the great patrons of Jaina religion and were constantly referred to in Jaina literature as the devout followers of Mahavira. The sixth Princess Jyeshtha and the seventh Princess Chandana remained unmarried throughout their lives and devoted their energies in the propagation of Jaina religion. In fact Chandana entered the ascetic order formed by Mahavira and eventually became the head of the female ascetics of the order.

The first Princess Trishala was married to King Siddhartha, the Ganaraja of Kundhapura (Vaishali), who belonged to the Kshatriya clan of the Jnatrikas. King Siddhartha hailed from Kashyapa Gotra and was the son of King Sarvartha. According to another version, Trishala was sister of King Chetaka and not daughter of King Chetaka.

Three Periods of Holy Life

Mahavira's life may be divided into three periods. The first discovers him in the enjoyment of the royal grandeur of his father and leading a pious life of a Shravaka or a house-holder. In the second he is deeply immersed in the religious meditation, Dhyana, and severe bodily mortification, of which Yoga is but a form, in order to prepare himself for the great work of a religious preacher which has given a lasting permanancy to his name. In the beginning of this period we find him disgusted with the worldly pleasures and determined to know the truth by meditation. At the end of it we find him the master of the truth, a Kevalin. In the third period we find him preaching his gospel to his pupils and the men of the world and bearing all the hardships that a religious preacher has to suffer, thus realising his doctrines in his right conduct, Samyak-charitra. His birth and Nirvana being added to these make the five great points of his life described so beautifully in the Jaina Shastras, and known as the five Kalyanakás.

Then we begin with the early life of Mahavira. As a matter of fact, the early lives of great men, great in the real sense of the word, are always wrapped up in mystery. Superstitious men as we are, we are likely to invent by our conjectures, myths and miracles, and connect them with the early epochs of the lives of great men. Common people are easily led to believe any thing that is said by the more refined among them. It is how the lives of great men grow mysterious. Mahavira's early life is also looked upon as a sort of mysterious thing, but the spell is easily broken if we subject it to a little scrutinising and comparative study of the Jaina Shastras. Thus we see that both the Digambaras and the Shvetambaras assert that Mahavira led the life of a Shravaka, a layman, for thirty years living with his father and mother in Kundalpura, The difference is only in the details.

The Kalpa-sutra is silent about this. It only says that the Venerable Ascetic Mahavira had lived thirty years in Videha when his parents went to the world of the gods (i. 6. died), and he with the permission of his elder brother and the authorities of the kingdom fulfilled his promise, i.e. became a Sanyasi. This does not throw any light upon the kind of life that he led during these thirty years.

The Acharanga-sutra, another Shvetambara work like the Kalpa-sutra, however, clears, this to some extent. It says that "the Venerable Ascetic Mahavira, after his intellect had developed and the childhood had passed away, lived in the enjoyment of the allowed, noble, fivefold joys and pleasures: (consisting in) sound, touch, taste, colour and smell". This, too, does not satisfy our curiosity, and we learn from it only that he had developed his intellect in his childhood and nothing more than this. The latter half of the above quotation asserts that Mahavira, in the very prime of his youth, passed his time in the enjoyment of senses and not in the spiritual study of his Self and thus preparing himself for the great mission of his life.

Of course this does not mean that he was addicted to, or a slave of, these pleasures: (consisting in) sound, touch, taste, colour and smell; otherwise it would not be reasonable to expect from him the performance of the great mission of his life, of reviving the decayed frame of ten religion of the Tirthankaras by promulgating their doctrines throughout the whole of Northern India. He lived in the enjoyment of these pleasures only as far as it is allowed. But the Digambara Acharyas do not allow him the enjoyment of any worldly pleasures at all. From them we learn that in his very eighth year he had taken the vow of observing the twelve Prattmas or the rules of conduct of a Shravaka or a layman. He was pious from his very childhood, and never deviated from the paths of integrity and virtue.

His very mission of life was to give an example of an ideally noble life and thus teach the world to become good, by practically showing them how to lead it and not by mere precepts. It has been just remarked that the life of a man to a great extent depends upon the kind of instruction given in childhood.

The nurse is the first educator of men, hence the importance of having good nurses for the nourishing and the educating of children. "Give your child to be educated by a slave," said an ancient Greek, "and instead of one slave, you will then have two". King Siddhartha knew the necessity of providing children with good nurses, and he, therefore, employed the services of the best nurses in the country.

From the Shvetambara Shastras we learn that he was attended by five nurses: a wet nurse, a nurse to clean him, one to dress him, one to play with him, one to carry him. The Digambaras hold that he was attended by the Chhappan Kumarikas of the Ruchakadwipa. Who these nurses were and where this island Ruchaka is, cannot be ascertained now. But we can say that great care was taken of his nursery and early education.! From his childhood we pass to his boyhood, and about this we leara from both the authorities that, in addition to his leading the life of a strict Shravaka, he took great interest in out-door games and martial exercises.

He used to go to the royal gardens of his father with his playmates and with the sons of his father's "ministers and amuse himself there with several kinds of feats of strength and physical exercises. He had a handsome and symmetrical body and a magnetic personality. He was a man of great courage and supreme valour. He is never said to have lost his courage even on the occasions requiring great strength of body and the mind.

The Digambara Shastras tell us an anecdote illustrating his supreme valour and perseverance. It runs thus:

> "One day, while playing with his friends in the garden of his father, Mahavira saw an elephant, maidenhead ferocious on account of the juice issuing from his temples, coming towards him. All his companions, boys as they were, being wonder-struck and afraid of the impending danger deserted him and ran off. Without losing a moment, Mahavira — went near the elephant, caught his trunk with his strong hand and ascended his back at once".

The Miracles

This looks somewhat like a miracle and an impossibility. The belief in the miraculous power of the master bears witness to the holy awe of the first disciples and reflects their religious enthusiasm". Thus we see that every sect has some miracle — connected with its founder to illustrate the great might and valour of the man. It is possible, then, that the Jainas, too, following the popular custom, might have invented this story to illustrate the unlimited valour (Ananta veerya) of the last of their twenty-four Tirthankaras. But we cannot call it entirely an invented miracle. It is possible in all probability.

Formal Education

From this we come to his education, the real part of a man's life. Curious enough to remark that both the Digambaras and the Shvetambaras say nothing about it. They assert that Mahavira had brought with him 'a highly (though not fully) developed spiritual nature from his previous births, and, therefore, he was wiser than the wisemen of his age. The Digambara Shastras say that from hie very childhood he possessed the mati, shruti and the avadhi gyan or three of the five kinds of knowledge. In the Kalpasutra we read that 'he possessed supreme, unlimited, unimpeded knowledge and intuition.' Thus we see that both the authorities assert the same thing with only this difference that one says him to possess the Avadhigyan and the other says that he was in possession of the Abhogika gyan which is inferior to the Avadhi knowledge. But all this does not satisfy us. We want to know if education was imparted to him in the modern way. We would know if he could read and write. We wish to be imformed of his skill in learning. But, perhaps, the Acharyas did not think it necessary to educate Mahavira who was a born instaurator of all knowledge. However, this may not convince the modem readers, and we have to assume that Mahavira was really educated in the palace of his father.

In the preceding pages much has been said about the childhood, the boyhood, the education and the bodily valour of Mahavira. We see that there is not much difference in the description of these as given by the two sects. The facts differ a little, but the kind of life that he led is the same in both.

However, when we come to his youth, we find that there is a real and wide difference between the opinions of the two sects. The Digambaras hold that Mahavira was never married and led the life of a Brahmachari in his youth and was disgusted with the world from his very boyhood. On the other hand the Slivetambaras assert that he was married to a charming princess Yashoda belonging to the Kaundinya gotra, but they say nothing about the parents and the relations of this princess. They further say that Mahavira had a daughter Anojja or Priyadarshana. She was married to Jamali, a pupil of Mahavira, and had a daughter called Seshavati or Yashovati.

As to his having an uncle, an elder brother, and a sister, the Digambaras do not admit it. As to his parents both assert the same. As to his posterity the Digambaras say nothing about it.

3

Renunciation of the World

Evidently, Lord Mahavira was disgusted with the world and had a mind to become a Sanyasi from his very boyhood; but he was kept from doing so by the remonstrances of his parents. We have no testimony to show whether or not he was brooding upon his early idea of renouncing the world all along. According to the Digambara Acharyas it was in his thirtieth year that one day, while meditating upon his Self, all of a sudden he reflected upon his age which he knew through his threefold knowledge to be of only seventy-two years, and this reflection reminded him of his long cherished wish of becoming a Muni. This shows that the idea of renunciation was out of his mind at least for sometime, but he had not totally given it up and when still on the verge of manhood he determined to leave the world and become a Nirgrantha Muni. The same authority further says that his parents were still living and would not allow him to give up his princely amusements and pleasures and be a Sanyasi. His mother, an affectionate woman as she was, came to him and said, "Vardhamana, Prince, you are still a young man; you have never been exposed even to the light of the sun; how will you bear the scorching rays of the sun?

Your delicate body and mild limbs will not bear the hardships of strict Digambara Diksha, you must live with your parents in the Royal Palace and help your father in the management of his kingdom".

But Mahavira would not now be kept back and explained to his mother that the world is like an illusion in which we short-sighted mortals see things different from what they are. He told her that every man, after passing the life of a Shravaka should leave the Raga and become a Sanyasi so that he may attain Nirvana. Through his remonstrances his mother, though with some reluctance, gave her consent, and Mahavira became a Muni in his thirtieth year.

Decision to Renounce the World

From the Shvetambara point of view, he had thought of renouncing the world several times, but his devotion to his old parents and the love of his young wife stood in his way. When his parents died, then he 'perceived with his supreme unlimited knowledge that the time of his Renunciation had come.' But his elder brother would not allow him to do so. Vira, "said he, "the deaths of our parents are still fresh in our memories; your leaving us this time would simply render our bereavement more unbearable and painful. "Mahavira lived for two years more in the palace with his brother and after that time with the consent of those in power entered the spiritual career and thus fulfilled his promise in his thirtieth year".

Now from both these sources we learn that Mahavira became a Muni in his thirtieth year only with this difference that from the Digambara point of view his parents were living at that time and the idea of Renunciation came suddenly to him, while from the Shvetambara point of view his parents were dead and he was brooding upon the idea all along.

Further they agree in asserting that this took place on the tenth day of the latter half of Margashirsha (Magsir). When he determined to renounce the world, he began to distribute his wealth which according to the Acharanga-sutra, amounted to three hundred and eighty-eight corers and eighty lakhs of gold. This appears to be somewhat exaggerated. However, it is possible that he might have distributed his wealth among his subjects.

The authority quoted above further says that he fasted for two days and a half before leaving his home. On the tenth day of the latter half of Magsir in the afternoon he left his palace and "marched to a place outside the Kshatriya part of his capital Kundalpura, being carried on his palanquin, Chandraprabha, which only a thousand men can carry, and being followed on his way by a train of all kinds of men raising a shout of victory and praising him with swift and soft words". The place to which he was carried and where he performed his first penance was a park known as the Sarthi Khanda according to the Digambaras and Gnatri Shanda or the Shandavana of the Gnatris according to the Shvetambaras. There he had his palanquin stopped. A special throne, known as the Pandushila or the five daises placed one over the other, each of the upper one being somewhat smaller than the lower one so as to make one able to climb above, was erected there.

This was ornamented, surrounded on all sides by garlands and had a sandal or an Ashokan tree over it. Mahavira took his seat upon this dais below the sandal tree, took off his ornaments, garlands and finery, etc. and entered the state of houselessness. He then renounced the twenty-four Parigrahas "or the attachments and assumed the twenty-eight Miil-gunas"' or the chief qualities of a monk.

Thus he adopted the holy conduct of Jaina Nirgrantha Muni. Then followed a very bold and a trying ceremony known as the Keshalochana ceremony which, as is the custom, requires a man who wishes to enter the spiritual order of the Jaina Munis, to "pluck out with his right and left (hands) on the right and left (sides of his head) his hair in five handfuls". The process is not of cutting or shaving the hair of the head as is the custom with the Hindu Sanyasis, but it is of plucking it out in handfuls. No doubt it requires a great courage and a strong will to do it and only those can do it who have no love with their flesh and bones, who are really disgusted with the world and who have completely mastered their passions. It is said that if a man hesitates from doing so at the time of the ceremony, he is disqualified to enter the sacred order. Obviously the custom is a trial of a man's courage and fortitude, and Mahavira is said to have passed it very successfully.

Hard Life of a Muni

He tore out the hair of his head without shrinking from the severe trial. It is also said that Mahavira possessed the Manha paryaya Oyan at this time. Then he paid obeisance to all the Siddhas who had attained Nirvana before him, and then formed the following resolution: I shall for twelve years neglect my body and abandon the care of it; I shall with equanimity bear, undergo, and suffer all calamities arising from divine powers, men or animals. He now reached the period in the life from which he begans to lead that houseless and hard life of a Jaina Muni in which he had to travel from place to place, except in the rainy season, all the eight months of summer and winter, preaching and teaching the people as he travelled, and performing severe bodily mortification for the destruction of the karmas and the attainment of kevalgyan. A very interesting and precise description of this part of his life is given in the Jaina Shastras mentioning the places which he visited and where he preached to the people the doctrine of Jainism during the couise of his travels through the greater part of India. Though both the sources of our information, the Digambaras and the Shvetambaras, declare that he travelled and performed penance for twelve years before the attainment of Kevalgyan, yet there is much discrepancy between the accounts given by the two.

Thus the Acharanga-sutra says that Mahavira, soon after his Diksha or "the Renunciation" and after having formed the resolution of leading a devoted life of a Jaina Muni, neglecting his body, arrived in the village of Kummara, and then began his travels from that place. It does not say anything about the places which he visited.

The Kalpasutra does not mention his first visit to Kummar; but it says that he stayed the first Chaturmasa or the rainy season of four months in Asthika-grama,''' three rainy seasons in Champa and Phristi-champa, and the rest of the eight in Vaisali and Vanijagrama. But this does not contradict the fact of his going to Kummar. It is possible that Mahavira might have first visited Kummar and then commenced his travels beginning with his first rainy season stay at Asthikagrama. Travelling for the Jaina Munis is prohibited for four months of the rainy season for fear of killing the insects and such other small creatures as are seen specially in that season and thereby committing Hinsa which is strictly to be avoided by the Jainas. In compliance with this Agya (order)

Mahavira had to stay at one place during the rainy seasons and thus the fact of his staying in different places in different rainy seasons as given by the Kalpasutra is possible. Let us now see what the Digambara Granthas say about this. In the Mahavira Purana we read that he did not attain the fourth Gyan just at the time of his renunciation. Just after his renunciation he performed constant meditation for six months in which he had to be quite motionless.

Still he did not attain the fourth kind of knowledge. He had to undergo bodily mortification several times before he got it. At the end of six months he is said to have gone to a place called Kulpura.

Kuladhipa, the ruler of that place, paid his respect to his venerable guest; and it is at this place that Mahavira had his first Parana or meal at the end of a fast of six months. From this place he went to the city of Dashapura. Kula, the King of that place, came to see him and having gone round him three times and having washed his feet with his own hands offered him milk and rice for his breakfast.

Having partaken of his hospitalities, Mahavira returned to the forest. He then visited several places and then began to perform twelve kinds of penances. Through this he obtained eight kinds of Riddhis and many kinds of Siddhis. There he had to bear the twenty-two Parishahas. He then observed the five Mahavritas, the five Samitis, the three Guptees and the eighty-four Uttara Gunas. He again visited several places. Once he went to Ujjain and there began his penance at a cemetery. Here a test of his perseverance was made by a certain Rudra, who, being struck with Mahavira's wonderful power of bearing bodily pain and of forbearance, at last came to liim and asked his pardon for the mischief he was intending to do him. We shall give this anecdote later on. From Ujjain, Mahavira went to Kaushambi,''' and then again returned to the forest and entered his self-meditations. It was now that he attained the fourth, the Manhparyaya Gyan. Then he is said to have observed the vow of silence for twelve years and to have performed severe penance. This shows that Mahavira performed his penance for twelve years at one place and the above mentioned travels were made before this time. This fact brings us to an unexpected difficult. We have already learnt that Mahavira renounced the world on the tenth day of the first half of Magsir in his thirty-first year, i.e. when he was thirty years, seven months and twenty-seven days old. He is then said to have performed penance for six months. So that, before commencing his meditations he was about thirty years and two months old, he was in his thirty-second year when he began his Dhyana.

Twelve Year Stay

He is said to have remained in his Dhyana for twelve years. This shows that at the time of attaining Kevalgyan he was about forty-three years and two months old, i.e. he attained Kevalgyan in his forty-fourth year. But it is further stated that it was on the tenth day of the latter half of Vaishakha when he was forty-two years old, i.e. he obtained Kevalgyan in his forty-third year.

Thus there is a difference of about one year between the two computations. Moreover, this does not take into account the time for which he travelled before entering his Dhyana. However, this difficulty can be overcome by supposing that Mahavira's renunciation took place in his thirtieth year and not when he was thirty years old. It was what perhaps the Digambara Acharyas meant to indicate.

Further, we learn from Bhagawati that Mahavira met Gosala two years after his Renunciation at a place called Nalanda, near Rajgriha, and the two ascetics lived together for six years in Paniyabhumi. Now this is not consistent with the facts given above. According to Kalpasutra, Mahavira went to Paniyabhumi after his obtaining Kevalgyan and stayed there only" for one rainy season.

There is a further discrepancy between the two authorities about the mode of his life during these years. In the Kalpasutra it is said that, after his Renunciation, Mahavira, wore clothes for a year and a month, and after that time he walked about naked. On the other hand, Mahavira Purana says that he had abandoned the twenty-four Parigrahas, and as clothes were one of them, he had to abandon them too.

After the end of his twelve years' penance he obtained Kevalgyan. Both the Digambaras and the Shvetambaras assert that this took place in his forty-third year on the tenth day of the latter half of Vaishakha near a place called "Grimbhakgrama" on the northern bank of the river Rijkult not very far from Parasnatha hills. They also say that this took place in the field of a certain farmer Samaga or Samaka. Mahavira at that time was sitting upon a Ratna Shila below a Sal tree in a squatting position with joined heels, exposing himself to the heat of the sun. He had to perform severe meditation there at the end of which, having destroyed the four Ghatiya Karmas, he reached the highest knowledge and intuition called Kevala, which is infinite, supreme, unobstructed, complete and full.

Thirty Year Wandering and Preaching

Now, it was the end of the second great period in the worldly career of Lord Mahavira. In the beginning of this period of twelve years he was a Sanyasi, disgusted with the world, determined to renounce it and attain the ever-lasting life of bliss and happiness, Nirvana, by a constant study of his Self and by performing severe bodily mortifications or Yoga.

At the end of this period he was in the full realisation of his hope, a Jina or a conqueror of the Karmas, the eight great enemies of the soul, and a Kevalin, that is, an omniscient lord comprehending all objects; he could know all conditions of the world and the thoughts of men. His knowledge pervaded all things; and by reflecting on his self and the world he had reached the highest intuition and knowledge. Such was our Lord Mahavira as we find him in the beginning of the third great period in his life. From this begins the third great act in his life.

This period comprises thirty long years of travels and preachings. He having known the great Law, proceeds to teach the same to all the human beings in this world. The whole of this period was spent in travelling and preaching except in the rainy seasons when for fear of killing small creatures and thereby committing hinsa he had to suspend his mission and to pass four months in one place under the patronage of some mighty chief. In fact, it was a life of hard work and severe austerities. He passed it 'in teaching his religious system and organising his order of ascetics', which as we shall see later on, was patronised by the mighty Kings of northern India. Mahavira was convinced of the necessity of his penances in the last twelve years of his life and did not think his years wasted, for he knew that it was through his penances that he had obtained the nine avdhis and the Ananta Chatushtaya.

It may be remarked here that there is not much difference between the accounts of this period as given by the Digambara and the Shvetambara Acharyas. The difference, if any, is of details rather than that of main outlines. Before commencing his travels there is one fact worthy of note.

First Pupil

Soon after his obtaining Kevalgyan, Mahavira was visited by Gautama Tandrabhuti who became his first pupil and was raised to the position of the head Ganadhara or a Chief Pontiff. His story is one of great interest, and we will give it later on. He followed his master for the last thirty years of his life and obtained Kevalgyan at the very time when Mahavira attained Nirvana. Mahavira began by first preaching to Gautama, then to the people around him, and then he began his travels.

Long Tours

He travelled through many parts of India, and preached the high doctrines of Jainism and Nirvana to people professing different creeds and religions. It was his earnest desire that people should give up their wrong beliefs and follow the true path to happiness. He preached on both the sides of the Ganges. First he preached in Magadha and the country round Kundalpura, where he was received with due greeting.

From Magadha he proceeded to Behar where he visited Shravasti, Vaishasti and many other places. He is said to have extended his travels as far as the foot of the Himalayas. In the Kalpasutra a list is given containing the names of the places where he passed his rainy-seasons. According to that authority "he stayed four rainy seasons in Vaisali and Vanijagrama', fourteen in Rajgriha and the suburb of Nalanda, six in Mithila, two in Bhadrika, one in Alabhika, one in Paniyabhumi, one in Shravasti, and the one and the last in Papa in King Hasthipa's office of the writers."

Now we see that some of these names do not occur in the Mahavira Purana; but there is not much difference. There it is also mentioned that he travelled and preached throughout the countries of northern India. In Videha he was patronised by Chetaka, the ruling chief of that country.

Kunika, the King of Anga, also welcomed the great preacher. He is said to have gone even to Kaushambi. Shataneeka, the ruler of the place, had heard much about his preachings and severe penances. He paid high reverence to the great preacher and entered his holy order. During these thirty years, Mahavira is said to have converted to Jainism Magadha, Bihar, Prayag, Kaushambi, Champapuri and many other powerful states in the north of India. But the place where he spent a large part of his life and where he was much loved by the people was Rajgriha, the then metropolis of Magadha.

Shrenika, the powerful King of that place, was one of the greatest champions of Jainism and a staunch follower of Mahavira. They are said to have met each other under very auspicious circumstances. When Mahavira went to Rajgriha he put up at Mount Vipulachala in the vicinity of the country. King Shrenika, hearing the happy news of the arrival of the great preacher in his capital, went to see him with all his ministers and whole of his army. He was charmed with the divine splendour of the Lord and of Samosaran or the great religious assemblage. Having paid his due greetings, he took his seat in the gallery reserved for men. He is said to have put sixty thousand questions to Mahavira and all of them were answered by Gautama Indrabhuti at the command of his master. To our great misfortune no account, not even a very small one, has been left of this interesting discussion. Shrenika was satisfied with the answers and entered the holy order of our Lord. It is said that Gautama also related the previous births of Shrenika and his relations.

Some few remarks may be made here upon Mahavira's method of preaching. He did not travel from place to place like an ordinary Sadhu unaccompanied by any one. On the other hand he was followed by many men who had entered his order. His order was known as the Samosaran. This consisted of about fourteen thousand Munis according to both the Digambaras and the Shvetambaras.

Where-ever they went a magnificent hall of audience was erected for them, containing many galleries for different orders of men. They had among them many Arjikas or nuns too. The pillars of the hall were set with jewels and Mahavira used to sit upon a costly throne of diamonds and rubies and pearls. Such was the Samosaran, they say, in which Mahavira used to preach wherever he went.

It is said that Mahavira preached to the people in his Anakshari language 'which was unintelligible to the people. Gautama, who was specially sought for this purpose, explained it to them in Magadhi.

Another thing worthy of note is his doctrine of conversion. He paid no regard to caste or section. His order was open to all kinds of men who would hear him and profess the doctrines of Jainism. Gautama Indrabhuti, the head of the order, was a Brahmin at first. We thus see that Mahavira converted men of all castes to Jainism.

Thus travelling from place to place, with the whole of his order of ascetics, preaching the Karma philosophy to the people, and converting countries after countries to Jainism under the mighty patronage of the Kings of those countries, Mahavira passed the last thirty years of his life.

Widespread Travels

From this analysis of the various kingdoms and republics of Eastern India, it would appear that Mahavira's reformed church gained followers practically all over the vast stretches of the country. The references in the Jaina texts enable us to draw a complete map of Lord Mahavira's travels and to recount the names of some of his prominent followers during the period of his propagation of the faith. The following is the list of the places where he stayed for the successive rainy seasons after the attainment of *Kevala-Jnana*.

It has been stated above that Mahavira attained the *Kevala* while sitting in meditation in a field outside the town *Jrmbhikagrama* and that he made his first converts and established the *Sangha* at a *Samavasarana* near the place of *Somilacarya's Yajna*.

From there the Lord proceeded to *Rajgrha,* the capital of *Magadha,* where he initiated the Princes *Meghakumar* and Nandisena into the order of monks, gained numerous lay followers including *Sulsa, Abhayakumar,* and the King Srenika (Bimbisara) himself. The first rainy season he spent at Rajgrha.

After the rains were over, the Lord turned towards Videha, and passing through many villages ultimately reached Kundagrama, his birth place. The town of Kundagrama seems to have been divided into two settlements, a Ksatriyakunda where Mahavira's father had lived and a *Brahminakund* where lived *Devananda,* Mahavira's Brahmin foster-mother and her husband by name Rsabhadatta. Mahavira made his stay in Brahminakund and there converted to his order the Brahmin Rsabhadatta and his wife Devananda. It was on this occasion that on the sight of Mahavira Devananda had that sight of Mahavira Devananda had that sudden material emotion to which reference has been made earlier in this book. Another important convert at Kundagrama was the Ksatriya Jamali who joined the order with his five hundred companions. This Jamali later on organised a schism in the Jaina church. From Kundagrama Mahavira proceeded to Vaisali, where he passed the second rainy season.

On the completion of the 2nd rainy season the Lord proceeded towards the Vatsa country. The ruler of Vatsa, Satanika, had died and the kingdom was administered by the widow, Queen Mirgavati, on behalf of her minor son Udayana. At Kausambi, the capital of Vatsa, Mahavira held a public audience and converted to his order the Queen Mirgavati and an aunt of the King, by name Jayanti. From there, he proceeded further to Kosala, where at Sravasti a number of sympathisers and followers were gained for the Jaina faith. The rainy season was passed at Vanijyagrama in Videha, to which Mahavira returned from Kosala. At Vanijyagrama in Videha, to which Mahavira returned from Kosala. At Vanijyagrama, the merchant *Ananda* and his wife *Sivananda* accepted the Sramanopasak vows. *Ananda* became one of the loyal and highly trusted followers of the Lord.

From Vanijyagrama Mahavira repaired at the end of the rainy season to Magadha, where after roaming about the kingdom for several moths he settled down for the rainy Season at Rajgrha.

Among the new converts this year there were the merchants Dhanya and Salibhadra.

Campa was the next place, which the Lord visited on the completion of the rainy season. Here he converted the Prince Mahacandra Kumar. From Campa he proceeded to the province of Sindhu Sauvira, where Udayana was ruling over Vitabhaya. It has been already explained how this Udayana was related to Mahavira through his wife Prabhavati. The journey to Sindhu Sauvira was very difficult, involving travel in desert areas and hard country; but Mahavira went to the place in order to give to King Udayana *Diksa* as a "*Sramanopasaka*". Returning from Sindhu-Sauvira, he spent the rainy season at Vanijyagrama.

After the rainy season, a visit was paid to Benares and certain other places in the kingdom of Kasi, where numerous followers were gained for the Jaina church. For the rainy season, the Lord returned to Rajgrha. At Rajgriha he spent a highly fruitful season King Srenika had proclaimed that he would personally undertake to feed and otherwise overlook the dependents of anybody who desired to join Mahavira's order of monks. As a result of this proclamation, thousands of people joined the order and Mahavira stayed on at Rajgriha giving *Diksa to* the comers for sometime even after the finishing of the rainy season. Enraged, probably at the success of Lord Mahavira's ministry, Gosala Mankhaliputra, of whom mention has been made already, began his public criticism of Mahavira's faith, although unsuccessfully, in the course of an argument with Ardraka, a monk of Mahavira's order. The rainy season was spent by Mahavira again at Rajgriha.

Having spent two rainy seasons at Rajgrha, Mahavira proceeded towards Vatsa country, visiting on the way Alabhiya in the kingdom of Kasi. At Kausambi he converted Queen Mirgavati and several Queens of Canda Pradyota. From here he proceeded towards Videha, and spent the rainy season at Vaisali.

On the completion of the rainy season he went to Mithila, thence to Kakandi, Sravasti, and the republics of the west, and made numerous conversations. The rainy season was passed at Vanijyagrama.

From here Mahavira proceeded after the rainy season to Magadha, where there was the famous meeting between his followers and the monks of Prasva's order. As a result of discussion of the several points of difference between the practices of the two orders, Mahavira's leadership of the Jaina community was accepted by all. The rainy season was spent at Rajgrha.

From Rajgrha, Mahavira repaired at the end of the season to the Western kingdoms, but returned to Vanijyagrama for spending the next rainy season.

The next year was marked by the occurrence of the first schism in the community, when Jamali separated from the Lord with a small band of his companions. Mahavira himself repaired to Kausambi, then to Rajgrha, where he spent the next rainy season; then after the end of the rains to Campa, where after the death of Srenika, his son, Kunik, had transferred his capital. From Campa he turned towards Mithila and spent the next rainy season there.

It was when Mahavira proceeded to Sravasti after the rainy season that he had his famous encounter with Gosala, who after separating from Mahavira had continued to hang about the city claiming among his followers the potter-woman *Halahala* and the minstrel Ayampul. Gosala had of course, claimed for himself the status of a Tirthankara, so that arose the anomaly of two *Tirthankaras* staying at the same town. When questioned about it, Mahavira denounced Gosala and stated in a public audience that he was not a Tirthankara nor a true believer, whereupon got enraged, and visited Mahavira for a religious discussion. The discussion was, of course, inconclusive, but two disciples of Mahavira who intervened were burnt up by his fiery power. Gosala attempted to burn Mahavira himself, but was unsuccessful. The after-effects of Gosala's fiery attack were, however, felt by Mahavira and he suffered great pain later on. The rainy season was passed at Mithila.

From Mithila, Mahavira went towards Kosala-Pancala, visiting Sravasti, Ahicchatra, Hastinapur and other towns, and returned for the next rainy season to Vanijyagrama. The last few rainy seasons were spent at Rajgrha, Vanijyagrama, Vaisali, Vaisali again, Rajgrha Nalanda, Vaisali, Mithila, Rajgrha, Nalanda, Mithila, Mithila again, Rajgrha, until at the age of 72 he attained Nirvana on Kartika Amavasya at Pavapuri.

Many a Disciple

Mahavira succeeded in attracting a large number of disciples, both men and women, and organised his community into four orders. Chief among his followers were fourteen thousand monks, at the head of whom stood the eleven Ganadharas, and thirty-six thousand nuns, at the head of whom was Candana. These included "three hundred sages who knew the fourteen Purvas, who though not Jinas came very near them, thirteen hundred sages who were possessed of the *Avadhi*-knowledge and superior qualities; seven hundred Kevalins; seven hundred who could transform themselves; five hundred sages of mighty intellect; four hundred professors who were never vanquished in disputes; seven hundred male and fourteen hundred female disciples who reached perfection; and eight hundred sages in their last birth," During Mahavira's own lifetime nine of the Ganadharas attained Kevalajnana. Two survived him, Gautama and Sudharma, and as Gautama attained Kevala-*jnana* just as Mahavira breathed his last and obtained *Nirvana*, Sudharma became the head of the Order.

From Sudharma it is possible to trace a whole of succession of the leaders of the order right up to the present time. Mahavira's third order consisted of laymen. They were householders who did not actually renounce the world but who could and did keep his rules in a modified form, while their alms supported the professed monks. As Mrs. Stevenson says, the genius for organisation which Mahavira possessed is shown in nothing more clearly than in the formation of this and the order of laywomen.

The laymen are said to have numbered during Mahavira's lifetime one hundred and fifty-nine thousand men; according to the Digambara version the number given is one hundred thousand; the laywomen numbered three hundred and fifty-eight thousands.

In one of the well-known Jaina Agamas, *Uvasagadasao*, the names of ten of the more important lay followers of Mahavira are given. Vanijyagrama, Campa, Baranasi, Alabhiya (or Alai), Kampilyapura, Polasapura, Rajagrha and Sravasti are mentioned as the important ones along the places that were visited by the Venerable Ascetic Mahavira. The town of Campa had near it the shrine of Purnabhadra, Vanijyagrama, the shrine called Dutipalasa.

Baranasi the Kosthaka shrine; Alabhiya, the garden called Sankhavana; Kampilyapura, the garden Sahasramravana: Polaspura, a garden known by the name of Sahasramravana; Rajgrha, a shrine called Gunasil; and Sravasti, the Moshthaka shrine. In Vanijyagrama the great lay disciples of Mahavira and the lay supporters of his order were Ananda and his wife Sivananda; in Campa; Kamadeva and his wife Bhadra; in Baranasi. Culanipiya and his wife Syama, and Suradeva and his wife Dhanya; in Alabhiya, Cullasataka and his wife Bahula; in Kampilyapura, Kundakolita and his wife Pusya; in Polasapura, Sakadalaputra and his wife Agnimltra; in Rajgrha, Mahasataka; and in Sravasti, Nandinipriya and his wife Asvini, and Salatipiya and his wife Phalaguni. These lay disciples are all mentioned as persons of opulence and influence, and as those noted for their piety and devotion. Ananda of Vanijyagrama is described as householder who "possessed a treasure of four *kror* measures of gold deposited in a safe place, a capital of *four* kror measures of gold put out on interest, a well stocked estate of the value of four *kror* measures of gold, and four herds, each herd consisting of ten thousand herds of cattle". He "was a person whom many Kings and Princes and merchants made it a point to refer to, and to consult, on many affairs and matters needing advice in short, on all sorts of business. He was also the main pillar, as it were, of his own family, their authority, support, mainstay and guide. In short, he was a cause of prosperity to whatever business he was concerned with". Even the Buddhist texts bear testimony to numerous rich householders being among he lay disciples of Mahavira.

The Enlightenment

After Gosala's withdrawal, Mahavira continued his wanderings and practice of asceticism alone. Gosala proclaimed himself a Jina and started collecting followers after acquiring supernormal powers, but Mahavira persisted in his search. From Siddhartha grama he went to Vaisali and thence to Vanijyagrama, where he was visited by Ananda, a wealthy merchant of the place and then travelled to Sravasti (which has been identified with Sahet-Mahet on the south bank of the river *Tapti*) for his tenth *chaturmas*.

On the expiry of the tenth *chaturmas* began the sad episode of *Sangamaka,* the tempter-god, who made his appearance and began his attack, which in its various forms lasted for about six months. The eleventh chaturmas was spent at Vaisali and the twelfth at Campa. The interval between the eleventh and twelfth was marked by the famous *abhigrah* at Kausambi, which took five months and twenty-five days to be fulfilled and meant a forced fast for Mahavira of this duration.

During the thirteenth year, in the second month of summer, in the fourth fortnight, the light (fortnight) of *Vaiskha,* on its tenth day, called *Suvrata,* in the *Muhurta* called *Vijaya,* while the moon was in conjunction with the asterism *Uttarapalguni,* when the shadow had turned towards the east and the first wake was over, outside the town *Jrmbhikagrama,* on the northern bank of the river *Rjupalika,* in the field of the householder Samaga, under a *Sala* tree, in a squatting position with joint heels exposing himself to the heat of the Sun, with the knees high and the head low, in deep meditation, in the midst of abstract meditation, he reached the complete and full, the unobstructed, unimpeded, infinite and supreme, best knowledge and intuition, called *Kevala*".

Kevalin

On the attainment of *Kevala jnana,* says the *Kalpautra,* the Venerable Ascetic Mahavira became omniscient. "He knew and saw all conditions of the worlds, of gods, men and demons; whence they came, whither they are born as men or animals or became gods or hellish, beings, the ideas, the thoughts of their mind, the food, doings, desires, the open and secret deeds of all the livings in the whole world; the Arhat, for whom there is no secret, knew and saw all conditions of all living beings in the world, what they thought, spoke, or did at any time".

It is notable that frequently in the course of audience and in his preaching after this great event he would refer to the earlier existence of a person or what one was going to be in the next birth; this extended vision of the past, resent and future became obviously an essential attribute of Mahavira's personality. Even the Buddhist texts always refer to him as possessing such vision.

It would be helpful in this connection to understand the Jaina theory of knowledge. According to Jainism, consciousness is the very essence of the soul, not a mere characteristic of it. The soul (*jeev*) can know unaided everything direct and exactly as it is. Of consciousness, there are two manifestations, perception (*darshan*) and knowledge (*gyan*). The former is simple apprehension, the latter conceptual knowledge. In the former details are not perceived, in the latter they are; *darshan* is a perception of generalities (*samanya*) of things without particularities (*vishaish*). There can be no *jeeva* without consciousness or cognition, as there can be no consciousness without a *jeeva*. Incidentally, this is a point which illustrates the distinction of Jainism from Buddhism, where not the mind but only states of consciousness are admitted as real. The fact that the knowledge which a *jeeva* actually has is fragmentary in its character is due to the obstruction caused by Karma, which interferes with its power of cognition. The *Karmas* which obscure the different kind of *jnana* are called the knowledge- obscuring (*jnanavaranr*) those which obscure the different varieties of *darsan* are called the perception-obscuring (*darshanavaranr*) karmas. The different kinds of *jnana* recognised by Jainism are: (1) matigyan which is ordinary cognition obtained by normal means of sense perception. It includes remembrance (*smriti*), recognition (*Prtyabhigya*), induction based upon observation (*tark*), and deductive reasoning (*anuman*) and it is acquired by means of the senses and mind; (2) *shrut* or testimony, i.e. knowledge derived though signs, symbols, or word; (3) *Avadhi* which is direct knowledge of things even at a distance of time and space. It is knowledge by clairvoyance, limited by and coextensive with the material object of the knowledge; (4) Manpryadirect knowledge of the thoughts of others, a telepathic knowledge of others" minds; and (5) *Kaival* perfect knowledge comprehending all substances and their modifications. The last three categories of knowledge are direct in the sense that they are derived without the medium of senses and mind.

Darshan or Perception is of four kinds; perception through visual sensations (*chakshudarshan*), perception through non-visual sensations, perception through the faculty of Avadhi or clairvoyance (*Avadhidarshan*), and lastly *Kevaldarshan* perception through Kevala or infinite perception, which is unlimited and apprehends all general reality.

All accounts of Mahavira's life are agreed that he possessed a highly active and clever mind from the very beginning. He is mentioned to have possessed from his very childhood the *Mati, Sruta and Avadhhi jnana;* the*Svetambara* books say that he was in possession of *Abhogika-Jnana,* which is inferior to the *Avadhi* knowledge but is essentially of the same class. Direct knowledge of the thoughts, he obtained while renouncing the world and adopting the career of an ascetic. The *Kalpasutra* refers to his having perceived with "his supreme unlimited knowledge and intuition" that the time of his renunciation had come. Now he came to acquire Kevala-*jnana, Kevala-darsana,* and approximation to the perfect condition of the soul. Perfect knowledge is completely free from doubt (*sanshey*), perversity (*viprya*), and indefiniteness (*andhyavaseya*). It is absolute apprehension without media, 'soul-knowledge," knowledge par excellence which is higher than all the other varieties of normal and supernormal knowledge. Such knowledge, of course, comprehends knowledge of the soul itself, for contrary to the *Nyaya-Vaisesika* theory which believes that knowledge reveals only external relations but not itself, the Jaina *Siddhanta* asserts that in knowing any object the soul knows itself simultaneously. After the attainment of *Kevala-jnana* a *jeeva* may lead an active life, but the activity would not taint him, would exert no fresh *Karmic* influence of the obstructive type upon the soul. During the period between Enlightenment and actual death the person is termed as "*Arhati*" at actual liberation he becomes a "*siddha*". The Stage of Arhat-ship corresponds roughly to the Hindu ideal of *jivanmukti.*

The concept of such absolute and perfect knowledge may not be unique to the Jainas but their ways of attainment of knowledge are certainly unique. The *Upanisadic* seers drew a distinction between lower knowledge and higher knowledge, the higher knowledge being conceived as the knowledge by which alone the imperishable being is reached. The Greek philosophers also drew a similar distinction between Doxa and Episteme, between opinion and truth (or knowledge). Plato, in his Republic, brought out the distinction by means of a parable. "Imagine human beings living in a sort of underground den, which has a mouth wide open towards the height, and behind them a breastwork such as marionette players might use for a screen; and there is a way beyond the breastwork along which passengers are moving, holding in their hands various works of art, and among them images of men and animals, wood and stone, and some of the passers of talking and others silent. They see nothing but the shadows which the fire throws on the wall of the caves, to these they give names; and if we add an echo which returns from the wall, the voices of passengers will seem to proceed from the shadows. They are ourselves, and to us, brought up in the limited-atmosphere of such a den from our childhood, "truth is just nothing but the shadows of the images". But the released from the prison of the den and compelled suddenly to go up, we can gradually have a clear view of the Truth, perceiving at first only shadows and reflections in the water, then recognising the moon and the stars, and beholding finally the sun "in his own proper place". Thus, their knowledge will come to have clearness of certainty and rescue itself from the cloudiness of opinion".

Incidentally, this parable of Plato also presents a theory of knowledge, which is wholly akin to the Jain theory. Knowledge is not something which has to be put into the soul and which was not there before. "The power is already in the soul; and as the eye cannot turn from darkness to light without the whole body, so too when the eye of the soul is turned round, the whole soul must be turned from the world of generation into that of being".

Jina

The attainment of *Kevala-Jnana* was achieved by Mahavira after a prolonged practice of profound meditations and austerities for over twelve years, and this entitled him to be called the *Jina* (conqueror). It may be mentioned that Buddha also led a life of austerities of six years, but that he thought these years wasted and his penance's useless for attaining his end; while Mahavira was not only convinced of the necessity of his penance's and thought them essential for obtaining perfection, but persevered in some of them even after becoming a Tirthankara. In Mahavira's view, "the full blaze of omniscience" in the *jiva* is impossible of accomplishment without the practice of a regulated course of self-discipline and the conquest of *karmas.* The Karma in Jaina *Siddhanta* is recognised as a substantive force, matter in a subtle form, which builds up a special body, called *Karmana-*

sarira and which retards the inherent radiance of the soul. "As heat can unite with iron and water with milk, so *karma* unites with the soul". The kind of matter fit to manifest *karma* fills all cosmic space, and it has the peculiar property of developing the effects of merit and demerit. Except in final release the soul is always in connection with matter, and the Karma forms the link between the two.

The *Jaina Siddhanta* recognises eight kinds of *karma*. (1) *Gyanavaranr* which obscures right knowledge of detail and prevents our receiving mental illumination. It may not only impede us in gaining true knowledge, but may actually give rise to false and hurtful knowledge and misuse of intellectual powers. (2) *Darshanavaranr* which obscures right perception and prevents our having general comprehension of things. (3) *vaidniye* which obscures the bliss-nature of the soul and causes us to experience either the sweetness of worldly pleasures *sukhvaidniye* or the bitterness of misery (*Dukhvaidniye*). In the Jaina view, it is not only evil action but also good action that has to be worked off before one can obtain liberation. (4) *mohneeya* which obscures the right attitude of the soul towards faith and right conduct and prevents us from speaking and thinking clearly, which in short "bemuses all our faculties". (5) *Ayoo* which determines the length of time a *jiva* must spend in the form with which is *Karma* has endowed him. (6) *nam* which determines the peculiar body of the soul with its general and special qualities and faculties. (7) *Gotra* which determines the nationality, caste, family, social standing, etc. (8) *antray* which causes such energy in the soul as obstructs the performance of good action when there is a desire to do so. It causes hindrances in life and has the effect of "muddling away every opportunity that life offers". These *Karmas* are classified into the *Ghatii*, which are particularly obstructive to the accomplishment of the natural perfections of the pure soul and which can only be destroyed by great labour and effort, and the *Aghati*, which are not very injurious and can be more easily destroyed. The *Ghati karmas* are *gyanvaran, darshanavaranr, mohniye* and *antrayeand* once they are burnt up in the burning glow of austerities, the *Aghati* can be snapped as easily as a piece of burnt string.

This is clearly admitted in the analysis of the fourteen steps (*ghunrsthan*) by which a *jiva* is supposed to ascend to the state of liberation. The analysis of these stages through a developing soul passes is but one instance of "the amazing knowledge of human nature which *Jaina* ethics display". Deliverance is impossible so long as the soul is bound by and does not fully annihilate the *Ghati-karma*, but once freed from the *Ghati-karma* the soul may retain its connection for sometime with the *Aghati-kamras* without being effectively bound by them. In the ladder of the fourteen steps, the first step (*miyhyatv*) is when the soul is completely under the influence of *Karma* and does not know its true good at all. From the first step, either through the influence of the past good *karma* or in response to some external stimulus, the soul obtains a glimpse of the true faith and thus immediately rises to the fourth stage (*avirat*) when although unable to take those vows which help in the fight against *Karma*, it can, if it likes, control the grossest form of anger, conceit, intrigue and greed, the four *anantanubandhee kasayas*. In the absence of active effort to control these passions, there may be a falling back of the soul to the second stage (*sasvdan*) which is characterised by a very faint sense of discrimination between what is false and what is true, and from here to either further descent to the first stage or gradual ascent to the third *mishr* which typifies a state of uncertainty, one moment knowing the truth and the next doubting it. The second and the third steps are thus merely transitional and transitory; it is the fourth step, which is really stable after the first stage.

The distinguishing mark of the fourth stages is that the soul has belief in the path of liberation but is unable to observe the rules of conduct for attaining liberation; the thought-activity characterising this stage is that the soul has destroyed excessive anger, pride and greed but not entirely escaped from their influence. In this stage, the *Jiva* however develops the power of curbing anger (*Prasam*), the realisation that the world is evil (*sanvaig*), the capacity for non-attachment (*nirvaid*), compassion (anucampa) and true faith (astikya). In the fifth stage (*Daishvarti*) the desire to realise the objective by the proper regulation of conduct first manifests itself, and the individual takes partial vows, e.g. the vow not to drink intoxicant or eat flesh (*madyamanstyag*) or to keep all twelve vows of a householder

(*Shremanropasek*) or to maintain absolute chastity, etc. The sixth stage (*Premet*) can be ascended by a professed ascetic, who renounces all worldly objects, and who controls even the slight passions. But as yet the *jiva* remains slack in concentration. By further effort the soul mounts to the seventh stage (*Apremat*) when renouncing all carelessness, it becomes fully absorbed in spiritual contemplation. From the seventh stage onwards the path of ascent follows two different routes, (1) the route in which the several right-conduct-deluding *karmas* become quiescent and controlled, and (2) the route in which they get actually destroyed. Thus the eighth stage (*Apoorvkerenr*) marked by an absolute control or conquest of pride and consequently by an unusual intensification of the power of meditation and concentration. That is the beginning of the first *Sukla-dhyana* pure concentration and gives a joy to the *jiva* the like of which he has never experienced before. The ninth stage is marked by an absolute control or conquest of deceit and consequently, by a special thought activity of still greater purity. The tenth stage (*Sookshemsampraye*) is marked by an absolute control or conquest of greed the last of the great passions. From the tenth stage the soul that has followed the route of actual destruction of the *karmas* directly mounts to the twelfth stage which is characterised by complete freedom from all the *Ghati-karmas* and which inevitably leads to the attainment of *Kevala-jnana;* but the ascetic who has followed the route of merely controlling the karmas instead of destroying them has to pass through the eleventh stage (*Upshantmoh*) which is a really critical experience. The subsided *karma* may at any time "like a flood burst its dam, and force of its current may carry the soul far down the slope he has been climbing, depositing him on either the sixth or the seventh step, or even on the lowest".

There is no falling back from the twelfth stage, because the *Ghati-karmas* have already been destroyed; and although the *Aghati-karmas* still persist, they have little power to bind the soul and "can be snapped as easily as piece of burnt string". So limited the fact is the power of the *Aghati-karma* that at death a soul passes at once through the two remaining stages and enters *Moksa* without delay. The thirteenth stage (*Senyogikaiveli*) is that of a vibrating perfect soul, that is to say, when the soul has after the destruction of the obstructive *karmas*, obtained the *Kevala* but continues to retain its human body; and the fourteenth and last stage (*Ayogi kevali*) is that of the vibration-less perfect soul, that is to say, when the perfect soul is leaving its human body in order to proceed to *Moksa* there to reside for ever in perpetual peace and bliss above the land called *Siddhasila*.

Tirthankara

Mahavira was now in the Thirteenth stage of his spiritual career. He had purged away all his *Ghati-karmas* and had consequently attained *Kevala-jnana* and *Kevala-darsana*. Now he devoted himself to the noble task of the active propagation of the truth and for this purpose of organising the community or *Tirtha*, he assumed the role of the *Tirthankara*.

The difference between a *Tirthankara* and any other *Kevalin* consists in just this, that the *Tirthankara* is master of a special *Nama-Karma*, which gives him a position of peculiar respect and eminence and makes him responsible for the organisation and establishment of a *Sangha*. Most *Kevalins* in the *Sayogikevali* stage go about preaching truth; but it is-only a *Tirthankara* who forms the *Tirthas* (or fords) by means of which a *jiva* can cross this *samsara* over to the other side (i.e. *Moksa*). It was in the organisation of the *Jaina sangha* that the *Tirthankara* Mahavira showed his real abilities. He welded together into the *Sangha* the ascetic as well as the layman, and men as well as women, prescribed for all their respective duties, and provided for a rigid discipline and rigorous form off control. In the Buddhist *Sangha* laymen were not originally connected with the clergy: Buddha's church was a church of monks and nuns only and no attempt was ever made to organise a quasi-church of lay-brothers and lay-sisters, or to establish an organic relationship between the clergy and the laity. But Mahavira welded together the two sections of the Order, the clergy and the laity, and accorded to the latter a definite and honourable place in the ecclesiastical scheme and made it incumbent upon them, both as a duty and as an act of merit, to support the clergy by giving alms liberally. As there was a *de jure* relationship involved in the concept of the clergy, so was a *de jure* relationship involved in the concept of the laity; as there was definite procedure for the initiation of the monks and nuns, so a special procedure was prescribed for the initiation of lay disciples of the *Sramanopasaka* variety. Above all, the laity was enjoying to be exclusive in their loyalty and patronage. Intercourse with adherents of a rival creed was disapproved, as is clear from the following declaration made by Ananda, a newly converted disciple of Mahavira: "Truly, Reverend sir, it does not befit me from this day forward to praise and worship any man of a heretic community or any of the Devas or objects of reverence of heretic community or without being first addressed by them to address them or converse with them; or to give them or supply them with food and drink or delicacies or dainties except it be by the command of the King or the community or any powerful man or a deva or by the orders of one's elders or by the exigencies of living".

For initiation into the *Sangha*, a layman was required first to renounce five faults (*atichar*), first, doubt, secondly, the desire to belong to another faith, thirdly, misgivings about the reality of the fruits of *Karma (Vichikitsa)*, fourthly, praise of hypocrites (*Parprshansa*) and fifthly, all association with them (*Sansatvan*). That done, he was to take the twelve lay vows. (1) The vow never intentionally to destroy a *jiva* that has more than one sense. This vow would not prevent a King leading any army in defence of his kingdom; but it forbids the killing of weak creatures and of acting as agent provocateur. It forbids animal sacrifice. (2) The vow never to indulge in falsehood or exaggeration (*sthooolmrishavadviremenrh*). This vow enjoins commercial honesty and forbids rash speech, of secrets relating to one's wife, giving false evidence, forgery, etc. (3) The vow never to steal (*Sthooladetadanviremanr*), the vow including stealth from a house, highway-robbery, misappropriation of funds, etc. (4) the vow of chastity (*Savdaranstosh*) by which a man promises to be absolutely faithful to his own wife at all times and never to allow any evil thoughts in his own mind about other women. The vows may be infringed by such activity as evil talk, excessive sexual indulgence, match- making and match-brokerage, unfaithfulness before marriage, and consummating marriage with a girl before she has attained her puberty. (5) The vow of limitation of possessions (*parigreh parimanr*), by which a man promises that he will never allow himself to retain more than a certain fixed quantity of houses and fields, gold and silver, cash and corn, servants and cattle, furniture and plenishing. These five vows are called the five *Anuvratas* and they resemble in their subject matter the five great vows a monk takes. If layman keeps all these five vows and also abandons the use of intoxicants, animal food, and honey, he is entitled to be called a *Sravaka*. The next three vows are called the *Gunavratas*, for they help the keeping of the first five vows. (6) (*Digviriti*) which sets bounds to one's travels and thus helps to curtail sin by restricting the area in which one can sin. (7) (*Bhogopbhogenriman*) which imposes a limit on the number of things a man may use and is intended thus to help people to keep their vows against lying, covetousness and stealing. (8) (*Anarthdandvirti*) by which a man vows not to think evil of others, nor to persuade people to do evil, nor to be careless about keeping or using weapons. The keeping of these vows which need not to be taken by ascetics but only laymen, would help the curtailment of sin by limiting the motive for sinning.

The remaining four vows are called *Siksavratas*, for they tend to encourage the laity in the performance if their religious duties. By the 9th vow *samayik* a man promises to perform *Samayika*, that is to say, to spend at least forty eight minutes every day in meditation, thinking no evil of anyone, but being at peace with all the world, to meditate on what heights one's soul may reach. By the tenth vow (*daishviramanr*) he promises for one particular day to still further contract the limits he has undertaken not to transgress, possibly binding himself during that day not to go outside the village or the house, to have only one meal or to drink nothing but water.

The eleventh vow (*poshdopvas*) is of special significance as connecting the laity closely with the ascetics; it compels the layman to spend at least twenty-four hours every month as a monk, observing celibacy, and committing no sort of sin, touching neither food, water, fruit, betelnut, ornaments, scents, nor any sort of weapon. The twelfth vow (*Atithisanvibhag*) encourages the laity to support the ascetic community by giving food, water, etc.

A definite procedure for initiation was also prescribed. The person who is desirous of being initiated tells a *Guru*of his wish. The *guru* reads out he vows and gives him an instruction on each one and its infringements. The layman assents to the instruction and fixes the limits under various vows for himself. Every year he must confess to the ascetic who happens to be available the infractions of the vows and accept the penance given. The vows may be taken for the whole life or for a limited period of time, on the expiry of which they may be taken afresh.

As in the case of a *Sravaka,* so for an ascetic there is a definitely prescribed procedure for initiation (*prvrjya*) An ascetic is usually initiated into the order with the permission of his guardians after a certain period of probation, during which he receives preliminary training at the hands if a *guru,* which may last from several days to one or two years.

At the end of the probationary period, the novice is initiated into monkhood, the ceremony of initiation being fairly elaborate and highly solemn. After being led in a great procession, the candidate takes off his jewels and clothes, plucks his hair by the hand, and solemnly takes up the five great vows and the life of a homeless wanderer.

The five great vows of the ascetic are:

- *Ahimsa,* never to destroy any living thing. In order to keep this vow, the ascetic is expected to be careful in walking, watchful in speech so as to not give rise to quarrels or murders, and cautious in his whole daily conduct. He must be careful as to the alms he receives that they can contain no living insects, etc.
- *Asatya -tyaga,* never to indulge in untruthfulness. The five*bhavanas,* or strengthening clauses to this vow supply a remarkable psychological analysis of the causes which lead to untruthfulness. They condemn speech without deliberation, speech in anger, speech when moved by avarice, or by fear, and speech in fun. One should respect the vow of truthfulness by always avoiding jesting, greed, cowardice, and anger and by thinking before speaking.
- *Asteya vrata,* never to steal. A monk must ask permission of owner before occupying any one's house; he must repeat such a request from time to time. A junior monk must always show to his *guru* whatever he has received in alms and then eat it after receiving his permission.

- *Brahmacaryavrata,* to remain chaste always. A monk is enjoined not to talk about a woman, or look at the form of a woman, or live in the same building as a woman lives in. He must not recall to mind, the former amusement and pleasure woman afforded him when he lived in the world; nor must he eat or drink to excess, or partake of too highly spiced dishes.
- *Aparigraha vrata,* never to have attachment for anything or any person. "Renouncing liking for pleasant touch, taste, smell, from or word, and for all the objects of the five senses, renouncing hatred for unpleasant things, these are the ways to maintain the vow of *Aparigraha*".

Apart from the maintenance of these five great vows the discipline of the ascetic's daily life is very rigid. Getting up at about four o'clock, before sunrise, he performs the daily *pratikrmanr* which is a form of confession of the sins of the past night, then carries out *pratilaikhan* a daily search for any insect life that may be sheltering in his clothing, etc. and after that attends to the list of his morning duties, which include, preaching, begging for alms, auricular confession to the Guru, study of the scriptures and mediation. There are innumerable rules that should be observed when begging, and they differ from sect to sect but all sects agree in only taking what may be reasonably considered to be left over after the needs of the household have been satisfied, and in refusing things specially prepared for the ascetic, In the afternoon *pratilaikhan* is performed again and so the evening *pratikarmanr* which now is a confession of sins for the day.

The individual ascetic formed an integral part of the *Sangha,* which was given by the Master a Constitution and a code of laws. Dūring his own lifetime Mahavira attracted a large number of disciples, both men and women. He collected an excellent community of fourteen thousand monks, thirty six thousand nuns, one hundred and fifty nine thousand laymen and three hundred and fifty-eight thousand lay women. At the head of these were eleven *Gaadharas* or chief disciples. This was an important item in the organisation of the *Sangha*. Mahavira had seen in the case of Gosala what special temptations and dangers beset ascetics in their wandering life. He had made the life of his own ascetics fairly full. Unlike the Buddhist *Sramanas*, who had a lot of free time and were often guilty of indolence or indulged in dissension's, disputes and strifes, Mahavira's Nirgrantha ascetics had plenty of work to do by way of the practice of austerities, penance's and fasts, besides meditation and the daily routine of duties, to keep them engaged.

Anyhow, he insisted on his was the case with the Buddhist *sramanas*. But he also resolved to combat the degenerating tendencies inherent in all monastic orders by a strong organisation and detailed set of regulations, and above all, as we have mentioned above, by organically connecting it with the lay element in society. This gave to the Jaina *Sangha* "a roof in India which the Buddhists never obtained, and that roof firmly planted amongst the laity enabled Jainism to withstand the storm that drove Buddhism out of India".

The *Sangha* as well as the controlling *Ganadharas* and their succeeding *Acharya* were not law-makers in any sense of the term. The fundamental truths and the law were recognised to have been formally and finally enunciated by Lord Mahavira. The *Sangha* had only to apply and expound his regulations, and that was provided to be done by the general assembly of all the monks resident in a particular locality under the ultimate supervision of the Ganadhara or Acharya.

The procedure was likely to raise an insuperable problem, such as faced. Buddhism itself when its band of disciples grew into a large spiritual force preaching and begging throughout all India and even beyond it; the problem was to effectively administer the spiritual regency in church-government in which the centre of gravity lay within the circumference, within the small corps of brethren dwelling in the same circuit. The Jaina *Sangha* also rapidly grew, both in numbers and in the area of its activity. From Bihar its influence spread to *Kalinga* and from there presumably to South India on one side and to the Mathura, Gujarat and the Punjab on the other.

Yet the spiritual regency of the Jainas has continued to be administered right up to this day with an honesty, a rigour, and a desire not to lose grip of the fundamental truths enunciated by the Master, which is wholly antique in the annals of any religion with such long history.

The anxiety to stick to the original doctrine as closely has enabled Jainism to weather the storms that in India wrecked so many of the other faiths. "The inflexible conservatism of the Jaina community has probably been the chief cause of its survival during period of severe affliction; for there can be little doubt that the most important doctrines of the Jaina religion have remained practically unaltered since the first great separation in the time of Bhadrabahu, about 300 BC. And although a number of less vital rules concerning the life and practices of the monks and laymen, which we find recorded in the holy scriptures, may have fallen into oblivion or disuse, there is no reason to doubt that the religious life or the Jaina community is now substantially the same as it was two thousand years ago. It must be confessed from this that an absolute refusal to admit changes has been the strongest safeguard of the Jainas".

4

Ascetic Life of Mahavira

All biographies of Mahavira are agreed upon on one point, namely, that he led the life of a householder for thirty years. With what mental attitude this period of life was lived, of that we have no certain knowledge. Certain Digambara books suggest that Mahavira lived his life as a house-holder in a normal manner, taking a healthy interest in his environment and enjoying the many opportunities of work and play afforded to him by his exalted station in society, until all of a sudden in his thirtieth year he began to reflect and meditate and feeling dissatisfied with the prospect of an "unending mundane existence" made up his mind to renounce the world.

The Svetambara accounts, on the other hand, depict Mahavira as having been an unusually reflective lad from the very beginning. Even in his early youth he seems to have thought of renouncing the world, but he was always prevailed upon by his affectionate parents to change his resolve. Nor did Mahavira desired to hurt his parents, if he could help it. It appears that Mahavira's parents were quite assiduous in making attempts to engage the boy's mind in worldly things and in creating around him a luscious atmosphere of amusement and pleasure. Fairly early in life he was married to a charming Princess, Yasoda, belonging to the Kaundinya *gotra*.

On the question of Mahavira's marriage there is a fundamental difference of detail between the Digambara and Svetambara accounts. While the Svetambara books distinctly mention that Mahavira lived married life for about 10 years and begot a daughter named Anojja or Priyadarsana, the Digambara books deny the fact of marriage altogether. But from a critical study of the several old biographies of Mahavira, it is possible to establish that the Digambara view is based upon a misconstruction of certain verses in the *Paumacariya* and*Avasyaka Niryukti*. These books give in a comparative form the various details about the life of the Tirthankaras; with reference to their status at the time of renunciation these books mention that the other Tirthankaras renounced the world after having been actual rulers over their states, Vasupujya (the 12th Tirthankara), Malli (the 19th Tirthankara), Nemi (the 22nd Tirthankar), Parsva (the 23rd Tirthankara), and Mahavira were still *kumar* (i.e. Princes).

Mali Arithnaimee paso veero ya vasupunjay (57)
Aiai kumarsiya gayaho nigya jinrvarinda
Saisa vi hu rayanro puhee bhotunr nikhanta (58)

-Padmachriam

Veeram aritoothanaimee pasem malim cha vasupunjam cha
Aiai mutoonr jinrai avsaisa asee rayanro
Raikulaisu vi jaya visudhvanyaisu khtiykulaisu
Na ya ichhiyabhisaya kumarvsami pviya

-Avashykaniryukti

The same couplets, in Sanskrit, have been repeated in the Digambara books such as *Padma-Purana* and*Harivamsa-Purana*.

Vasupoojyo bhaveero mali pasharvo yadutam
Kumara nirgata gaihat prithveepatyoparai

-Padyapuran 20.67

Nishkrantivrasupoojysy malairnaimijinantyo
Panchanan tu kumarakhyan ragyan -shaishjinaishanam

-Harivanshpuranr 60.214

It is clear that the word kumar in these verses has been interpreted in its other meaning of "celibate" by the later Digambara *acaryas;* but it is also obvious that this meaning will not possibly bear in the context. There is no particular reason in these circumstances to disbelieve the facts of Mahavira's marriage. It is possible, however, that the marriage when made was against his own inclination and desire and was made in difference to the wishes of the parents; but that he lived a marriage life for several years and became father seems to be well-founded.

The Digambara and Svetambara versions differ also on another point, whether in the thirtieth year of Mahavira's life when he actually renounced the world his parents were alive or dead. The Svetambara accounts mention hat Mahavira had made a promise to his mother that he would not renounce the world so long as the parents were alive. This would seem to follow quite logically from what has been said before about Mahavira's leaning towards ascetic life and the parent's objection to his renouncing the world and taking up an ascetical career and from the further fact that Mahavira was naturally a dutiful and considerate son, although strong in his determination at the same time. The story goes that Mahavira's parents died when he was in his twenty-eighth year, that "perceiving that the time of his renunciation had come" he repeated his desire to enter the Order to his elder brother who was now the eldest member of the family, and that the brother dissuaded him from acting on that desire forthwith, for "the deaths of our parents are still fresh in our memories, your leaving us at this time would render our bereavement the more unbearable and painful". Mahavira lived for two years more in the palace and then "with the consent of those in power entered the spiritual career". The Digambara books, on the other hand, mention that Mahavira's parents were alive at the time when he renounced the world, that they tried first to dissuade him from his resolve but yielded in the end when they found that Mahavira was definitely bent upon executing it.

Renunciation of the Material World

Be that as it may, the fact remains that disgusted with the non-finality of the things of the world and persuaded by a desire to search for the ultimate Truth, on the tenth day of *Margasirsa* Mahavira formally renounced all his secular bonds, left his silver, gold and riches, quitted and rejected his real, valuable property, distributed his wealth in presents, set out for the life of a homeless monk. The great event has been somewhat poignantly described in the *Kalpasutra*.

> "In that period, in that age, in the first month of winter, in the first fortnight, in the dark (fortnight) of *Margasirsa*, on its tenth day, when the shadow had turned towards the east and the (first) *Paurusi* was full and over, on the day called *Suvrata*, in the *Muhurta* called *Vijaya*, in the palanquin *Candraprabha*, Mahavira was followed on his way by a train of gods, men, and *asuras*, and surrounded by a swarm of shell-blowers, proclaimers, *pattivalas*, courtiers, men carrying others on the back, heralds, bell beaters. They praised and hymned him with kind, pleasing, sweet and soft words.............
>
> "Then the Venerable Ascetic Mahavira-gazed on by a circle of thousands of eyes, praised by a circle of thousands of mouths, extolled by a circle of thousands of mouths, extolled by a circle of thousands of hearts, being the object of many thousands of wishes, desired because of his splendour, beauty, and virtues, pointed out by a circle of thousands of forefingers, answering with (a greeting) of his hands a circle of thousands of jointed hands of thousands of men and women, passing along a row of thousands, of palaces, greeted by sweet and delightful music, as beating of time, performance on the *Vina*, *Turya* and the great drum, in which joined shouts of victory, and the low and pleasing murmur of the people; accompanied by all his pomp, all his splendour, all his army, all his train, by all his retinue, by all his magnificence, by all his grandeur, by all his ornaments, by all the tumult, by all the throng, by all subjects, by all time-beaters, by the whole seraglio, adorned with flowers, scented robes, garlands, and ornaments, and under the

> continuous din and sound of trumpets, with great state and splendour, with a great train of soldiers, vehicles, and guests, under the sound, din, and noise of conches, cymbals, drums, castanets, horns, small drums, kettle drums, *Muajas*, *Mrdangas*, and *Dundubhis*, which were accompanied at the same time by trumpets-went right through Kundapura to a park called the *Sandavana* of the *Jnatrkas* and proceeded to the excellent tree *Ashoka*. There under the excellent tree Ashoka he caused his palanquin to stop, descended from his palanquin, took of his ornaments, garlands and finery with his own hands, and with his own hands plucked out his hair in five handfuls. When the moon was on conjunction with the asterism *Uttaraphalguni*, he after fasting two and a half days without drinking water, put on a divine robe, and quite alone, nobody else being present, he tore out his hair and leaving the house entered the state of houselessness".

Change of Mind

Mahavira's ascetic life before his attainment of the highest spiritual knowledge lasted for more than twelve years. Since his parents were lay disciples of the Order of *Parsva*, it would be justified to infer that he began his novitiate as an ascetical member of the same Order. At the same time it appears that he did not abide rigorously by all the specified rules of the Order: there is a tradition current in Jaina literature that a Tirthankara does not adopt a guru and, presumably, the prevailing practice of an earlier Tirthankaras Order. There seems to be no doubt that the monks of Parsva's Order wore clothes.

In the *Uttaradhyayayana sutra* there is an account of a meeting between Kesi, a young *Sramana* of the school of Parsva, and Gautama, the chief disciple of Mahavira, in which "knowledge and virtuous conduct were for ever brought to eminence and subjects of the greatest importance were settled". The matter that had been occasioning controversy was hat Parsva's law recognised only four vows and permitted the wearing by the monks of an under and an upper garment, while Mahavira's law enjoined five vows and forbade the wearing of clothes altogether; and Gautama explained away the difficulty by stating that "the various outward marks of religious men introduced to distinguish them do not count towards final liberation but only knowledge, faith and right conduct. In conformity with the rules of Parsva's Order, Mahavira also wore clothes for a year and a month, but then adopted nudity and stuck to it throughout the rest of his life. The Digambara tradition credits him with having adopted nudity from the start.

His habits of life during this period may be briefly mentioned. He went about naked and without any outfit of any kind. He did not even possess a bowl for collecting food, which he collected in the hollow of his hands. He completely neglected his body and abandoned care of it. Many insects crawled on his person, bit him and caused him pain, but he bore it with patience. People were shocked at the sight of him; they shouted at him and at time even struck him. He bore everything patiently and with equanimity. For days and months he would observe silence and remain absorbed in his own thoughts.

The Digambara tradition mentions that he observed the vow of silence for twelve years, but that is possibly an exaggeration. He avoided men as well as women, often gave no answers to questions put to him and omitted to return greetings. Diversions of all kinds he positively avoided.

The ascetic life of Mahavira strongly contrasted with the probationary period in Buddha's life. The Buddha created an agreeable impression wherever he went; he was welcomed by teachers like Alara Kalama and Uddaka Ramaputta and their pupils, and even when he followed a graduated course of austerities and consequently reduced himself to a mere skeleton, skin and bone, he did not arouse the hostility of the onlooker.

Mahavira's troubles were partly due to his unkempt appearance and partly to his somber silence and look of grim determination. Not without justification do the Jaina accounts say that unusually large for a Tirthankara was Mahavira's share of the defilement of Karma which he had to suppress before obtaining enlightenment.

Penances

Mahavira performed a very prolonged course of severe penance for twelve years for the destruction of the karma. This course of penance's comprehended "uninterrupted meditation, unbroken chastity, and the most scrupulous observance of the rules concerning eating and drinking". The account of his *sadhana* given in the Acaranga is literally soul -stirring.

He mediated day and night, undisturbed and non-perturbed Avoiding women and giving up the company of householders, he realised singleness. He lodged in workshops, assembling places, manufactories, shed of straw, towns, garden-houses, in cemeteries and burial grounds, or at the foot of a tree, wherever shelter was available. He did not care for sleep for the sake of pleasure and slept only for short hours.

In winter when cold winds blew, he did not seek sheltered places or kindle wood or seek to cover himself with clothes. In the cold season he mediated in the shade, in summer he exposed himself to the heat. He would mediate with his eyes fixed on a square space before him of the length of a man or in some of the posture without the smallest motion. While mediating he would concentrate on the things above, below, or beside. He meditated free from sin and desire, not attached to sounds or colours, and never acted carelessly. Being averse from the impressions of the senses, he spoke very little and was always calm.

"Thoroughly knowing the earth-bodies and water-bodies and fire-bodies and wind-bodies, the lichens, seeds and sprouts" and comprehending "that they are, if narrowly inspected, imbued with life", he avoided all kinds of sin and abstained from all sinful activities. He did not use another's robe, nor did he eat out of another's vessel. He did not rub his eyes or scratch his body. Knowing measure in eating and drinking he was not desirous of delicious food, nor had he a longing for it". For more than a couple of years he led a religious life without using cold water. He completely abstained from indulgence of the flesh; whether wounded or not, he took no medical treatment. He lived on rough food-rice, pounded jujube and beans. Sometimes he ate stale food. He accepted moist or dry or cold food, old beans, old pap, or bad grain, whatever was available. But where there were hungry crows or thirsty beings or other beggars standing in his way, he would go past that place without begging alms. He kept fasts; sometimes he ate only the sixth meal, or the eighth, or the tenth, or the twelfth; sometimes he did not drink for half a month or even for a month or for more than two months or even six months.

In accordance with the rules of the order he wandered about unceasingly, except for the four months of the rainy season. During the rest of the year, he lived in villages only a single night and in towns only five nights. He was indifferent alike to the smell of ordure and the sweet scent of sandal, to straw and jewel, dirt and gold, pleasure and pain, his world and the world beyond, to life and death. His mind was completely free from attachment. Circumspect in his thought, words and acts, he moved without wrath, pride, deceit and greed. Like water in a vessel, he was unattached in the midst of sin.

During the course of his travels, he visited the pathless country of the Ladhas, in Vajjabhumi and in Subbhabhumi; and here his troubles were endless. The rude natives of the place attacked him and set dogs to bite him, but he did not use as much as a stick to keep off the dogs. He endured the abusive language of the rustics and bore pain, free from desire. "When he approached the village the inhabitants met him on the outside and attacked him, saying "Get away from here". He was struck with a stick, the fist, a lance, hit with a fruit, a clod a potsherd. Beating him again and again many cried. When he once sat without moving his body they cut his flesh, tore his hair under pains, or covered him with dust. Throwing him up they let him fall, or disturbed him in his religious postures". But like a hero at the head of a battle, bearing all hardships he proceeded on his path wholly undisturbed.

Extensive Travels

The Jaina books give a precise description of Mahavira's wanderings during this period of over twelve years, the various places he visited and the several contacts he formed. The *Kalpasutra* and the *Bhagavati* supplement, and do not as certain scholars are inclined to think, contradict, each other; together help to frame a complete picture of his travels from place to place.

Kummaragrama may be supposed to be the starting point of Mahavira's travels. The *Acaranga* mentions that renunciation implied the quitting of "the northern Ksatriya part of the place Kundapura" and arrival in the village Kummara, which was presumably a suburb of Kundagrama. From Kummara he moved on to the settlement of Kollaga (situated close to Nalanda), where he was hospitably received by the Brahmin Bahula. After roaming about in that area for some six months, Mahavira ultimately came to Asthigrama to spend his first rainy season there. The commentary on the Kalpasutra refers to Vardhamana as the former name of Asthigrama; Dr. BC Law is inclined to identify it with modern Burdwan. On the way to Asthigrama Mahavira had the first taste of those bitter experiences, which were going to be such a common feature of his Sadhaka life, (i) of hostility towards him of the *parivrajaka* sects living in north India at time, and (ii) of his persecution at the hands of various tempter gods in a similar way to the temptation of the Buddha by the traditional *Mara*. On both these a few words may be parenthetically added.

In the 6th century BC North India generally and the north-eastern provinces in particular were buzzing with ascetic life. A whole legion of ascetic orders was flourishing in these regions. Scholars are of the opinion that asceticism has its roots in the Vedas; the centre of *Vedic* religion is the *Rsi* (seer) who is capable of a direct realisation of Truth by practice of *Tapasaya* or asceticism. There is no doubt that asceticism received great encouragement in the age of the Aranyakas and the *Upanisads* when, dissatisfied with growing rituals and superstition under the aegis of the priestly class, serious-minded people openly questioned the prevailing intellectualism of religion and retired to the forests in their search for the highest knowledge and for a new world of experience.

The *Sruti* practice of asceticism was accordingly regularised into a system in the *Smrtis*, which made it obligatory upon every *Hindu* to devote the latter part of his life to the two *ashrams* of *Vanaprastha* and*Samnyasa*. It may be mentioned that the Brahminical system did not confine asceticism only to elderly people or advanced householders; even youths could be permitted to take up the ascetic career, if they wanted to shun the world in their quest for the Ideal, such youths being known as the *naishthik* *brahamchari*. Thus in the normal *brahminic* system quite about half of society would be wandering about as mendicants and ascetic in pursuit of Truth under the guidance of chosen teachers. This floating mass of houseless population was organised into different orders or sects in accordance with the different systems of doctrines and discipline they followed. The Buddhist text *Udana* bears testimony to the fact that the characteristic feature of the religious life of India during this period was a multiplicity of ascetic groups, secretaries of *Sramanas* and *Brahminas, parivrajakas,* followers of different *dittis* (viewpoints), *darshan* system, gyanti (beliefs), *ruchi* (aims), and *ashray* (organisations)", the Jaina texts also mention numerous sects and schools, with their own beliefs and practices, existing in the country at the time. In his introduction to the *Acaranga*, Jacobi has elaborately compared the rules and religious practices of *Brahminic* and *Sramanic* ascetics, and stated his conclusion that certain rules were commonly observed by most of the ascetic orders, for instance, (1) the injunction that the *Bhiksu* must station himself in a fixed retreat during the rains, (2) the injunction that the Bhiksu must not store up articles of consumption, nor kill life, and (3) various rules regarding beggings, etc. *Tapas* (or austerities), in some form or other, it appears, was common to particularly all orders. But Mahavira was now giving a new meaning to the term, which conflicted with all its prevailing notions and which raised the practice of *tapsaya* to a spiritual height, unattained and not even intended to be attained, by any of the existing *parivrajaka* orders.

Mahavira's idea of *tapas* was that of self-restraint with regard to the body, speech and mind; in his view, austerities had to be inward as well as outward, and fasting, absolute chastity and unmitigated meditation were its several forms. The practice of austerities or penance's was to be restored to as a means of wearing out and ultimately destroying the effect of sinful deeds committed in former existence's, and the practice of the threefold self-restraint, of the body, speech and mind, as a means of stopping the production of new *karmas*. As justified forms of penance's, Mahavira was prepared to recognise only *anshan* (fasting), *unrodaree* (limiting the food that one eats), *bhikshacharya* (eating only begged food), *rasparityag* (abstaining from special items of food which one most enjoys, *kaeyklaish* (bodily austerity), *Pratisanleenta* (avoidance of temptation by control of senses and mind), *Prayishchit* (confession and penance), *vinay* (reverence), *veyivritay* (service rendered to the aged and the helpless), *swadhyai* (the study of the scriptures), *dhyan* (meditation), *Kayotsarga*(feeling and showing absolute indifference to the body and its needs). He gave no honoured place to practices like the tending of a fire the exorcising of evil spirits; the performance of *agnihotras;* the taking of regular bath; the living under water, or in caves, or on trees; the eating of roots, leaves, moss, flowers or bark of trees, or of grass; the besmearing of body with ashes, etc. just the practices in which the other *parivrajaka* orders had gloried.

It appears that Parsva's monks had been fairly lax in their morals and discipline, but they were far more regulated in their conduct than the other *parivrajakas,* for there is an occasional mention in the Jaina texts of the weaker spirits in Parsva's order finding it hard to observe the rules and consequently joining the othe r*parivrajaka* sects with less rigorous rules of discipline. But it is certain that the austerities prescribed by Mahavira for himself, and later on for the members of his Order, presented an infinitely harder code of penance's and were combined with a far more rigorous discipline of ethical and spiritual conduct than was prevalent in any *parivrajaka* sect at that time; and there is no doubt that Mahavira earned the hostility of the other sects for doing so.

As regards the persecution of Mahavira by the tempter-gods, it is a reminder of the story of Mara in Buddha's life. Mara is looked upon in Buddhist literature as the supreme lord of all evil, the chief seducer to evil thought, word and deed. He is supposed to have followed the Buddha step by step and watched for a moment of weakness to over-power his soul and deflect him from the pursuit of knowledge. As a god of evil he is not associated with that gloomy tragedy with which we are accustomed to fancy the diabolical, deadly foe of good surrounded; and as seducer his methods of work are fairly commonplace, "appearing at one time as a Brahmin, at another as a husband man, at another as an elephant King, and in many other different forms" in order to shake Buddha's life.

Instead of the traditional Mara, however, Jaina books speak of different gods appearing at different times and the methods of their attack are not always non-violent as in the case of Mara, but comprehend elaborate bodily pain and torture. The first encounter with the temper-god in Mahavira's life took place on the ever of his firs *chaturmus*. While on the way to *Asthigrama*, he came across a small temple dedicated to the God *Sulapani*, which used to be left completely untenanted at night but where Mahavira decided to stay and meditate. He suffered frightful tortures at the hands of the god in the course of his meditation at night. But the real battle with temptations took place in the eleventh year of his *sadhaka* life, when *Sangamaka*, another temper-god, set about his task with a view to confuse Mahavira and, if possible, to shake him from his search for Truth, followed him step by step for a period of six months giving him all sorts of torture and creating all conceivable difficulties in his way in order to overpower his soul in a moment of weakness. Adopting the garb of a disciple of Mahavira, he started committing theft in a house, got caught, put the blame upon his guru and had him severely beaten. He had Mahavira arrested on suspicion of being a spy. Several times he made Mahavira's excursions for alms fruitless by various devices he had him ridiculed by people with derisive gestures; and gave him troubles in a hundred other ways. But Mahavira remained steadfast, bore all his trials with fortitude, and therefore the god was ultimately obliged to depart.

Meeting with Gosala

Mahavira's second *chaturmus* was spent in Nalanda, a suburb of Rajagrha. While here he was met by Gosala Mankhaliputra (or Maskariputra), the Ajivakas teacher. Gosala was then wandering about in the country showing pictures to the people, and was attracted by Mahavira owing to his extra-ordinary self-restraint and impressive habits of medication and by the fact that a rich householder of Rajagrha, by name Vijaya had shown respect and hospitality towards Mahavira. Possibly another factor, Mahavira's capacity to prophesy things correctly, also helped to increase Gosala's keenness, as it certainly helped towards the diffusion of Mahavira's influence and following in the later part of his career. The Jaina books mention that Gosala approached Mahavira with a request that he may be adopted as his disciple, but that Mahavira declined his request, presumably because he at once sensed the great difference between their temperaments. Gosala's request was repeated on two later occasions and on each successive occasion with greater earnestness, and was ultimately granted by Mahavira. It appears that from this time onwards, Mahavira and Gosala lived and travelled together for period of six years. The third and the fourth *chaturmas* were spent at Campa, at different quarters of the same town. After the fourth chaturmas for a short period, they seem to have trekked into the Ladha country, which they visited again in the ninth year. The fifth and the sixth chaturmas were spent at Bhaddila, the capital town of the Mallas; the seventh at a place in the kingdom of Magadha; and the eighth at Rajagrha. In the ninth year Mahavira travelled again into the Ladha-desa and stayed there for over six months; in the absence of any settled retreat to spend the rainy season he had to wander about during the period. Presumably Gosala was with him this time also, although the fact that no incidents are mentioned of his use of his undeniably harsh tongue during the sojourn in *Ladha-desa* is somewhat remarkable. On return from Ladha country, while they were travelling from *Kumaragrama* to *Siddharthagrama*, they met the ascetic Vesayana, who was seated with upraised arms and upturned face in the glare of the Sun while his body was swarming with lice. Gosala jesting and indiscreetly asked whether this man was a sage or a bed of lice. Provoked at this, Vesayana attempted to strike Gosala with his super-normal powers, but was shielded by Mahavira. Gosala, however, was so impressed with the fact of the possession of supernormal powers that he felt inclined to give up Mahavira's company and to devote all his energies to the practice of the severest penance's with a view to acquire these powers, and after that he proclaimed himself a Jina and founded the order of the *Ajivakas*.

On the Gosala episode, the opinions of the scholars are very different and highly conflicting. Gosala figures in the early tradition of Buddhism as an independent leader of thought, the head of an order, of a following, the teacher of a school, well known and of repute as a sophist......a man of experience who has long been a recluse; there is no suggestion made of his personal relation with Mahavira. From the point of view of thought and belief, the Jaina and the Ajivakas sects are undoubted allied, having many points in common between them. In the immediate background of both were the teachings of Parsva, Parsva being honoured by both as the last but one Tirthankara, while Mahavira and Gosala were sharply divided in their claim to the position of the last Tirthankara. The eight *Mahanimittas* of the Ajivakas canon were in fact extracts made from the Ten *Purvas,* which are recognised as the literary authority of the sect of Parsva. The commonness of their tradition and the fact that Gosala proclaimed himself a Jain and was recognised as a teacher for at least two years before Mahavira, were considered by Jacobi and Barua as adequate reasons for advancing the somewhat fanciful opinion that contrary to the Jaina account Mahavira was a disciple of Gosala for sometime. Such an opinion is clearly unfounded for if Gosala had ever been Mahavira's teacher, it is presumable that the Buddhist texts would have at least recorded something to that effect, and anyhow Gosala would have put forward that claim when he visited Mahavira to upbraid him for calling him his own disciple.

Thus, even if the Bhagavati version of the relationship between Mahavira and Gosala is not accepted a reversal of that relationship cannot surely be accepted at all. That the Bhagavati account may be somewhat exaggerated is warranted by the fact that neither in the *Acaranga* nor in the *Kalpasutra* is there any mention of Gosala. It may also be mentioned that the *Digambara* accounts of Mahavira's life also do not refer to his contact with Gosala. What appears on the basis of available materials to be well- founded is that Mahavira and Gosala did not have a teacher and disciple relationship at all. It is highly doubtful that Mahavira had started taking disciples before his attainment of Enlightenment. Mahavira and Gosala were just two associates in a common concern, two *sadhakas* who lived together for six years in asceticism. Later on there sprang up acute differences of opinion between the two. They separated from each other and became irreconcilable opponents, fighting out their differences generally through their followers.

5

Attainment of Nirvana

The three phases of the great exercise have been performed and there remains very little to be said as an epilogue. Birth and death, like the opposite poles in a magnet, are always seen together. One is never found without the other. They are constantly following the soul like two police men attending a prisoner between them. He who is born must die some day or other, and he who is dead must be born in some form or other. Night and day, like a black and a white mouse, are always trying to gnaw with their sharp teeth, the slender rope of our life. They must succeed some day or other, and their success is nothing but the end of that life. Such end must come to each of us, but the end of that noble life of our Lord was not an ordinary one. He passed "never to come again". It was a death which liberated his soul for ever from his two great enemies, birth and death. This is what the Jainas mean by saying that he attained Nirvana.

The Final Goal

Nirvana, as already explained, is the goal in the long race of every man's life. It is what the gods and men are alvrays struggling to reach at in their repeated births. It was for the attainment of this Nirvana, the condition of unlimited happiness, unimpedable valour, and liberation from all the cares and miseries of this world, that Mahavira had to pass through so many repeated births and deaths, and, as we learn from the Jain a Shastras, it was for this purpose that he came to this world. Whatever it may be, he obtained it at the end of his life, and a description of the manner in which he obtained it will be found interesting.

As to the place where he died all the sources of our information assert the same thing. In the Kalpasutra and in the Buddhist works he is said to have died at Papa. In the Digambara Shastras and in the modern times, too, it is known by the name of Pavapuri. The place has been thus described by Mr. J. L. Jaini:

A small hamlet of moderate dimensions, and of mud-houses mostly, Pavapuriji is a place lovely in its simple surroundings and lovelier still in its sacred traditions. There are several dharmashalas (resting-places) for Jaina pilgrims. There are about half a dozen temples erected by the Shvetambaras and Digambaras. Many pilgrims of both sexes proceed to the place chiefly on the Divali occasion, the day on which Lord Mahayira attained Nirvana and then up to the month of March, when the attendance begins to fall. The main temple, which contains the charanaa, sacred foot-impressions, of Lord Mahavira, stand in the middle of a tank, covered with lotus leaves and other aquatic plants of various kinds. Many fish float in the water and make a very funny sight by their incessant flitting. Sometimes a bigger fish would attack a shoal of smaller fish and make them dart down into the water in great confusion. At present no lotuses are blooming in the tank but it is easy to imagine how charming the tank must look when white and red lotuses dot its surface and the fish dance in its pellucid depths through the mazes of the lotus-stems.

The sun also may then be imagined as converting every stray drop of water that the ever-busy tails of the fish have cast on to a lotus, into a pearl of the most beautiful pink colour. The insulated temple of our last Lord is reached by a bridge of stone. In the temple itself is a low chamber, facing the east are 3 niches; the central one, the largest of the three, contains the foot-impressions of Lord Mahavira; the niche on the right of it, of his disciple Gautama Swami; and that on the left those of Sudharmacharya.

Hastipal, the ruler of this place, was, as we have already learnt, a patron of Mahavira, and he had made great arrangements for the reception of the great preacher. Almost all the ruling chiefs of the country had assembled there.

Then came the seventh day. It was the fifteenth day of the first half of Kartika when the moan was in conjuaction with the asterism Svati. Mahavira was sitting upon a high diamond throne in the centre of a magnificent hall specially erected for his preaching in the forest in the vicinity of a large tank. All men from the beggar to the mighty King, were round him. They had formed themselves into twelve societies consisting of the different grades of society. 'It was a dark night and hence the whole of the hall had to be illuminated with the brightest light. His pupils were all around him excepting Gautama ladrabhuti, who is said in the Shvetambara Shastras, to have been on a mission.

For the whole night he was preaching to them. In the fourth prahar of the night all men fell asleep. Mahavira, through his Saklagyan saw that his end was come. He assumed a particular position known as the Samparyanka, and attained Nirvana just when it was twilight. In the morning when the people got up they saw to their great sorrow that their Lord was gone. There was no help. They began to grieve but Gautama comforted them. Then they celebrated his cremation with great pomp.

The news of his death reached far and wide and the people had illuminations and sabhas in several places. They thought it more worthy to rejoice than to weep on the occasion of the liberation of their Lord from the bonds of this world. It is said that the modern festival of Divali took its rise from this great incident. The word Divali is a corruption of the Sanskrit word dipavali which means a "row of lamps". It refers to the illumination that is held every year on the Divali festival.

This is illumination but the imitation of the great illumination held on the occasion of the death of Mahavira. The people have forgotten the great incident which gave rise to this national festival, but they have tenaciously stuck to it through so many centuries. It is also said that the modern Hoi or Hatri, worshipped after same days of Divali, is also an imitation of the great hall at Pavapuri in which Mahavira breathed his last.

Approximate date of Nirvana

The last bat not the least point about Mahavira that remains to be specially mentioned is the date of his salvation or the year of his death which in all probability is a most important point in the life of a great man. It may be remarked, before proceeding to enter into a serious discussion upon the more than one sources of our information concerning this matter, that it is difficult or rather impossible to give a final judgement upon this subject in a book like this which comes from the pen of an ordinary student who does not claim any share in the research work of the modern scholars. The demonstrations that are brought forward in the following few lines are not, as some one is likely to suppose, the result of any research work on his part. On the other hand all information on this point is a secondary one, being due to and only to the unceasing labours of scholars like Prof. Jacobi and Dr. Hoernle whose learning and tact should be admired and respected by every student of antiquity.

It has been observed above that there are many facts to show precisely the year in which Mahavira died. In the first place we learn from the sacred books of the Buddhists that Mahavira was a contemporary of Buddha. Thus in Mahavagga and Mahaparinibhana Sutta, the two great Buddhist works, Mahavira is said to have been a contemporary of Buddha. He is mentioned by his Prakrit name Nataputta. He is spoken of as one of the six opponent teachers of Buddha. Prof. Jacobi cites in his translation of the Jaina Sutras, besides the above quoted books, the Anuguttara Nikaya, Samanaphala Sutta of the Digh Nikaya, Sumangala Vilasini, a commentary by Buddhaghosha on Brahmagala Sutta of the Digh Nikaya, and the Magghima Nikaya, all of which show that Mahavira was a great opponent of Buddha. "In the Magghima Nikaya it is related that the Nigantha Nataputta made Abhayakumara engage in a disputation with Buddha. The question was so adroitly formed that whether the answer was Yes or No, it involved Buddha in self-contradiction. But the plan did not succeed, and Abhaya was converted by Buddha.'" He wanted to pay Buddha a visit, but Nataputta tried to dissuade him from it, because the Niganthas' held the Kriyavada, while Buddha taught the Akriyavada, Siha, however, setting his master's prohibition at naught, went to Buddha on his own account, and was, of course, converted by him". Again in the Maghima Nikaya 35, a disputation between Buddha and Sakkaka, the son of a Nigantha, is narrated. From the same authority we learn that this Sakkaka was not himself a Nigantha. He boasts himself of having vanquished Nataputta in disputation. Now whatever the truth of these traditions, they put beyond doubt the fact that Mahavira and Buddha lived and preached at the same time.' This means that Buddha was born before the death of Mahavira. Now Buddha, according to the western scholars, was born about 557 BC. Therefore Mahavira's Nirvana must have taken place many years after this date. This is all we know from the Buddhist works. We learn nothing as to the priority of one over the other.

The Jaina Shastras, however, make this point a little clearer. The following gatha occurs in the Darslianasara written by Devauanda Acharya in Sambat 990 at Ujjain.

The admiration for Mahavira which we have in modern times is not due only to Jaina literature and the Jaina Acharyas, but it is due to a great extent to the faith which his followers and pupils had in him; and to say something about his followers will not be out of place. It may be safely remarked that the Digambaras and the Shvetambaras who differ so much from each other about many facts in the life of Mahavira, are almost of one opinion as regards the statement about his followers and the difference, if any, is very slight.

Excellent Community of Followers

The excellent community of Mahavira in his life-time was a large one and used to travel with, him from place to place. It consisted of four orders, each having its own head and different rules of life. The first order consisted of fourteen thousand members who were known as the Munis or the Shramornas. They held the highest position in the whole community and had very strict rules of living for them. These rules are given in the Jaina Shastras. Further, this order was divided into nine Ganas or schools each of them being under one head who was known by the name of Ganadhara or a teacher of one school. There were eleven such Ganadharas who were the first and the chief disciples of Mahavira like the twelve apostles of Christ. Seven of these had the charge of one school each, and the remaining four taught the remaining two schools, two of them together having the charge of one school. The names of these Ganadharas or the Sthaviras are as follows: I. Indrabhuti of the Gautama-gotra, whose Gana (school) consisted of five hundred Shramanas (Munis). II. Agnibhuti of the Gautama-gotra who had the charge of five hundred Munis. III. Vayubhuti of the Gautama-gotra who instructed five hundred Munis. IV. Arya-Vyakta of the Bharadvaj-gotra whose school consisted of five hundred Munis. V. Sudharma of the Agni-Veshyayana gotra. He had the charge of five hundred Munis. VI. Mandikaputra or Manditputra of the Vashistha-gotra who instructed two hundred and fifty Shramanas. VII. Mauryaputra of the Kashyapa-gotra whose order had two hundred and fifty Munis. Akampita of the Gautama-gotra and IX. Achalvrata of the Haritayana-gotra. Both of them instructed together three hundred Shramanas each. X. Maitreya XI. Prabhas. Both were of the Kandinya-gotra and had the charge of three hundred Munis each.

This shows that there were nine Ganas at the head of which there were eleven Ganadharas. It is also said that Indrabhuti was the chief disciple of Mahavira and exercised an authority over other pupils. Of these eleven, only Indrabhuti and Sudharma survived Mahavira, obtaining their salvations after his Nirvana. We will know more about tbem shortly. The rest died in his life-time as Kevalins.

From the above list we learn that there were only four-thousand and two hundred Munis, but it has been stated that there were in all fourteen thousand Munis. Perhaps the rest lived as apprentices, and were not taken in the order. This division of the Munis is according to their Ganas. There is a further classification according to their merits and spiritual attainments.

According to Kalpasutra among these there were three hundred sages who knew the fourteen Purvas and the twelve Angas of the Jina-Vani; thirteen hundred sages who were possessed of the Avadhi-knowledge and superior qualities; seven hundred Kevalins; seven hundred Mimis who could transform themselves, and, though no gods, had obtained

Riddhis or the powers of gods; five hundred sages who could know the thoughts of all beings; four hundred professors who used to discuss with men of other religions, and who will never be defeated; seven hundred male and fourteen hundred female disciples who were perfect; and eight hundred other sages. These make together only six thousand and eight hundred. The rest of them perhaps were of inferior merits. According to the Digambaras there were three hundred Munis who knew by heart the twelve Angas and the fourteen Purvas; thirteen hundred Munis possessing Avadhi-knowledge; seven hundred Kevalins or those who had Kevalgyan; nine hundred sages who could transform themselves'''; five hundred munis who had the four kinds of knowledge; twelve hundred professors; and nine thousand and nine hundred ordinary Munis. This, too, gives in all fourteen thousand and eight hundred Munis which is greater than the other number by eight hundred.

The eleven pupils of Mahavira were all converts to Jainism and, as such, they strictly adhered to the cause. They were greatly attached to their Lord. The story of Gautama Indrabhuti, the chief disciple, is a very interesting one. He was the son of a Brahmin named Vasumati. He is said to have been a learned pandit and a writer of Hindu Granthas. He was very proud of his learning.

Once upon a time a certain old man went to him and said, "O, Revered Sir, my Guru, Mahavira, gave me a poem, but before explaining it to me he entered his deep meditations. No one can explain me its meaning. 1 have heard much about your learing that you are well versed in the Vedas and the Puranas. I think I can not live without having explained to me the meaning of this poem. I hope, therefore, that you will be kind enough to save my life by explainng to me the meaning of this sloka". Indrabhuti promised to comply with the Brahamaua's request provided the Brahmin promised him to become his pupil on his having explained him the meaning of the sloka. The Brahmin promised to do so, and read the sloka to Gautama. It ran thus:

Gautama fell into confusion. He could not know what is meant by the three Kalas and the six Dravyas. He could not understand the Panchastikaya, the seven Tattvas and the six Leshyas. And he could not give a wrong explanation, for he was afraid of Mahavira. He, therefore, thought it proper to come to

Mahavira and there explain the meaning of the sloka as he understood it, so that he may not be charged with the guilt of having explained the sloka wrongly. Having thus concluded he went to Mahavira with his five-hundred pupils and his two brothers Vayubhuti and Agnibhuti. In the way he began to think that if he could not explain it in the absence of Mahavira how would he be able to explain it in his presence, but his brother induced him to go there. On his first seeing Mahavira, he was struck with the spiritual valour of the great Yogi. His pride went off and he saluted Mahavira by falling before him and then requested him to preach to him. Mahavira explained to him the doctrines of Jainism. Being struck with the truth of the doctrines and the learning and wisdom of the Lord, he left his home, became a Muni and entered the order of Mahavira.

His 500 pupils and 3 brothers did the same. He remained faithful to his master throughout his life. Mahavira was greatly pleased with him and hence raised him by and by to the position of a Ganadhara with his two brothers, and then to that of the chief Ganadhara. When Mahavira died he is said to have been on a mission to convert somebody. He became a Kevalin just when Mahavira died. After Mahavira he was the leader of the order. He died twelve years after, having lived fifty years as a monk, and altogether ninety-two years.

Another disciple who survived Mahavira was Sudharma. The Pattavali of the Kharataragachha states that he was the son of a Brahmin. He succeeded Indrabhuti to the position of the chief Gauadhara. He was a great preacher. The well known Jambu-Swami was one of his pupils. He was succeeded by Jambu-Swami, who was the last Kevalin and obtained his salvation at a place near Muttra.

From the order of the Munis we come to that of the Arjikas or the nuns. This is said to have consisted of thirty-six thousand nuns. These were the women who had entered the order of Mahavira. They are distinguished from ordinary women by the fact that they are not allowed to mix in worldly matters. They are female Munis. They have strict rules of conduct like the Munis. At the head of these nuns was Chandana. In the Digambara Shastras she is said to have been the daughter of Chetaka, the mighty ruler of Vaishali or Vishalpura. Further we learn from Kalpasutra that Chetaka was the maternal uncle of Mahavira. Thus Chandana must have been the cousin of Mahavira. The Digambaras say that Chetaka was the father of Trisala. This shows that Chandana was Mahavira's mother's sister. Whatever it may be, one thing is clear that she was closely related to Mahavira. The anecdote, showing how she became an Arjika, runs thus:

"One day, Chandana had been to the pleasure gardens for taking a walk. A certain Vidyadhara, being fascinated by her beauty, took her off, but in the way, thinking of his wife, he left her in the forest. She was weeping there, when a certain hill-man came there and took her with him to Kaushambi and sold to a rich man named Vrishabhasena. The man kept her for sometime in his house, but as she grew young, his wife, Subhadra, became jealous of her beauty. Chandana was illtreated by this Subhadra in all kinds of ways.

She was given the worst kind of food to eat and wretched clothes to put on. Sometimes she was beaten too. After sometime it happened that Mahavira came to that place and began to preach there. She was disgusted with the world, became an Arjika and entered the holy order. By and by she was raised to the position of the head Arjika".

The third order consisted of one hundred and fifty-nine thousand lay votaries with Sankhasataka at their head. These lay votaries are called the Shravakas and correspond to the Grihasthas of the Hindus. The rules of conduct for this order were not so strict as those for the Munis. They were allowed to live with their wives and children with some limitations. The Digambara Acharyas give the number only as one hundred thousand.

The fourth order consisted of three hundred thousand female lay votaries or Shravikas with Sulasa and Revati at their head. In the Kalpa Hsatra their number is given as three hundred and eighteen thousand Shravikas.

Such were the four orders of which the community of Mahavira consisted in his life-time. After Mahavira they were led by Gautama Indrabhuti for twelve years and after him by Sudharma for twelve years. After Sudharma Acharya his head pupil Jambu Swami led the order for twenty-four years. A long list of such leaders is given in the Kalpasutra known as the list of the Sthaviras, and also in the Pattavalis.

Great Character

"Character is one of the greatest motive powers in the world", wrote one of the best writers of the last century, and strange it would seem, as it really does, how Mahavira did such a great work in his life, if nothing is said about his character. Great men are not great only because they were looked upon to be so by the surrounding people, but also because they have done great things. Character is one of the chief factors in the accomplishment of such deeds, and no man has ever become great, not what we ordinarily mean by great but really great, without being one of good character. It is rather a fruitless task to try to find out the elements which composed the real greatness of Mahavira, for he was a Tirthankara, and, as such, must have possessed almost all the forty-six qualities of an Arhat; but it would not be out of place to give a glimpse of some of them. The three great elements of the character of a great man are bodily valour, intellectual excellence and morality. Of the first Mahavira is said to have been possessed to a high degree or Ananta. He had a very strong and a well-formed body which was beautiful and fragrant and is said to have been seven cubits high and to have the yellow colour of gold. As a proof of this statement we have already learnt the anecdote of his having tamed a wild and a ferocious elephant while playing with his friends in a garden when he was a young Prince of eight years.

The auspicious mark of lion that is seen on his images in modern times might have perhaps been given to him to show his great bodily valour. It has already been noted that in the Shvetambara shastras he is said to have married and led the life of a house-holder for thirty years, while in the Digambara shastras he is said to have been one of the five Bal-brahmacharis.

Intellectual Excellence

As to his intellectual excellence there is nothing to show that he was regularly educated in the ordinary way. In the Jaina shastras knowledge is said to have been of five kinds. They are Mali, Shrut

Avadhiy Manahparyaya and Kevalgyan, Of these Mahavira is said to have been born with the first three. The fourth, as we have seen, he attained at the time of his Renunciation and the fifth one he obtained in his forty-third year. This is all we know about his education. He acquired learning through Yoga. He was also a great speaker. He always spoke the truth. As to his morality there is no doubt that he was a type of virtue. He was a great preacher, and knowing that example is better than precept, he did what he preached to others.

Principles of Gospel

He strictly followed the principles of the gospel that he preached, and observed them in his practice also. Forbearance is one of the ten high virtues with the Jainas, and Mahavira patiently bore the abuses and even the ill-treatment of the wild tribes of Vajra-Bhumi, and Shuddha-Bhumi, when he preached to them the doctrines of Jainism. He was never angry, and led a life which is a Jaina model of purity and piety. We have already learnt of his attachment to his parents. He did not only love them but was very obedient to them. Thus he is said to have intended to renounce the world several times, but would not do so against the wish of his parents. It is also said that he was greatly obedient to his elder brother. Nothing is so necessary as perseverance for one who wishes to become a great Yogi, and Mahavira is said to have been a man of great perseverance. Soon after his Renunciation, "it happened that a certain cowherd with his cows came to the place where he was sitting all absorbed in his meditation and calling upon Mahavira to look after his cows that he left to graze there, himself went away to the village. Mahavira being engaged in his meditations, could not hear him and the cows went astray. The cowherd, when he came back from the village, did not find the cows there, and began to reproach Mahavira and actually dealt two or three blows to him. Happily, some acquaintances of Lord Mahavira came there.

They rebuked the cowherd very much and informed him of the real character of the saint". The story, though illustrating the great mental powers of Mahavira, has somewhat the colour of absurdity. Mahavira, being the son of a great King and a noble saint, must have been known to all men, and specially to the subjects of his brother. The cowherd's not recognising Mahavira, who was the brother of the King of that state in which the cowherd lived, is a fact beyond our perception. However, as it stands, it shows that Mahavira was free from anger.

Somewhat similar anecdote is given in the Mahavira Purana. "Once he was deeply meditating upon himself at a cemetery called Devoktamukta near Ujjain. A certain Rudra in conspiracy with his wife, Parvati, intending to test Mahavira's perseverance began to interrupt him, but Mahavira did not leave his Dhyana and remained constantly absorbed in his meditation. Having completely satisfied themselves, Rudra and Parvati began to praise Mahavira". These were the great qualities of Mahavira which led him to do great things and in turn made him great.

Great Teacher

Mahavira was a great teacher. It is a misfortune that we have got no direct information regarding his gospel. All our information is secondary and comes from the Acharyas. The Acharyas say that whatever they say is the word of Sarvagya, but how are we to convince others of this truth in the absence of any direct proof? The history of the Jaina literature, as given by the Acharyas, is likely to make them hesitate from taking it for granted that they say the word of Sarvagya. However, the history of the evolution of the Jaina literature as it stands, is as follows:

The whole Jaina literature known as the Syadvad Agama is divided into two main divisions, the twelve Angas and the fourteen Angabahyashutras or the scriptures other than the twelve Angas. The last or the twelvth of the Angas consists of the five Parikramas, the Sutra, the Prathamanuyoga, the five Chulikas and the fourteen Purvas. All these form the twelvth Anga. This vast literature chiefly known as the Dwadashanga word of the Sarvagya has never been seen by any body, for it was never written down. It was preached by the Tirthankaras from time to time and was remembered by the people. Lord Mahavira taught the same thing to the people who were present in his sermons and who could understand the divine speech of their Lord. After Mahavira his Ganadharas, whose memory was the chief repository and means of continuance of the Siddhantas, used to promulgate the faith by word of mouth and tradition. Gautama Indrabhuti, Sudharma and Jambu Swami, the three consecutive Kevalins after Mahavira, held the pontifical chair for sixty-two years, and taking advantage of their highly trained memories, which could retain all the Agamas, propagated the traditions by word of mouth. These were followed by the five Shruta Kevalins who held the chair for hundred years. The memory of these was weaker than that of the Kevalins and hence they forgot the Angabahyas. Thus the knowledge of these Angabahyas was shut from the world.

Then came the eleven Ten-Purvins who remained pontiffs for about hundred and eighty-one years. They forgot four of the Purvas, and thus the four of the Purvas were no more known. These were followed by the five Eleven Angins who remained for hundred and twenty-three years. The memory of these was still weaker. They forgot all the fourteen Purvas and other parts of the twelvth Anga. Thus the twelvth Anga was no more known. Then came the four Four-Angins holding the chair for ninety nine years. They could remember only four Angas. But after them came the five One-Angins. They remained pontiffs for hundred and eighteen years. There memory was so weak that they forgot every thing but one Anga. Thus only one Anga was known to the world. But after them no one had the knowledge of even of one complete Anga. The Acharyas, seeing that their memory was growing weaker and weaker, thought it expedient to take advantage of the art of writing, and with the little knowledge of the Agamas left to them by the One-Angins, they composed the Shastras.

This took place about 57 AD. The above history is from the Digambara point of view. This tradition, notwithstanding our full faith in its reality, is not likely to appeal to the reason of a modern critical reader, who is likely to assume that this is an invention of the Jaina Acharyas with the object of giving a sacred authority and a colour of antiquity to all their writings, which are, as a matter of fact, of a later day composition. In the absence of any direct proof he can not believe that the Jaina Shastras are a true representation of what Mahavira taught, and even if he assumes that the original compositions of the Acharyas are based upon the information given by the One-Angins he can hardly believe that the whole Jaina literature, vast as it is the out-come of the original compositions which are said to have been drowned by Shankaracharya.

Nirvana (Salvation)

Mahavira attained nirvana at Pava in 527 BC at the age of 72. The Licchavis and Mallas were two peoples to whom the rise of Mahavira was an object of national pride, and accordingly, it is said in the Kalpasutra that when Mahavira died, the eighteen confederate Kings of Kasi and Kosala, the nine Mallakis and the nine Licchavis, instituted an illumination saying "Since the light of intelligence is gone, let us make an illumination of material matter!"

6

Mahavira's Five Great Vows

The Background

The age, Venerable Ascetic Mahavira, lived in happened the five most important moments of his life, when the moon was in conjunction with the asterism Uttaraphalguni. In Uttaraphalguni he descended from heaven, and having descended, he entered the womb of Devananda; in Uttaraphalguni he was removed from the womb of Devananda to the womb of Trishala; in Uttaraphalguni he was born; in Uttaraphalguni tearing out his hair, he left the house, and entered the state of houselessness; in Uttaraphalguni he obtained the highest knowledge and intuition, called Kevala, which is infinite, supreme, unobstructed, unimpeded, complete, and perfect. But in Svati the Venerable One obtained final liberation.

When in this Avasarpini era, the Sushama-sushama period, the Sushama period, the Sushamaduhshama period, and much time of the Duhshamasushama period had elapsed, seventy-five years nine and a half months of it being left; in the fourth month of summer, in the eighth fortnight, in the light fortnight of Ashadha, on its sixth day, while the moon was in conjunction with Uttaraphalguni, the Venerable Ascetic Mahavira descended from the great Vimana, the all-victorious and all-prosperous

Pushpottara, which is like the lotus amongst the best and highest flowers, and like the Svastika and Vardhamanaka amongst the celestial regions, where he had lived for twenty Sagaropamas till the termination of his allotted length of life, divine nature and existence among gods. Here, forsooth, in the continent of Jambudvipa, in Bharatavarsha, in the southern part of it, in the southern brahminical part of the place Kundapura, he took the form of an embryo in the womb of Devananda, of the Jalandharayana gotra, wife of the Brahmin Rishabhadatta, of the gotra of Kodala, taking the form of a lion. The knowledge of the Venerable Ascetic Mahavira was threefold: he knew that he was to descend; he knew that he had descended; he knew not when he was descending. For that time has been declared to be infinitesimally small.

Then in the third month of the rainy season, the fifth fortnight, the dark fortnight of Ashvina, on its thirteenth day, while the moon was in conjunction with Uttaraphalguni, after the lapse of eighty-two days, on the eighty-third day current, the compassionate god Indra, reflecting on what was the established custom with regard to the birth of Tirthankaras, removed the embryo from the southern brahminical part of the place Kundapura to the northern Ksahtriya part of the same place, rejecting the unclean matter, and retaining the clean matter, lodged the fetus in the womb of Trishala of the Vasishtha gotra, wife of the Kshatriya Siddhartha, of the Kashynpa gotra, of the clan of the Jnatris, and lodged the fetus of the Kshatriyani Trishala in the womb of Devananda of the Jalandharayana gotra, wife of the Brahmin Rishabhadatta, of the gotra of Kodala, in the southern brahminical part of the place Kundapuri. The knowledge of the Venerable Ascetic Mahavira was threefold: he knew that he was to be removed; he knew that he was removed; he also knew when he was being removed.

In that period, in that age, once upon a time, after the lapse of nine complete months and seven and a half days, in the first month of summer, in the second fortnight, the dark fortnight of Chaitra, on its thirteenth day, while the moon was in conjunction with Uttaraphalguni, the Kshatriyani Trishala, perfectly healthy herself, gave birth to a perfectly healthy boy, the Venerable Ascetic Mahavira.

In that night in which the Kshatriyani Trishala, perfectly healthy herself, gave birth to a perfectly healthy boy, the Venerable Ascetic Mahavira, there was one great divine, godly lustre originated by descending and ascending gods and goddesses of the four orders of Bhavanapatis, Vyantaras, Jyotishkas and Vimanavasins; and in the conflux of gods the bustle of gods amounted to confusion.

In that night, the gods and goddesses rained down one great shower of nectar, sandal powder, flowers, gold, and pearls.

In that night the gods and goddesses (of the above mentioned four orders) performed the customary ceremonies of auspiciousness and honour, and his anointment as a Tirthankara.

Upwards from the time when the Venerable Mahavira was placed in the womb of the Kshatriyani Trishala, that family's treasure of gold, silver, riches, corn, jewels, pearls, shells, precious stones, and corals increased. When the parents of the Venerable Ascetic Mahavira had become aware of this, after the lapse of the tenth day, and the performance of the purification, they prepared much food, drink, sweets, and spices; and having invited a host of friends, near and remote relatives, they distributed, portioned out bestowed the above-mentioned materials to Shramanas, Brahmins, paupers, beggars, eunuchs, etc. and distributed gifts to those who wanted to make presents; then they gave a dinner to the host of friends, near and remote relatives, and after dinner they announced the name of the child to their guests: 'Since the Prince was placed in the womb of the Kshatriyani Trishala this family's treasure of gold, silver, riches, corn, jewels, pearls, shells, precious stones, and corals increased; therefore the Prince shall be called Vardhamana.

The Venerable Ascetic Mahavira was attended by five nurses: a wet-nurse, a nurse to clean him, one to dress him, one to play with him, one to carry him; being transferred from the lap of one nurse to that of another, he grew up on that beautiful ground, paved with mosaic of precious stones, like a Champaka tree growing in the glen of a mountain.

Then the Venerable Ascetic Mahavira, after his intellect had developed and the childhood had passed away, lived in the enjoyment of the allowed, noble, fivefold joys and pleasures: consisting in sound, touch, taste, colour, and smell.

The Venerable Ascetic Mahavira belonged to the Kashyapa gotra. His three names have thus been recorded by tradition: by his parents he was called Vardhamana, because he is devoid of love and hate.; he is called Shramana, i.e. Ascetic, because he sustains dreadful dangers and fears, the noble nakedness, and the miseries of the world; the name Venerable Ascetic Mahavira has been given to him by the gods.

The Venerable Ascetic Mahavira's father belonged to the Kashyapa gotra; he had three names: Siddhartha, Shreyamsa, and Jasamsa. His mother belonged to the Vasishtha gotra, and had three names: Trishala, Videhadatta, and Priyakarini. His paternal uncle Suparshva belonged to the Kashyapa gotra. His eldest brother, Nandivardhana, and his eldest sister, Sudarshana, belonged both to the Kashyapa gotra. His wife Yashoda belonged to the Kaundinya gotra. His daughter, who belonged to the Kashyapa gotra, had two names: Anojja and Priyadarshana. His granddaughter, who belonged to the Kaushika gotra, had two names: Sheshavati and Yashovati.

The Venerable Ascetic Mahavira's parents were worshippers of Parshva and followers of the Shramanas. During many years they were followers of the Shramanas and for the sake of protecting the six classes of lives they observed, blamed, repented, confessed, and did penance according to their sins. On a bed of Kusha-grass they rejected all food, and their bodies dried up by the last mortification of the flesh, which is to end in death. Thus they died in the proper month, and, leaving their bodies, were born as gods in Adhbuta Kalpa. Thence descending after the termination of their allotted length of life, they will, in Mahavideha, with their departing breath, reach absolute perfection, wisdom, liberation, final Nirvana, and the end of all misery.

In that period, in that age the Venerable Ascetic Mahavira, a Jnatri Kshatriya, Jnatriputra, a Videha, son of Videhadatta, a native of Videha, a Prince of Videha, lived thirty years amongst the householders under the name of Videha.

After his parents had gone to the worlds of the gods and he had fulfilled his promise, he gave up his gold and silver, his troops and chariots, and distributed, portioned out, and gave away his valuable treasure consisting of riches, corn, gold, pearls, etc. and distributed among those who wanted to make presents to others. Thus he gave away during a whole year. In the first month of winter, in the first fortnight, in the dark fortnight of Margashiras, on its tenth day, while the moon was in conjunction with Uttaraphalguni, he made up his mind to retire from the world.

A year before the best of Jinas will retire from the world, they continue to give awav their property, from the rising of the sun.

One crore and eight lacs of gold is his gifts at the rising of the sun, as if it were his morning meal.

Three hundred and eighty-eight crores and eighty lacs were given in one year.

The Kundaladharas of Vaishramana, the Laukantika and Maharddhika gods in the fifteen Karmabhumis wake the Tirthankara.

In Brahma Kalpa and in the line of Krishnas, the Laukantika Vimanas are eightfold and infinite in number.

These orders of gods wake the best of Jinas, the Venerable Vira: 'Arhit! propagate the religion which is a blessing to all creatures in the world!'

When the gods and goddesses, of the four orders of Bhavanapatis, Vyantaras, Jyotishkas, and Vimanavasins had become aware of the Venerable Ascetic Mahavira's intention to retire from the world, they assumed their proper form, dress, and ensigns, ascended with their proper pomp and splendour, together with their whole retinue, their own vehicles and chariots, and rejecting all gross matter, retained only the subtle matter. Then they rose and with that excellent, quick, swift, rapid, divine motion of the gods they came down again crossing numberless continents and oceans till they arrived in Jambudvipa at the northern Kshatriya part of the place Kundapura; in the north-eastern quarter of it they suddenly halted.

Shakra, the leader and King of the gods, quietly and slowly stopped his vehicle and chariot, quitely and slowly descended from it and went apart. There he underwent a great transformation, and produced by magic a great, beautiful, lovely, fine-shaped divine pavilion, which was ornamented with many designs in precious stones, gold, and pearls. In the middle part of that divine pavilion he produced one great throne of the same description, with a footstool.

Then he went where the Venerable Ascetic Mahavira was, and thrice circumambulating him from left to right, he praised and worshipped him. Leading him to the divine pavilion, he softly placed him with the face towards the east on the throne, anointed him with hundredfold and thousandfold refined oil, with perfumes and decoctions, bathed him with pure water, and rubbed him with beautifying cool sandal, laid on a piece of cloth worth a lac He clad him in a pair of robes so light that the smallest breath would carry them away; they were manufactured in a famous city, praised by clever artists, soft as the fume of horses, interwoven with gold by skilful masters, and ornamented with designs of flamingos.

Then the god decked him with necklaces of many and fewer strings, with one hanging down over his breast and one consisting of one row of pearls, with a garland, a golden string, a turban, a diadem, wreaths of precious stones, and decorated him with garlands, ribbons, scarves, and sashes like the Kalpavriksha.

The god then, for a second time, underwent a great transformation, and produced by magic the great palanquin, called Chandraprabha, which a thousand men carry. This palanquin was adorned with pictures of wolves, bulls, horses, men, dolphins, birds, monkeys, elephants, antelopes, sarabhas, yacks, tigers, lions, creeping plants, and a train of couples of Vidyadharas; it had a halo of thousands of rays; it was decorated with thousands of brilliant glittering rupees; its lustre was mild and bright; the eyes could not bear its light; it shone with heaps and masses of pearls; it was hung with strings and ribbons, and with golden excellent necklaces, extremely beautiful; its was embellished with designs of lotuses and many other plants; its cupola was adorned with many precious stones of five colours, with bells and flags; it was conspicuous, lovely, beautiful, splendid, magnificent.

This palanquin was brought for the best of Jinas, who is free from old age and death; it was hung with wreaths and garlands of divine flowers, grown in water or on dry ground.

In the middle of the palanquin was a costly throne covered with a divine cloth, precious stones and silver, with a footstool, for the best of Jinas.

He wore on his head a chaplet and a diadem, his body was shining, and he was adorned with many ornaments; he had put on a robe of muslin worth a lac.

After a fast of three days, with a glorious resolution he ascended the supreme palanquin, purifying all by his light.

He sat on his throne, and Shakra and Ishana, on both sides, fanned him with chowries, the handles of which were inlaid with jewels and precious stones.

In front it was uplifted by men, covered with joyful horripilation; behind the gods carried it: the Suras and Asuras, the Garudas and the chiefs of Nagas.

The Suras carried it on the eastern side, and the Asuras on the southern one; on the western side the Garudas carried it, and the Nagas on the northern side.

As a grove in blossom, or a lotus-covered lake in autumn looks beautiful with a mass of flowers, so did then the firmament with hosts of gods.

As a grove of Siddhartha, of Karnikara or of Champaka looks beautiful with a mass of flowers, so did the firmament with hosts of gods.

In the skies and on earth the sound of musical instruments produced by hundreds of thousands of excellent drums, kettle-drums, cymbals, and conches *was* extremely pleasant.

Then the gods ordered many hundreds of actors to perform a very rich concert of four kinds of instruments: stringed instruments and drums, cymbals and wind-instruments.

At that period, in that age, in the first month of winter, in the first fortnight, the dark fortnight of Margashiras, on its tenth day, called Suvrata, in the Muhurta called Vijaya, while the moon was in conjunction with the asterism Uttaraphalguni, when the shadow had turned towards the east, and the first Paurushi was over, after fasting three days without taking water, having put on the one garment, the Venerable Ascetic Mahavira, in his palanquin Chandraprabha, which only a thousand men can carry, with a train of gods, men, and Asuras left the northern Kshatriya part of the place Kundapura by the high way for the park Jnarri Khanda. There, just at the beginning of night, he caused the palanquin Chandraprabha to stop quietly on a slightly raised untouched ground, quitely descended from it, sat quitely down on a throne with the face towards the east, and took off all his ornaments and finer)'.

The god Vaishravana, prostrating himself, caught up the hunter and ornaments of the Venerable Ascetic Mahavira in a cloth of flamingo-pattern. Mahavira then plucked out with his right and left hands on the right and left sides of his head his hair in five handfuls. But Sakra, the leader and King of the gods, falling down before the feet of the Venerable Ascetic Mahavira, caught up the hair in a cup of diamond, and requesting his permission, brought them to the Milk Ocean.

After the Venerable Ascetic Mahavira had plucked out his hair in five handfuls, he paid obeisance to all liberated spirits, and vowing to do no sinful act, he adopted the holy conduct. At that moment the whole assembly of men and gods stood motionless, like the figures on a picture.

At the command of Shakra, the clamour of men and gods, and the sound of musical instruments suddenly ceased, when Mahavira chose the holy conduct.

Day and night following that conduct which is a blessing to all animated and living beings, the zealous gods listen to him with joyful horripilation.

When the Venerable Ascetic Mahavira had adopted the holy conduct which produced that state of soul in which the reward of former actions is temporarily counteracted, he reached the knowledge called Manahparyaya, by which he knew the thoughts of all sentient beings, with five organs, which are not defective, and possess a developed intellect, living in the two and a half continents and the two oceans. Then he formed the following resolution: I shall for twelve years neglect my body and abandon the care of it; I shall with equanimity bear, undergo, and suffer all calamities arising from divine powers, men or animals.

The Venerable Ascetic Mahavira having formed this resolution, and neglecting his body, arrived in the village Kummara when only one Muhurta of the day remained. Neglecting his body, the Venerable Ascetic Mahavira meditated on his Self, in blameless lodgings, in blameless wandering, in restraint, kindness, avoidance of sinful influence, chaste life, in patience, freedom from passion, contentment; control, circumspectness, practising religious postures and acts; walking the path of Nirvana and liberation, which is the fruit of good conduct. Living thus he with equanimity bore, endured, sustained, and suffered all calamities arising from divine powers, men, and animals, with undisturbed and unafflicted mind, careful of body, speech, and mind.

The Venerable Ascetic Mahavira passed twelve years in this way of life; during the thirteenth year in the second month of summer, in the fourth forthnight, the light fortnight of Vaishakha, on its tenth day, called Suvrata, in the Muhurta called Vijaya, while the moon was in conjunction with the asterism Uttaraphalguni, when the shadow had turned towards the east, and the first wake was over, outside of the town Jrimbhikagrama, on the northern bank of the river Rijupalika, in the field of the householder Samaga, in a north-eastern direction from an old temple, not far from a Sal tree, in a squatting position with joined heels exposing himself to the heat of the sun, with the knees high and the head low, in deep meditation in the midst of abstract meditation, he reached Nirvana, the complete and full, the unobstructed, unimpeded, infinite and supreme, best knowledge and intuition, called Kevala.

When the Venerable One had become an Arhat and Jina, he was a Kevalin, omniscient and comprehending all objects, he knew all conditions of the world, of gods, men, and demons; whence they come, where they go, whether they are born as men or animals, or become gods or hell-beings; their food, drink, doings, desires, open and secret deeds, their conversation and gossip, and the thoughts of their minds; he saw and knew all conditions in the whole world of all living beings.

On the day when the Venerable Ascetic Mahavira reached the Kevala, the gods of the four orders of Bhavanapatis, Vyantaras, Jyotishkas, and Vimanavasins descended from, and ascended to heaven.

Then when the Venerable Ascetic Mahavira had reached the highest knowledge and intuition, he reflected on himself and the world: first he taught the law to the gods, afterwards to men.

Five Great Vows

The Venerable Ascetic Mahavira endowed with the highest knowledge and intuition taught the five great vows, with their clauses, the six classes of lives to the Shramanas and Nirgranthas, to Gautama, etc.

First Great Vow

The first great vow, runs thus:

> I renounce all killing of living beings, whether subtle Or gross, whether movable or immovable. Nor shall I myself kill living beings nor cause others to do it, nor consent to it. As long as I live, 1 confess and blame, repent and exempt myself of these sins, in the thrice threefold way, i.e. acting, commanding, consenting, either in the past or the present or the future.

There are five clauses.

The first clause runs thus:

> A Nirgrantha is careful in his walk, not careless. The Kevalin assigns as the reason, that a Nirgrantha, careless in his walk, might with his feet hurt or displace or injure or kill living beings. Hence a Nirgrantha is careful in his walk, not careless in his walk.

This is the first clause.

Now follows the second clause:

> A Nirgantha searches into his mind. If his mind is sinful, blamable, intent on works, acting on impulses, produces cutting and splitting (or division and dissension), quarrels, faults, and pains, injures living beings, or kills creatures, he should not employ such

> a mind in action; but if, on the contrary, it is not sinful, then he may put it in action.

This is the second clause.

Now follows the third clause:

> A Nirgrantha searches into his speech; if his speech is sinful, blamable, etc. kills creatures, he should not utter that speech. But if, on the contrary, it is not sinful, then he may utter it.

This is the third clause.

Now follows the fourth clause:

> A Nirgrantha is careful in laying down his utensils of begging, he is not careless in it. The Kevalin says: A Nirgrantha who is careless in laying down his utensils of begging, might hurt or displace or injure or Jails all sorts of living beings. Hence a Nirgrantha is careful in laying down *his* utensils of begging, he is not careless in it.

This is the fourth clause.

Now follows the fifth clause:

> A Nirgrantha eats and drinks after inspecting his food and drink; he does not eat and drink without inspecting his food and drink. The Kevalin says: If a Nirgrantha would eat and drink without inspecting his food and drink, he might hurt and displace or injure or kill all sorts of living beings. Hence a Nirgrantha eats and drinks after inspecting his food and drink, not without doing so.

This is the fifth clause.

In this way the great vow is correctly practised, followed, executed, explained, established, effected according to the precept.

This is, the first great vow: Abstinence from killing any living beings.

Second Great Vow

The second great vow runs thus:

> I renounce all vices of lying speech arising from anger or greed or fear or mirth. 1 shall neither myself speak lies, nor cause others to speak lies, As long as I Hue, I confess and blame, repent and exempt myself of these sins in the thrice threefold way, in mind, speech, and body.

There are five clauses.

A Nirgrangtha speaks after deliberation, not without deliberation. The Kevalin says: Without deliberation a Nirgrantha might utter a falsehood in his speech. A Nirgrantha speaks after deliberation, not without delibertion.

This the first clause.

Now follows the second clause:

> A Nirgrantha comprehends and renounces anger, he is not angry. The Kevalin says: A Nirgrantha who is moved by anger, and is angry, might utter a falsehood in his speech. This is the second clause.

Now follows the third clause:

> A Nirgrantha comprehends and renounces greed; he is not greedy. The Kevalin says: A Nirgrantha who is moved by greed, and is greedy, might utter a falsehood in his speech.

This is the third clause.

Now follows the fourth. clause:

> A Nirgrantha comprehends and renounces fear; he is afraid. The Kevalin says; A Nirgrantha who is moved by fear, and is afraid, might utter a falsehood in his speech.

This is the fourth clause.

Now follows the fifth clause:

> A Nirgrantha comprehends and renounces mirth; he is not mirthful. The Kevalin says: A Nirgrantha who

is moved by mirth, and is mirthful, might utter a falehood in his speech.

This the fifth clause.

In this way the great vow is correctly practised, followed, executed, explained, established, effected according to practice. This is, the second great vow.

Third Great Vow

The third great vow runs thus:

I renounce all taking of anything not given, either in *a* village or a town or a wood, either of little or much, of small or great, of living or lifeless things. I shall neither take myself what is not given, nor cause others to take it, nor consent to their taking it. As long as I live, 1 confess and blame, repent and exempt myself of these sins, in the thrice threefold way in mind, speech and body.

There are five clauses:

The first clause runs thus:

A Nirgrantha begs after deliberation, for a limited ground, not without deliberation. The Kevalin says: If a Nirgrantha begs without deliberation for a limited ground, he might take what is not given.

This is the first clause.

Now follows the second clause:

A Nirgrantha consumes his food and drink with permission of his superior, not without his permission. The Kevalin says: If a Nirgtantha consumes his food and drink without the superior's permisison, he might eat what is not given.

This is the second clause.

Now follows the third clause:

A Nirgrantha who has taken possession of some ground, should always take possession of a limited

> part of it and for a fixed time. The Kevalin says: If a Nirgrantha who has taken possession of some ground, should take possession of an unlimited part of it and for an unfixed time, he might take what is not given.

This is the third clause.

Now follows the fourth clause:

> A Nirgrantha who has taken possession of some ground, should constantly have his grant renewed. The Kevalin says: If a Nirgrantha has not constantly his grant renewed, he might take possession of what is not given.

This is the fourth clause.

Now follows the fifth clause:

> A Nirgrantha begs for a limited ground for his co-religionists after deliberation, not without deliberation. The Kevalin says: If a Nirgrantha should beg without deliberation, he might take possession of what is not given.

This is the fifth clause.

This is the third great vow.

Fourth Great Vow

The fourth great vow runs thus:

> I renounce all sexual pleasures, either with gods or men or animals. I shall not give way to sensuality. As long as I live, 1 confess and blame, repent and exempt myself.

There are five clauses:

The first clause runs thus:

> A Nirgrantha does not continually discuss topics relating to women. The Kevalin says: If a Nirgrantha discusses such topics, he might fall from the law declared by the Kevalin, because of the destruction or disturbance of his peace.

This is the first clause.

Now follows the second clause:

> A Nirgrantha does not regard and contemplate the lovely forms of women. The Kevalin says: If a Nirgrantha regards and contemplates the lovely forms of women, he might fall from the law declared by the Kevalin.

This is the second clause.

Now follows the third clause:

> A Nirgrantha does not recall to his mind the pleasures and amusements he formerly had with women. The Kevalin says: If a Nirgrantha recalls to his mind the pleasures and amusements he formerly had with women, he might fall from the law declared by the Kevalin.

This is the third clause.

Now follows the fourth clause:

> A Nirgrantha does not eat and drink too much, nor does he drink liquors or eat highly-seasoned dishes. The Kevalin says: If a Nirgrantha did eat and drink too much, or did drink liquors and eat highly seasoned dishes, he might fall from the

law declared by the Kevalin. This is the fourth clause.

Now follows the fifth clause:

> A Nirgrantha does not occupy a bed or couch affected by women, animals, or eunuchs. The Kevalin says: If a Nirgrantha did occupy a bed or couch affected by women, animals, or eunuchs, he might fall from the law declared by the Kevalin.

That is the fifth clause.

This is, the fourth great vow.

Fifth Great Vow

The fifth great vow runs thus:

> I renounce all attachments, whether little or much, small or great, living or lifeless; neither shall 1 myself form such attachments, nor cause others to do so, nor consent to their doing so. As long as I live, I confess and blame, repent and exempt myself.

There are five clauses:

The first clause runs thus:

> If a creature with ears hears agreeable and disagreeable sounds, it should not be attached to, nor delighted with, nor desiring of, nor infatuated by, nor covetous of, nor disturbed by the agreeable or disagreeable sounds. The Kevalin says: If a Nirgrantha is thus affected by the pleasant or unpleasant sounds, he might fall from the law declared by the Kevalin.

If it is impossible not to hear sounds which reach the ear, the mendicant should avoid love or hate, originated by them. A creature with ears hears agreeable and disagreeable sounds.

This is the first clause.

Now follows the second clause:

> If a creature with eyes sees agreeable and disagreeable forms or colours, it should not be attached, to them.

Nirgrantha is thus affected by the pleasant or unpleasant forms, he might fall from the law declared by the Kevalin. This is the second clause.

Now follows the third clause:

> If a creature with an organ of smell smells agreeable or disagreeable smells, it should not be attached to them. So he falls from the law declared by the Kevalin.

This is the third clause.

Now follows the fourth clause:

> If a creature with a tongue tastes agreeable or disagreeable tastes, it should not be attached, to them. So he falls from the law declared by the Kevalin.

This is the fourth clause.

Now follows the fifth clause:

> If a creature with an organ of feeling feels agreeable or disagreeable touches, it should not be attached to them. So he falls from the law declared by the Kevalin.

This is the fifth clause.

In this way the great vow is correctly practised, followed, executed, explained, established, effected, according to the precept.

He who is well provided with these great vows and their twenty-five clauses is really Houseless, if he, according to the sacred lore, the precepts, and the way correctly practises, follows, executes, explains, establishes, and, according to the precept, effects them.

7

Precepts of Mahavira (Sermons)

Rules of Conduct

- Do not injure any living beings.
- All living beings love their own life, crave for pleasures, and are averse to pain; they dislike any injury to themselves; everybody is desirous of life, and to every living being, his own life is dean.
- One should treat all creatures as counterparts of one's own Self.
- This is the quintessence of the wisdom of the wise; Not to injure any living being. Non-injury to living beings should be regarded as the Samaya, i.e. the essence of the teaching of scriptures.
- Non-injury is the highest religion.
- If a man kills living beings himself, or causes others to kill them, or even if he merely consents to their killing, he increases his enmity towards living beings.
- Know and realise that all classes of living beings desire happiness. By hurting these beings, you harm your own souls.

- Impartiality or equanimity towards all living beings in the world, whether friends or foes, and life long abstention from injury to living beings, is a vow difficult to observe.
- The very first principle of religion is Ahinsha, i.e. non-injury to living beings, which must be observed very scrupulously and thoroughly. One should behave towards all living beings with proper restraint and control.
- Knowing that all the evils and sorrows arise from injury to living beings, and knowing further that it leads to unending enmity and hatred, and is the root cause of great fear, a wise man, who has become awakened; should refrain from all harmful activities.
- Do not kill living beings in any of the three ways (i.e. in mind, word or deed) if you seek your interest being free from desires of fruit and practising full self-control In this way many became perfect in the past, many become so at present and many others will become so:
- Any injury whatsoever to the material or conscious fatalities caused through passionate activity of mind, body or speech is Himsa.
- Assuredly, the non-appearance of attachment and other passions is Ahimsa, and their appearance is Himsa.
- Truth is the highest divine principle.
- O man ! Know that truth is the fundamental principle ! The wise man, who always abides by the commandment of truth, goes beyond death always injurious to living beings, whether for his own sake or for the sake of others, or out of anger or fear; he should also not force others to speak a lie.
- A wise man should never altar wards sinful 'or" condoning sin, whether out of anger, greed, fear or jest.
- Himsa comes in, certainly, in falsehood also.
- The third great sin is taking what is not expressly given, i.e. stealing; it causes heart-burning to others; endangers life; is sinful, alarming and scaring others, it is the cause

of greed for others' property, and it is the root-cause of greed; it is a vile and ignoble act, censured by the good; it the causes disruption among friends and dear ones, and gives rise to passions and hatred.

- To abstain from taking what is not given, even so much as a toothpick, etc.; and to accept only such alms as are free from all faults'; this is a difficult vow to observe.
- The taking of objects, which have not been given, is to be deemed theft, and that is Himsa because it is the cause of injury.
- Celibacy is the best among all the vows in the world.
- Celibacy is the root cause of excellent austerities, vows, knowledge, faith, conduct, righteousness and discipline.
- Among all the austerities, celibacy is the highest.
- Non-celibacy is the root of all sins, and a multitude of all great faults.
- A celibate monk should avoid a women, even though her hands and feet are cut off, her ears and nose are lopped off, and though she be a hundred years old.
- Sexual indulgence has root in desire and hence it is Himsa.
- To renounce all sense of possession with regard to wealth, corn and servants, to abstain from all harmful undertakings, and not to entertain any feeling of possession or attachment: this is a very difficult vow.
- He, who owns even a small property in living and non-living things, or consents to others possessing it, will never be delivered from misery.
- Immovable and movable property, wealth, corn and other perquisites-none of these is capable of freeing a man, from misery, who is suffering from the ripening of his actions.
- Every man should think that he has to depart certainly one day, leaving behind land, house, gold, sons, wife and relations -in fact leaving even his body.

- If somebody were to give the whole earth to one man, even then the man will not be satisfied; a greedy person is extremely difficult to be satisfied.
- Reading that wealth merely increases your sorrows and, worries, and the bonds of attachment or possession bring in their wake great dangers, you should bear the excellent yoke of religion, which will give you real pleasure, and will also bring you the great happiness of Moksha.
- Renunciation of all possessions is Ahimsa; and the appropriation of all possessions is Himsa.
- Misery is gone in the case of a man who has no delusion, while delusion is gone in the case of him who has no desire; desire is gone in the case of him who has no greed, while greed is gone in the case of him who possesses nothing.

Duties of Ascetics

- A monk who follows the order and commandments, who' gives proper respect to elders, and who acts according to his teachers' desires is a disciplined monk.
- When reprimanded, the wise monk should: not get angry; but he should have forbearance. He should avoid company, jokes and play with mean persons.
- Others may abuse a monk; but the monk should not be angry with them in return; because in that case the monk becomes like a child, the monk should not get angry.
- Self-restrained monk should withdraw with effort his mind directed to any desire or thought of injury, or any sinful act.
- In thought, words or deeds a monk should not undertake harmful activity to living beings, who live in this world, whether they are mobile or immobile.
- Well-dressed food quickly arouses passions; a monk, who is intent on practising celibacy, should always avoid such food.

- A monk, intent on practising the vow of celibacy, should abstain from ornaments, and should not do anything whatsoever to adorn or decorate his body in any manner.
- A monk should always abstain from the fivefold pleasant things (i.e. objects giving pleasures), viz. sounds, colours, smells, tastes, and touch.
- The ascetic life of those, who are intent on self-control, is comparable to living in heaven; while the life of those, who do not practise self-control, is like living in hell.
- Mortify yourself; give up the feeling of tenderness for the body; conquer desires and then you will realise that you have conquered all sorrow and misery; cut off all types of attachment, suppress hatred, and thus you will be happy in this worldly existence.
- He, who is desirous of storing, is a householder and not a monk.
- A monk should always concentrate on the highest and most pure type of meditation, be free from Nidana (i.e. carving for worldly or temporal gains in lieu of his austerities), should possess nothing, and move about in the world completely disregarding his body, till such time as death overtakes him.
- How can a monk, who cannot control his passions and who is swayed away by distracting thoughts and is discouraged at every step, can ever possibly practise the rules of asceticism?
- He, who abandons the evil thought of attachment to worldly objects, can alone give up possessions; he alone is a monk who has realised the real danger in the world, and who has no worldly attachments.
- A monk should not care for sleep, should avoid cutting jokes, should not take interest in the secrets of others, but should always be occupied and devoted to his studies.
- A monk is without any possessions, without egoism, without attachment, without vanity or conceit, he is impartial towards all living beings whether mobile or immobile.

- A monk is indifferent to success or failure, happiness and misery, life and death, so also to censure or praise, and honour or insults.
- The enlightened monks, who are completely disinterested in the world, who are keen on receiving alms from different places and not from one place only, and who are self-controlled, are like the bees; and that is why they are called the true monks.
- A monk should not eat for the sake of the delicious taste of the food, but far the sustenance of life and body, not being greedy for delicacies, nor eager for good fare, and restraining his tongue and being free from cupidity.
- If any body abuses a monk, he should not get angry with him.
- One who never tells stories that will incite quarrels, never gets angry, always controls his senses, and is calm and serene, who is always pursuing firmly the precepts laid down for observing self-control, is always unpurturbed, and never offends or insults others-he alone is a true monk.
- A monk should have compassion towards all beings, should be of a forgiving nature, should be restrained and chaste, and should avoid all sinful activities: He should move about in the world with all his senses properly controlled.
- A monk should not use words of censure behind the back of another, he should not use painful language in the presence of another; so also he should not use determinative expression as also unpalatable expression; a monk who behaves thus, is really a worthy one.

Practice of Religion

- Religion is the highest bliss is made up of abstinence from injury (to living beings), self-restraint and penance. Even gods bow down to him who has his mind always firm in religion.

- From the root grows up the trunk of the tree, from the trunk shoot up the branches, out of them grow the twigs and the leaves; and then there are produced flowers, fruits and juice. Similarly, obedience is the root of the tree of religion and the Liberation is the highest resultant (viz. the juice). It is by obedience that one gets quickly and completely renown and learning.
- While old age has not begun to ail, or disease has not grown, or senses have not failed, one should practise religion.
- Whatever day passes never comes back, in the case of a man practising irreligion, the days pass without bringing any fruit (i.e. benefits) to him.
- Whatever day passes never comes back; in the case of a man practising religion, the days pass bearing much fruit to him.
- In the case of living 1eings carried away on by the rapid current of old age and death, it is religion that stands as island, firm ground, refuge as well as the best shelter.
- This is the unchangeable, eternal and permanent religion expounded by the, linas. By means of this, the enlightened have reached perfection; others also Will reach perfection by it.

Theory of Karma

- All souls are susceptible to assimilating Karma particles, flowing from all the six quarters; the Karma binds the soul in all its parts, and the entire Karma-particles bind or cover the whole soul in every way.
- In this world, all living beings suffer individually for their deeds. For the deeds they have done, they obtain punishment or rebirth; none can escape the fruit of actions, except by suffering for it.
- In this world or in the next, the sinner suffers himself what he has inflicted on others a hundred fold or in some different form of punishment. Living beings in Samsara,

i.e. cycle of worldly existence, go on ever acquiring fresh Karma (by mind, speech or action), and suffer for their evil deeds.

- As a burglar caught in the breach of a wall, perishes by the act he himself had performed (viz. giving a breach in the wall), even to people, in this life and after death (i.e. in the next life), can never escape the fruit of actions performed by them.
- A man goes according to his Karma sometimes to the world of gods, sometimes: to hell; and sometimes to the Asura world (i.e. the world of demons).
- The relatives of a man will not act as relatives at, the time when the man is to reap, the fruit of his Karma which he has done in this worldly life for the sake of others, or in common for himself along with others.
- Neither his kinsmen nor his friends, nor his sons, nor his relatives are prepared to share his pain. He alone bears the pain himself. Karma follows invariably the doer alone.
- Therefore, a wise man should know the various subdivisions or types of these Karmas, and should also exert himself to prevent any new Karma and to destory the past Karmas.
- Just as a large tank, when its supply of water has been stopped, gradually dries up by the consumption of the water, and by evaporation, similarly 'the Karma of a well-controlled monk, acquired in crores of past births, is annihilated by austerities provided, however, that there is no further influx of bad Karma.
- Just as a dried gourd fruit, when it is covered with layers of soft clay, becomes heavy and sinks down in water, in the same way the soul becomes heavy because of the influx of Karmas, and sinks to (i.e. is born in) the lower types of births. But the same gourd - fruit, when it is freed from the thick layers of clay (-with the! clay - gradually being dissolved in water-) becomes light (or attains its natural lightness), and floats on the surface of water;'in

like manner, the souls devoid of all the Karmas, (attain their natural state), and go to the top of the world and reside there permanently.

Value of Self-control

- The body is said to be the boat and the soul is said to be the sailor. The Samsara, i.e. the worldly existence, is said to be the ocean which is crossed only by great sages.
- One must always guard one's soul from all evil, by having the sense-organs properly, controlled. In case the soul is not well-guarded; it takes 'to the path leading' to birth and, death; while if well-controlled, it becomes free from all worldly sorrows and misery.
- The Self alone should be subdued; for it is very difficult to subdue it; he who has subdued his Self becomes happy in this world as well as in the next.
- It is better, that I myself should subdue my Self-control and austerities, than be subdued by, others with fetters, rather corporal punishment.
- My, own Self is the river Vaitarani (i.e. river is hell with bitingly cold water); my own Self is the Kutashalmati tree (i.e. a tree in hell with sharp leaves); my own Self is the Kamadhenu, (i.e. the desire-yielding cow); and my own:, Self is the park Nandana (i.e. paradise).
- My own Self is the doer and un-doer of misery and happiness in this world; my own Self is my (best) friend or (worst) enemy, depending on whether it acts well or badly.
- A man may conquer thousands and thousands of invincible foes (but that is of no real consequence); his greatest victory is when he conquers only his own Self.
- Fight with your (own) Self; what is the good of fighting the external foes? By conquering one's Self by means of one's own Self, one obtains true happiness.
- The five senses, and (the four passions, viz.)- auger, pride, deception and greed, are all difficult to 'conquer; equally difficult it is to conquer one's own Self. But one who has

conquered his Self, has conquered everything else in the world.

- Having committed a wrong (or sin) knowingly or unknowingly, one should immediately revoke it, and should never repeat it a second time.
- The gods, the demons, the Gandharvas, the Yakshas, the Rakshasas and the Kinnaras-all bow down to a chaste monk who observes the difficult Self-Control.
- A man might give by way of charity, thousands of thousands of cows every month; but far better than him will be the man who may give nothing in charity, but only observes perfect Self -Control.
- Self-control is un-tasteful like eating a morsel of sand. And to practise life-long penance is as difficult as to walk on the edge of a sword.
- In this world nothing is really difficult for one who is free from desires.

  O man ! You better control and curb your own Self? Thus alone will you be free from all sorrows and misery:
- I beg pardon of all living beings; may all living beings pardon me. I bear friendship for all living beings; I bear no enmity to any.
- Anger destorys love, pride puts an end to modesty, deceit removes friends, while greed-destroys everything.

Way of Salvation

- Right faith, right knowledge and right conduct, these together constitute the path to liberation.
- Liberation comes soon to those desiring Self-advancement, when they exert ceaselessly in the threefold path of right belief, right knowledge and right conduct:
- One must by all possible means, first attain right belief, because only on the acquisition thereof, knowledge and conduct become right.

- Right knowledge, right faith, right conduct and austerities: Those who follow this fourfold path will attain the best state of existence, i.e. the final beatitude.
- By right knowledge one knows the true nature of things, by right faith one believes in them, by right conduct one controls the influx of Karma, and by austerities one attains purity.
- Without right faith, there cannot be right knowledge; without right. knowledge,' there can be no right or virtuous conduct; without virtuous conduct, there cannot be, release or freedom from Karma (i.e. release from bandage); and without release from Karmic bondage, there cannot be Nirvana (i.e. liberation).
- Having destroyed their past Karmas by means of Self-control and austerities, the sages proceed towards the goal of Moksha, which is free from all sorrows and misery.
- By the manifestation of perfect knowledge, by the avoidance of ignorance and delusion, by the destruction of love and hatred, one obtains Liberation which is full of pure happiness.

8

Doctrines of Mahavira

Rules of Conduct for Laymen

The householders are expected to observe twelve vratas, i.e. consisting of (A) five Anuvratas, i.e. small vows and (B) seven Shilavratas, i.e. supplementary vows. These vows form the central part of the ethical code and by their observance laymen can maintain constant progress in their spiritual career aimed at the attainment of final liberation.

Anuvratas: The five main vratas, i.e. vows, to be observed by all are: (i) Ahimsa, i.e. abstention from violence or injury to living beings,

- Satya, i.e. abstention from false speech,
- Asteya, i.e. abstention from theft,
- Brahmacharya, i.e. abstention from sexuality or unchastity, and
- Aparigraha, i.e. abstention from greed for worldly possessions.

If these vows are very strictly observed they are known as Mahavratas, i.e. great vows and naturally these are meant for the ascetics. Laymen, however, cannot observe the vows so strictly and therefore they are allowed to practise them so far as their conditions permit. Therefore, the same vratas, i.e. vows, when partially observed are termed as Anuvratas, i.e. small vows. For the fixing of these five vows in the mind, there are five kinds of Bhavanas i.e. attendant meditations, for each of the vows and every person is expected to think over them again and again. Further, every person must meditate that the five faults meant to be avoided in the vows are pain personified and are of dangerous and censurable character in this world. Moreover, every person must meditate upon the following four virtues which are based upon the observance of these five vows: (i) Maitri, i.e. friendship with all living beings,

- Pramoda, i.e. delight at the sight of beings better qualified or more advanced than ourselves on the path of liberation,
- Karunya, i.e. compassion for the afflicted, and
- Madhyastha, i.e. tolerance or indifference to those who are uncivil or ill behaved.

The observance of the five anuvratas and refraining from the use of wine, flesh and honey are regarded as eight Mulagunas, i.e. the basic or primary virtues of a house-holder. For minimising injury to living beings, complete abstinence of wine, flesh and honey is advocated and every householder must necessarily possess these eight primary or fundamental virtues.

These five vows form the basis of Jaina ethics. They give a definite outlook on life and create a particular type of mental attitude. The very essence of Jaina philosophy is transformed into action in the shape of observance of these five vows. Though the vows on their face appear to be mere abstentions from injury, falsehood, theft, sexuality and greed for worldly attachments, their implications are really extensive and they permeate the entire social life of the followers of Jainism.

Further, three things are enjoined in the matter of avoidance of the five faults of injury, falsehood, theft, etc. In the first place, a person should not commit any fault personally, secondly, he should not incite others to commit such an act, and, thirdly, he should not even approve of it subsequent to its commission by others. (i) Himsa, i.e. injury, has been defined as hurting of the fatalities caused through want of proper care and caution. But the meaning is not limited to this definition alone. Piercing, binding, causing pain, overloading and starving or not feeding at proper times, are forms of himsa and as such must be avoided. (ii) Asatya, i.e. falsehood, in simple terms, is to speak hurtful words. But spreading false doctrines, revealing the secrets and deformities of others, backbiting, making false documents, and breach of trust are all forms of falsehood and should be abstained from. (iii) Chaurya, i.e. theft, is to take anything which is not given. Imparting instructions on the method of committing theft, receiving stolen property, evading the injunction of the law (for example, by selling things at inordinate prices), and keeping false weights and measures are all forms of theft and one must guard oneself against them. (iv) Abrahma, i.e. sexuality, is also of several forms. Match making (i.e. bringing about marriages, as a hobby), unnatural gratification, indulging in voluptuous speech, and visiting immoral married and unmarried women are all forms of unchastity or sexuality and should be avoided. (v) Parigraha, i.e. greed for worldly possessions, consists in desiring more than what is needed by an individual. Accumulating even necessary articles in large numbers, expressing wonder at the prosperity of another, excessive greed, and changing the proportions of existing possessions are all forms of parigraha and should be discarded. This vow of aparigraha or parigrahaparimana recommends that a householder should fix, beforehand, the limit of his maximum belongings, and should, in no case, exceed it. If he ever happens to earn more than that, he must spend it away in charities, the best and recognised forms of which are distribution of medicine, spread of knowledge, provision for saving the lives of people in danger, and feeding the hungry and the poor.

Among these five main vows the utmost importance is given to Ahimsa, i.e. avoidance of injury. This noble principle of Ahimsa has been recognised by practically all religions but Jainism alone preaches the full significance of Ahimsa to such an extent that Jainism and Ahimsa have become synonymous terms. Jainism emphatically asserts that "Ahimsa Parmo Dharmah", i.e. Ahimsa is the highest religion. The philosophy of Jainism and its rules of conduct are based on the foundations of Ahimsa which has been consistently followed to its logical conclusion. That is why among the five main vows first place has been given to the observance of Ahimsa. Ahimsa is regarded as the principal vow and the other four vows are considered to be merely details of the first vow. It is emphasised that Himsa, i.e. injury, is included in falsehood, theft, sexual impurity and possession of goods. Thus all the main five vows are based on the principle of Ahimsa. That is why it is enjoined upon every person to avoid Himsa under any pretexts. Himsa, i.e. violence or injury, is considered of three kinds: (a) physical violence, which covers killing, wounding and causing any physical pain; (b) violence in words consists in using harsh words; and (c) mental violence implies bearing ill-feeling towards others. Further, Himsa may be committed, commissioned or consented to. A householder is unable to avoid all these in an ideal manner; so he is expected to cause minimal injury to others. In view of the routine life of the people, injury is classified under four heads: (i) first, there is Grharambhi Himsa, accidental injury in digging, pounding, cooking and such other activities essential to daily living; (ii) secondly, there is Udyami Himsa, i.e. occupational injury when a soldier fights, an agriculturist tills the land, etc. (iii) thirdly, there is Virodhi Himsa, i.e. protective injury, when one protects one's or other's life and honour against wild beasts and enemies; and (iv) fourthly, there is Sumkalpi Himsa, i.e. intentional injury, when one kills beings simply for killing themm as in hunting or butchery. A householder is expected to abstain fully from intentional injury and as far as possible from the rest. It is the intention or the mental attitude that matters more Than the act. So one has to take utmost care in keeping one's intentions pure and pious and abstain from intentional injury.

Shilavratas: Along with the five Anuvratas, i.e. small vows, there are seven Shilavratas, i.e. supplementary vows. Just as the encircling walls guard towns, so do supplementary vows protect Anuvratas. Therefore in order to practise the main Anuvratas, the Shilavratas also must be practised by the householders. The seven supplementary vows are as follows:

- Digvrata, i.e. taking a lifelong vow to limit his worldly activity to fixed points in all directions,
- Deshavrata, i.e. taking a vow to limit the above also for a limited area,

- Anarthadanda-vrata, i.e. taking a vow not to commit purposeless sins, or to abstain from wanton sinful activities,
- Samayika, i.e. taking a vow to devote particular time everyday to contemplation or meditation of the self for spiritual advancement,
- Proshadhopavasa, i.e. taking a vow to fast on four days of the month, namely, the two eighth and the two fourteenth days of the fortnight,
- Upabhoga-Paribhoga-Parimana, i.e. taking a vow everyday limiting one's enjoyment of consumable and non-consumable things, and
- Atithi-Samvibhaga, i.e. taking a vow to take one's food only after feeding the ascetics or, in their absence the pious householders.

Out of these seven Shilavratas, the first three are called Gunavratas, i.e. multiplicative vows, because they raise the value of the five main Anuvratas; and the remaining four are called Shikshavratas, i.e. disciplinary vows, because they are preparatory for the discipline of an ascetic life. Thus the five Anuvratas, the three Gunavratas and the four Shikshavratas constitute the twelve vows of a laymen. There are five aticharas, i.e. defects or partial transgressions, for each of these twelve vows and they are to be avoided by the observers of these vows.

The most significant feature of these twelve vows is that by practising these vows a layman virtually participates, to a limited extent and for a limited period of time, in the routine of an ascetic without actually renouncing the world. It is obvious that such practices maintain a close tie between the laymen and the ascetics as both are actuated by the same motive and are moved by the same religious ideals.

In addition to the above twelve vows a house-holder is expected to practise in the last moment of his life the process of Sallekhana, i.e. peaceful or voluntary death. A layman is expected not only to live a disciplined life but also to die bravely a detached death. This voluntary death is to be distinguished from suicide which is considered by Jainism as a cowardly sin. It is laid down that when faced by calamity, famine, old age and disease against which there is no remedy, a pious householder should peacefully relinquish his body, being inspired by a higher religious ideal. It is with a quiet and detached mood he should face death bravely and voluntarily. This Sallekhana is added to as an extra vow to the existing twelve vows of a house-holder. Like other vows, Sallekhana has also got five aticharas, i.e. partial transgressions, which are to be avoided by a householder.

These rules of right conduct prescribed for laymen have been conveniently divided into eleven Pratimas, i.e. stages or steps. These Pratimas form a series of duties and performances, the standard and duration of which rises periodically and which finally culminates in an attitude resembling monkhood. Thus the pratimas rise by degrees and every stage includes all the virtues practised in those preceding it. The conception of eleven Pratimas reveals in the best manner the rules of conduct prescribed for the laymen. The eleven Pratimas are as follows:

- Darshana Pratima, i.e. possessing the perfect, intelligent and well-reasoned faith in Jainism, that is, having a sound knowledge of its doctrines and their applications in life.
- Vrata Pratima, i.e. keeping up the twelve vows and the extra vow of Sallekhana.
- Samayika Pratima, i.e. worshipping regularly, in general for forty-two minutes, three times daily. Worship means self-contemplation and purifying one's ideas and emotions.
- Proshadhopavasa Pratima, i.e. fasting regularly, as a rule, twice a fortnight in each lunar month.
- Sachitta-tyaga pratima; i.e. refraining from eating uncooked vegetables, plucking fruits from a tree and the like.
- Ratri-bhukta-tyaga Pratima i.e. abstaining from food after sunset.
- Rahmacharya Pratima, i.e. maintaining sexual purity now assuming the strict aspect of celibacy and also not decorating one's person.

- Arambha-tyaga Pratima, i.e. abandonment of merelv worldly engagements and occupations.
- Parigraha-tyaga pratima, i.e. divesting oneself of Weald by dividing one's property among one's heirs and training generally to bear the hardships incidental to a life of asceticism.
- Anumati-tyaga pratima, i.e. increasing the rigour or living in the direction of asceticism and refraining even from giving advice on matters relating to family honour, business and the like.
- Uddishta-tyaga pratima, i.e. after renunciation of the householder's life, retiring into forest and adopting the rules laid down for the guidance of ascetics.

A householder is advised that according to his ability and environment he should proceed stage by stage and once he reaches the eleventh stage, he is fully prepared for practising the severe course of ascetic life.

Rules of Conduct for Ascetics

When a layman consistently observes the rules of conduct prescribed for the householders and especially attains all pratimas, he is qualified to become an ascetic. In this way there is a close link between the two social orders of laity and ascetics. The order of laymen (including laywomen) is preliminary and, in many cases, preparatory to the order of monks (including nuns). Because of this intimate relationship we find that the rules prescribed for laymen and ascetics do not differ in kind but in degree.

The same rules of conduct observed by laymen are to be followed by ascetics with the only difference that while laymen have to practise them partially or less rigorously, ascetics have to observe them fully and more rigorously. Thus the Anuvratas, i.e. small vows, of the householders become Mahavratas, i.e. great vows, when practised by ascetics. This is obvious because the ascetic stage signifies absolute renunciation of the world and the only objective in this stage is to concentrate energy on the attainment of Moksha, i.e. liberation. Asceticism is a higher course in spiritual training and it is in this stage real efforts are made for the stoppage of influx of Karmas and the shedding of existing Karmas with a view to attain liberation. Therefore very minute rules of conduct are prescribed for the ascetics and the latter have to observe them without any fault or transgression.

The stoppage of influx of fresh Karmic matter into the Atman or soul is known as Samvara and it is effected by following:

- three kinds of Gupti, i.e. control,
- five kinds of Samiti, i.e. carefulness,
- ten kinks of Dharma, i.e. virtues,
- twelve kinds of Anupreksha, i.e. meditations or reflections,
- twenty-two kinds of Parishaha-Jaya, i.e. subdual of sufferings, and
- five kinds of Charitra, i.e. conduct.

The Guptis: The flow of Karmas into the Atman or soul is caused by the activities of body, speech and mind; so it is quite necessary for the ascetics to keep these channels of influx under strict control, i.e. to observe the Guptis. The three guptis are regulations with reference to controlling one's inner nature, that is, they are dictated by the principles of self-control, (i) The first of them is Mano-Gupti, i.e. regulation of mind in such a way as to give room only to pure thoughts. (ii) The second Vag-gupti, i.e. regulations of speech and it consists in observing silence for a particular period or in speaking only as much as is absolutely necessary. (iii) The third is Kaya-gupti, i.e. regulation of one's bodily activity.

Samitis: It is just possible that even in performing the duties of an ascetic, the vows might be transgressed out of inadvertence. Hence as a precautionary measure the Samitis, i.e. acts of carefulness are prescribed. The Samitis are designed with a view to cultivate the habit of carefulness in accordance with the principle of Ahimsa, i.e. non-injury. The Samitis are prescriptions for the regulation of the movements of the body and are as follows:

- The Irya Samiti aims at regulation of walking, so as not to injure any living being.

- The Bhasha Samiti regulates the mode of speech with a view to avoid the hurting of other's feelings by use of offensive words.
- The Eshana Samiti regulates seeking or eating food so, as not to cause any injury to any living being.
- The Adana-Nikshepa Samiti regulates the actions of taking or using, and of putting away, anything whatsoever.
- The Utsarga Samiti regulates the movements connected with the answering of call of nature, etc. Both the three Guptis and five Samitis are sometimes grouped together under the name of "Ashta-Pravachana-Mata", i.e. "The Eight mothers of the Creed", on account of their fundamental character.

The Dharmas: It is mainly due to the Kashayas, i.e. passions, that the soul assimilates Karmas, hence the four passions of Krodha, i.e. angar, Mana, i.e. pride, Maya, i.e. deceptions and Lobha, i.e. greed, must be counteracted by cultivating ten Uttama Dharmas, i.e. Supreme virtues, as follows:

- Uttama-Kshama, i.e. supreme forgiveness,
- Uttama-Mardava, i.e. Supreme tenderness or humility,
- Uttama-Arjava, i.e. Supreme straight forwardness or honesty,
- Uttam-Shaucha, i.e. Supreme contentment or purity,
- Uttama-Satya i.e. Supreme truthfulness.
- Uttama-Samyama, i.e. Supreme Self-restraint,
- Uttama-Tapa, i.e. Supreme austerities,
- Uttama-Tyaga, i.e. Supreme renunciation,
- Uttama-Akinchanya, i.e. Supreme non-attachment, and
- Uttama-Brahmacharya, i.e. Supreme chastity.

These ten virtues together are termed as Dashalakshana Dharma, i.e. the ten observances.

***Anupreksha*s:** With a view to cultivate the necessary religious attitude, it is enjoined on the ascetics to constantly reflect on twelve religious topics know as Anupreksḥas, i.e. meditations. It is laid down that these Anupreksḥas should be meditated upon again and again. The twelve Anupreksḥas are as follows:

- Anitya anuprekshas, i.e. everything is subject to change or is transitory.
- Asharana anupreksha, i.e. unprotectiveness or helplessness. The feeling that soul is unprotected from fruition of Karmas, for example, death, etc.
- Samsara anupreksha, i.e. mundaneness. Soul moves in the cycle of existences and cannot attain true happiness till it is cut off.
- Ekatva anuprelcsha, i.e. loneliness. I am alone, the doer of my actions and the enjoyed of the fruits of them.
- Anyatva anupreksha, i.e. separatness. The world, my relation and friends, my body and mind, they are all distinct and separate from my real self.
- Ashuchi anupreksha, i.e. impurity. The body is impure and dirty.
- Ashram anupreksha, i.e. inflow. The inflow of Kar-mas is the cause of my mundane existence and it is; the product of passions.
- Samvara anupreksha, i.e. stoppage. The inflow of Karma must be stopped by cultivating necessary virtues.
- Nirjara anuprelcsha, i.e. shedding. Karmic matter should be destroyed or shaken out of the soul by the practice of penances.
- Loka anupreksha, i.e. universe. The nature of the, universe and its constituent elements in all their vast variety proving the insignificance and miserable nothingness of man in time and space.
- Bodhi-durlabha anupreksha i.e. rarity of religious, knowledge. It is difficult to attain right faith, knowledge and conduct.
- Dharma arzupreksha, i.e. reflection on the true nature of religion and especially on the threefold path of liberation as preached by the conquerors.

Sometimes these Anupprekshas, are termed as Bhavanas, i.e. contemplations.

The Parishaha-Jaya: With a view to remain steady on the path of liberation and to destroy the Karmic matter; ascetics should bear cheerfully all the troubles that might cause them distraction or pain. These troubles or hardships through which the ascetics have to pass are called the Parishahas, i.e. sufferings. There are twenty-two Parishahas which monks are expected to face unflinchingly. They are:

- Kslzut, i.e. hunger,
- Pipasa, i.e. thirst,
- Shita, i.e. cold,
- Ushna, i.e. heat,
- Damsharnashaka, i.e. insect-bite,
- Nagnya, i.e. nakedness,
- Arati, i.e. ennui, or disagreeable surroundings,
- Stri, i.e. seg passion,
- Charya, i.e. walking too much,
- Nishadya, i.e. continuous sitting in one posture,
- Shayva, i.e. resting on hard earth,
- Akrosha, i.e. abuse,
- Vadha, i.e. beating,
- Yachana, i.e. begging,
- Alabha, i.e. disappointment from getting no food,
- Roga, i.e. disease,
- Transplants, i.e. thorn-pricks,
- Mala, i.e. body dirt and impurities,
- Satlcarapur Qskara, i.e. disrespect shown by men,
- Prajna, i.e. non-appreciation of learning,
- Ajnaraa, i.e. persistence of ignorance, and

- Adarshana, i.e. slack belief, for example, on failure to obtain supernatural powers even after great piety and austerities begin to doubt the truth of Jainism and its teachings.

These Parishahas Should be ever endured without any feeling of vexation, by the ascetics who desire to get rid of all cause for pain.

The Charitra: The ascetics are also expected to strive to observe five kinds of conduct as follows:

- Samayika, i.e. equanimity,
- Chhedapasthapaiaa,
- Parilrara-Vishuddhi, i.e. pute arid absolute non-injury,
- Suk.rhma-Samparziya, i:e.'all but entire freedom from passion, and'
- Yathakyata, i.e. ideal and passionless conduct.

These five kinds of conduct help to- maintain the spiritual discipline of the ascetics,

Along with Samvara, i.e. the stoppage of the influx of Karmic matter into the soul, the ascetics have to strive to effect Nirjara, i.e. the gradual removal of Karmic matter from the soul if they have to proceed further on their path of liberation. The main way to Nirjara' i.e. shedding of the Karmas; is the observance of Tapa, i.e. penance or austerities, which is included in the tight-conduct. Tapa, i.e. penance is two fold, viz. (a) Badaya Tapa, i.e. external austerities, referring to food and physical activities and (b) Abhyantara Tapa, i.e. internal austerities, referring to spiritual discipline. Each of these 2 types of Tapas is of six kinds.

- The Bahya Tapa: The six external' austerities are as follows:
  - Anashana, i.e. fasting,
  - Avamodarya, i.e. eating less than one's fill, or less, than one has appetite for,
  - Vritti-Parisamkhyand, i.e. taking a mental vow to accept food from a householder only if certain conditions are fulfilled without letting any one know about the vow,

— Rasa-Parityaga, i.e. daily renunciation of one or more of six kinds of delicacies namely, ghee (i.e. clarified butter), milk, curds, sugar, salt and oil.

— Vivikta-Shayyasana, i.e. sitting and sleeping in a secluded place, devoid of animate beings, and

— Kayalesha, i.e. mortification of the body so long as the mind is not disturbed.

- The Abhyantra Tapa: The six kinds of internal austerities are:

— Prayashchitta, i.e. expiation or confession and repentance of sins,

— Yinaya, i.e. reverence or modest behaviour,

— Vaiyavrtya, rendering service to other saints,

— Svadhyaya, i.e. study of scriptures,

— Vyutsarga, i.e. giving up attachment to the body, and

— Dhyana, i.e. concentration of mind.

These external and internal penances show what a rigorous life of self-denial the ascetics have to lead. The ascetic is to sustain the body with minimum feeding and to take maximum work from it in the attainment of his spiritual ideal. In Jainism an elaborate technique of fasting has been evolved and the ascetic is trained all along his career so efficiently that when the hour of death comes, he accepts voluntary fasting and gives up the body as easily as one would throw off the old garment. The ascetic has always to take exercise in fasting by observing series of fasts differently arranged.

Among the internal penances special significance is attached to Dhyana, i.e. meditation, because it is considered as the most important spiritual exercise whereby alone the soul can make progress on the path to liberation and can destroy all the Karmas. Attachment for beneficial and aversion from harmful objects have to be given up to attain concentration of mind, which is the prerequisite of successful meditation. It is always emphasised that the Shukla Dhyana i.e. pure meditation, ultimately leads the soul to liberation because in Shukla Dhyana, an attempt is made for complete cessation of physical, verbal and mental activities. When the entire stock of Karmas is exhausted by following the rules of conduct laid down by Jaina ethics, the soul shoots up to the top of the universe where the liberated souls stay for ever.

Philosophical Doctrines

Since Tirthankara Mahavira was the 24th Tirthankara in the uniterrupted succession of Tirthankaras of the Jaina tradition beginning from the lst Tirthankara Rishabhadeva, he preached the doctrines which were already propounded by his 23 predecessors. Parshvanatha, the 23rd Tirthankara flourished 250 years before Tirthankara Mahavira and during his lifetime Parshvanatha did propagate the basic doctrines of Jainism to the benefit of mankind. But after Parshvanath the conditions of life considerably changed and common people were found holding various beliefs and observing several practices which were completely opposed to the beliefs and practices laid down by Jaina religion.

Hence there was a dire necessity to bring back the common masses to the right path advocated by the Jaina Tirthankaras. This urgent need was met by Tirthankara Mahavira during the sixth century B. C. by emphasising the age-old principles of Jainism to all categories *of persons* scattered over different parts of India. Tirthanhara Mahavira continued his preaching tour for 30 years till he attained Parinirvana. In this mission of propagation of his doctrines and of conversion of people to the Jaina way of life, 'Tirthankara Mahavira was highly successful because people were greatly impressed by his divine voice, oratorical powers, sublime personality, and sincerity of purpose and were firmly convinced about the utility of adopting the Jaina way of life. Thus the doctrines preached by Tirthankara Mahavira were essentially the doctrines of Jainism.

The basic principle in the philosophical doctrines of Tirthankara Mahavira is that 'Sat', i.e. reality is uncreated that it is characterised by 'Utpada', i.e. origination or appearance, 'Vyaya', i.e. destruction or disappearance. Further, every object of reality is found possessed of infinite characters, both with respect to hat it is and what it is not. It has its 'paryayas', i.e. modes and 'gunas', i.e. qualities, through which persists the essential substratum through all the times. The basic substance with its qualities is something that is permanent, while the modes or accidental characters appear and disappear: In this way both change and permanence are facts of experience.' For example, the soul or spirit is eternal with its inseparable character- of consciousness, but at the same time it is subjected to accidental characters like pleasure and pain and super-imposed modes such as body, etc. both of which are changing constantly. The gold, for instance, with its colour and density is something that is permanent though it is subjected to different shapes at different times.

Further, the philosophical doctrines assert that in this world 'dravyas' i. e. the substances, are real as they are characterised by existence. The substances are six in number and they can be broadly divided into two major categories, viz. Viva', i. e. living and 'ajiva', i. e. non-living.

Viva Dravya

The jiva means Atman i. e. soul or spirit. The jiva is essentially a unit of consciousness and there is an infinity of them. The whole world is literally filled with them. The souls are substances and as such they are eternal. Their characteristic mark is intelligence, which can never be destroyed. The soul is ever all perfect and all powerful. But by ignorance it identifies itself with matter and hence all its troubles and degradations start.

The souls are of two kinds, viz. (a) 'samsarin', i. e. mundane or baddha', i.e. those in bondage, and (b) 'siddha', i.e. liberated or 'mukta' i.e. those that are free. Mundane souls are the embodied souls of living beings in the world and are still subject to the cycle of Birth. On the other hand, the liberated souls are those who have reached Nirvana or 'Mukti' i. e. freedom from being em bodied. It means that the liberated souls will be embodied no more. Such liberated souls dwell in the state of perfection at the top of the universe and they have no more to do with worldly affairs. The liberated souls also accomplish absolute purity and in their pure condition they possess four attributes known as 'Ananta-Chatushtaya', Infinite Quaternary, viz.

ananta-darslaana', i.e. infinite perception,

'ananta- a', i. e. infinite knowledge,

ananta-virya', i.e. infinite power and

'ananta-sukha', i.e. infinite bliss.

Thus the most significant difference between the mundane and the liberated soul consists in the fact that the former is permeated with subtle matter known as 'Karma'; while the latter is absolutely pure and free from any material alloy.

The mundane souls are of two kinds, (1) Sthavara, i.e.. the immobile or one-sensed souls, that is, having only the sense of touch; and (2) Trasa, i.e. the mobiles or many-sensed souls, that is, having bodies with more than one sense organ. The former are associated with earth, water, fire, wind and plants, and the latter differ among themselves according to the number of sense-organs.

Ajiva Drayas

The non-living substances are of five kinds, namely, (i) Pudgala, i.e. matter, (ii) Dharma, i.e. medium of motion, (iii) Adharma, i.e. medium of rest, (iv) Akasha, i.e. space and (v) Kala, i.e. time.

Though all these are characterised by existence, the Constitution of time is slightly different: it -has no existence in space, but is made up of partite units. The matter is the non-living stuff possessed of sense-qualities with varied functions and forms; the principles of motion and rest facilitate all movements and static states in this physical universe; all these substances are accommodated in space; and it is the principle of time that marks continuity or change.

The doctrines of Jainism emphasise that these six jiva and ajiva dravyas, i.e. living and non-living substances, are externally existing, uncreated and with no beginning in time. As substances they are eternal and unchanging, but their modifications are passing through a flux of changes. Their mutual co-operation and interaction explain all that we imply by the term 'creation'. Hence the doctrines of Jainism do not admit any intelligent 'Creator' who can be credited with the making of this universe.

Further, the doctrines of Jainism not only state that the whole universe can be divided into jiva and ajivadravyas, i.e. the living and the non-living substances, but also explain the nature and interaction of these two elements. It is asserted, in short, that the living and the non-living, by coming into contact with each other, forge certain energies which bring about birth, death and various experiences of life; this process could be stopped, and the energies already forged destroyed, by a course of discipline leading to salvation. A close analysis of this brief statement shows that it involves the following seven propositions:

- that there is something called the living;
- that there is something called the non-living;
- that the two come into contact with each other;
- that the contact leads to the production of some energies;
- that the process of contact could be stopped;
- that the existing energies could also be exhausted; and
- that the salvation could be achieved.

These seven propositions are called the seven tattvas or realities in Jaina philosophy. These tattvas are termed as follows:

- Jiva, i.e. living substance.
- Ajiva, i.e. matter or non-living substance,
- Ashrava, i.e. the influx of Karmic matter into the soul,
- Bandha, i. e. bondage of soul by Karmic matter,
- Samvara, i. e. the stopping of Ashrava,
- Nirjara, i.e the gradual removal of Karmic matter, and
- Moksha, i.e. the attainment of perfect freedom.

(i) and (ii) Jiva and Ajiva. Out of these seven tattvas, the first two deal with the nature and enumeration of the eternal substance of nature, and the remaining five with the interaction between these two substances, viz. soul and matter. (iii) Ashrava: The third principle Ashrava signifies the influx of Karmic matter, into the Constitution of the soul. Combination of Karmic matter with Jiva is due to Yoga. Yoga is the activity of mind, speech and body. Thus Yoga is the channel of Ashrava. The physical matter which is actually drawn to the soul cannot be perceived by the senses as it is very fine. (iv) Bandha: When the Karmic matter enters the soul, both get imperceptibly mixed with each other. Bandha or bondage is the assimilation of matter which is fit to form Karmas by the soul as it is associated with passions. The union of spirit and matter does not imply a complete annihilation of their natural properties, but only a suspension of their functions, in varying degree, according to the quality and quantity of the material absorbed. Thus, the effect of the fusion of the soul and matter is manifested in the form of a compound personality which partakes of the nature of the both, without actually destroying either. The causes of Bandha are five, viz.

- Mithyadarshana, i.e. wrong belief or faith,
- Avirati, i.e. vowlessness or non-renunciation,
- Pramada, i.e. carelessness
- Kashaya, i.e. passions, and
- Yoga, i.e. vibrations in the soul through mind, speech and body.

(v) Samvara: Effective states of desire and aversion, and activity of thought, speech or body are the conditions that attract Karmas, good and bad, towards the soul. When those conditions are removed, there will be no Karmas approaching the Jiva, that is complete Samvara sort of protective wall shutting out all the Karmas is established round the self. Thus Samvara is the stoppage of inflow of Karmic matter into the soul. There are several ways through which the stoppage could be effected. (vi) Nirjara: Nirjara means the falling away of Karmic matter from the soul. The soul will be rendered free by the automatic falling out of the Karmas when they become ripe. But this is a lengthy process. The falling away may be deliberately brought through the practice of austerities. Thus Nirjara is of two kinds. The natural maturing of a Karma and its separation from the soul is called Savipaka Nirjara and inducing a Karma to leave the soul, before it gets ripened by means of ascetic practices, is called Avipaka Nirjara. (vii) Moksha: Moksha or liberation is the freedom from all Karmic matter, owing to the non-existence of the cause of bondage and the shedding of all the Karmas. Thus complete freedom of the soul from Karmic matter is called Moksha. It is attained when the soul and matter are separated from each other. The separation is effected when all the Karmas have left the soul, and no more Karmic matter can be attracted towards it.

Doctrine of Karma

The fundamental principles of Jaina Philosophy entail the doctrine of Karma. These principles assert that mudane souls exist in this world from time eternal in association with matter. Of course, the character of this association or bondage is freely and constantly being changed; but the fact and condition of the bondage of the soul by matter persists through all these changes. This association leads to further contact and so the cycle goes on till the association is severed in such a manner as to avoid any fresh contact.

This contact of soul with matter takes place in this manner. The soul is surrounded by a large volume of fine and subtle matter called Karma. When the soul tries to do any thing, then instantly the surrounding particles of matter cling to it just as the particles of dust stick to the body be smeared with oil. Like water in milk these particles of matter get completely assimilated with soul and remain in this condition throughout life as well as in its migrations from one body to another. The connection of soul and matter is real; otherwise in a pure state the soul would have flown to the highest point in the universe as the soul is the lightest of all substances. As this connection or bondage is effected by the Karma or deed or activity of the soul, the subtle matter which combines the soul is termed as Karma.

Thus the Karma is something material and it produces in the soul certain conditions, just as a medical pill, when introduced into the body, produces therein manifold effects. The Karmic matter remains with the soul and binds it in the circuit of births as gods, men, denisens of hell and subhuman beings. Since the presence of Karmic matter in the soul is the cause of cycle of births and deaths and of all conditions of life, the soul must be made free from the Karmic matter. For this the influx of Karmic matter must be stopped by cultivating pure thoughts and actions; and the stock of existing Karmic matter must be consumed by the practice of religious austerities.In this way when the Karmas are completely destroyed the soul becomes liberated with all its potential qualities fully developed. This liberated and perfect soul is an embodiment of infinite bliss and other qualities. It should, therefore, be the aim of every individual to achieve this perfect and natural condition of soul by one's own efforts. In this regard the Jaina philosophy clearly asserts that the attainment of the freedom of the soul from the Karmic matter entirely depends on one's own proper deeds or actions and not on the favours of human or divine beings. Just as the interacting eternal substances (viz. Dravyas) postulated in Jainism admit no Creator, so also the inviolable law of Karma makes man the master of his destiny and dispenses away with the favourite theistic idea that some divinity bestows on man favours and frowns.

Doctrines of Nayavada and Syadvada

According to Jaina philosophy, as noted above, the object of knowledge is a huge complexity constituted of substances, qualities and modifications, extended over past, present and future times and infinite space, and simultaneously subjected to origination, destruction and permanence. Such an object can be fully comprehended only in omniscience, which is not manifested in the case of worldly beings who perceive through their organs of senses. But the senses are the indirect means of knowledge, and whatever they apprehend is partial like the proverbial perception of an elephant by seven blind persons; each one touches only a part of the animal and concludes that the animal is like a log of wood, like a fan, like a wall, etc.

The ordinary human being, therefore, cannot rise above the limitations of his senses; so his apprehension of reality is partial and it is valid only from a particular point of view known as Naya. Thus as Nayas are modes of expressing things, there can be number of Nayas through which reality could be expressed. For example, when different kinds of gold ornaments are described from the point of view of the modes or modifications of gold, it is termed the Paryayarthika-naya or the Paryaya-naya, i.e. the modal point of view, and when gold ornaments are described with regard to their substance, i.e. gold, and its inherent qualities, it is termed the dravyarthika-naya or the dravya-naya, i.e. the substantial point of view. On the same lines, in spiritual discussions, the things could be described from vyavahara-naya, i.e. the common-sense of practical point of view and also from nishchaya-naya, i.e. the realistic point of view. In this way the system of describing reality from different points of view is known as Nayavada it is not enough if various problems about reality are merely understood from different points of view. What one knows must be able to state truly and accurately. This need is met by the doctrine of Syadvada or anekantavada, i.e. many-sided view-point. The object of knowledge is a huge complexity covering infinite modes; human mind is of limited understanding; and human speech has its imperfections in expressing the whole range of experience. Under these circumstances all our statements are conditionally or relatively true. Hence every statement must be qualified with the term 'Syat', i.e. 'somehow', or in a way, with a view to emphasise its conditional or relative character. In this way on the basis of anekanta-vada or Syadvada, while describing a thing seven assertions, seemingly contradictory but perfectly true, can be made in a following manner:

- Syadasti, i.e. showhow it is,
- Syannasti, i.e. somehow it is not,
- Syadasti-nasti, i.e. somehow it is and it is not,
- Syadavaktavyam, i.e. somehow it is indescribable,
- Syadasti cha avaktavyam cha, i.e. somehow it is and is indescribable,
- Syannasti chk avaktavyam cha, i.e. somehow it is not and is indescribable, and
- Syadasti nasti cha avaktavyam cha, i.e. somehow it is not and is indescribable.

For example, a man is the father, and is not the father and is both-are perfectly intelligible statements, if one understands the point of view from which they are made. In relation to a particular boy he is the father; in relation to another boy he is not the father; in relation to both the boys taken together he is the father and is not the father. Since both the ideas cannot be conveyed in words at the same time, he may be called indescribable: still he is the father and is indescribable; and so on. Thus, this doctrine of Anekantavada is neither self-contradictory nor vague or indefinite; on the contrary, it represents a very sensible view of things in a systematised form.

Further, this doctrine of anekantavada is also called the doctrines of Sapta-bhangi, i.e. the doctrine of sevenfold predication, because these seven possible modes of expression can be used while describing a thing.

Doctrine of the Path to Liberation

From the basic principles of Jaina philosophy, it is evident that the inherent powers of the soul are crippled by its association with karmic matter and that is why every person is found in an imperfect state. The Jaina philosophy also asserts that real and everlasting happiness will be obtained by a person only when the Karmas are completely removed from the soul and that even though man is imperfect at present, it is quite possible for him to rid himself of the Karmas by his own personal efforts without any help from an outside agency. The highest happiness is to escape from the Cycle of Births and Deaths and be a liberated soul, that is, to obtain Moksha.

This word is full of sorrow and trouble and it is quite necessary to achieve the aim of transcendental bliss by a sure method. When the goal has been fixed the next question arises regarding the way how to achieve that objective. To this question Jainism has a definite answer. It emphatically states that Samyag-darshana, i.e. right belief, Samyagnana, i.e. right knowledge, and Samyag-Charitra, i.e. right conduct, together constitute the path to liberation. Right belief, right knowledge and right conduct are called Ratnatraya, or the three jewels, in Jaina philosophy. These three are not different paths but form together a single path. These three must be present together to constitute the path of liberation.

Since all the three are emphasised equally, and since the Moksha marga, i.e. the path of liberation, is impossible without the comprehension of all the three, it is obvious that the Jaina philosophy is not prepared to admit any one of these three in isolation as means of salvation. That is why it is emphatically laid down that for attaining liberation all the three must be simultaneously pursued. It is contended that just as to effect a cure of a malady, faith in the efficacy of a medicine, knowledge of its use, and actual taking of it, constitute the three essential things together, so also to secure emancipation of the soul, faith in the efficacy of Jainism, its knowledge and its actual observation, from the three quite indispensable things together. The path of liberation is at times compared to a ladder with its two side poles and the central rungs forming the steps. The side poles are right belief and right knowledge and the rungs or steps are the gradual stages of right conduct. It is possible to ascend the ladder only when all the three are sound. The absence of one makes the ascent impossible. Thus a simultaneous pursuit of right belief, right knowledge and right conduct is enjoined upon the people. The ethical doctrines of Jainism, both for the householders and the monks, are based on this path of liberation comprising (i) right belief, (ii) right knowledge and (iii) right conduct.

Right Belief

Of the three jewels, right belief comes first and forms the basis upon which the other two jewels rest. It is laid down that one must, by all possible means, first attain right belief or the basic conviction on the fundamentals; because only on its acquisition, knowledge and conduct become right. Right Belief means true and firm conviction in the seven tattvas, i.e. principles of Jainism as they are and without any perverse notion.

The belief that the Jaina Tirthankaras are the true Gods, the Jaina Sastras, i.e. the sacred books, the true scripture, and the Jaina Saints the true Preceptors, is called Right Belief. The possession of Right Belief or faith by a person is always considered most essential in his efforts to achieve liberation.

It is specifically asserted that asceticism without faith is definitely inferior to faith without asceticism and that even a low caste man possessing right faith can be considered as divine being. In this way the right belief is given procedence over right knowledge and right conduct because it acts as a pilot guiding the soul towards Moksha, i.e. liberation.

Right Knowledge

On attaining right belief it is considered desirable to strive after right knowledge. Although right belief and right knowledge are contemporaneous, there is yet a clear relation of cause and effect between them, just as there is between a lamp and its light. Right knowledge is that knowledge which reveals the nature of things neither insufficiently, nor with exaggeration, nor falsely, but exactly as it is and that too with certainty. Such knowledge must be free from doubt, perversity and vagueness. Jainism insists that right knowledge cannot be attained, unless belief of any kind in its opposite, i.e. in wrong knowledge, is banished.

Right Conduct

Right Conduct includes the rules of discipline which restrain all censurable movements of speech, body and mind, weaken and destroy all passionate activity and lead to non-attachment and purity. Right induct presupposes the presence of right knowledge which presupposes right belief. Therefore it is enjoined upon the persons who have secured right belief and right knowledge to observe the rules of right conduct as the destruction of Karmic matter can be accomplished only through the right conduct. Right Conduct is of two kinds, viz. Sakala-Charitra, i.e. perfect or unqualified conduct and Vikala-Charitra, i.e. imperfect and qualified conduct, and of these two kinds the unqualified one is observed by ascetics who have renounced worldly ties and the qualified by laymen still entangled in the world.

Ethical Doctrines

Along with laying down the path to liberation, Jainism has also prescribed the definite rules of conduct to be followed both by the householders and the ascetics. All these rules are directed towards the main aim of achieving freedom of the soul from the Karmic matter, i.e. attaining liberation. The rules of conduct have been so designed that all persons would be in a position to follow them. Accordingly the rules of conduct have been divided into two categories, viz.

- Sagara-dharma, i.e. those prescribed for laymen, and
- Anagara-dharma, i.e. those prescribed for ascetics.

It is obvious that the rules for the laity are less rigid than those for the saints because the laymen have not renounced worldly activities for eking out their livelihood.

Propagation of the Doctrine

The last thirty years o his life. Mahavira spent in the propagation of his doctrine. He travelled through many parts of India, preaching and converting people to his faith, stopping as before for the four months of the rainy season at one place. It is possible to reconstruct a complete account of his travels from the names of the places where he passed his rainy seasons, mentioned in the Jaina texts.

Conversation of the Ganadharas

The Lord attained the *Kevalajnana* while sitting in meditation under a *Sala* tree in the field of the householder Samaga outside the town Jrmbhikagrama. Immediately on the attainment of *Kevalajnan*, there is a Jaina tradition, the Tirthankara holds a public conference in *Samavsarana* and preaches the doctrine, making converts. But Mahavira made no converts in his first public audience. This in *Svetambara* Jaina texts is regarded as having been a very "unusual occurrence". Probably the reason was because the public was nor available at the spot to listen to his preaching. The *Digambara* tradition does not admit the holding of the first *samavasarana* in the field of *Samaga* immediately of the attainment of *Kevalajnana*.

Knowing that a big *Yajna* had been organised by a *Brahmin Somilacarya* at a place at some distance from *Jrmbhikagrama*, he moved on to that place and held his second public audience there. He explained his own doctrine of the, *Karma, Asrava, Bandha, Nirjara* and *Moksa* and then went on to say that "four things of paramount value are difficult to obtain here by a living being; human birth, instruction in the Law, belief in it and energy in self-control. The Universe is peopled by manifold creatures, who are in this *samsara* born in different families and castes for having done various actions. Sometimes they go to the world of gods, sometimes to the bells, sometimes they become *Ksatriyas*, or *Candalas* or *Bukkasas*, or worms and moths, or (insects called)*Kunthu* and ants. Thus living beings of sinful actions, who are born again and again in ever-recurring births, are not disgusted with the *samsara*, but they are like warriors (never tired of the battle of life). Living beings bewildered through the influence of their actions, distressed and suffering pains, undergo misery in non-human births. But by the cessation of *Karman*, perchance, living beings will reach in due time a pure state and be born as men. And though they be born with a human body it will be difficult for them to hear the Law, having heard which they will do penance's, combat their passions and abstain from killing living beings. And though, by chance, they may hear the Law, it will be difficult for them to believe in it; many who are shown the right way, stray from it. And though they have heard the Law and believe in it, it is difficult for them to fulfill it strenuously; many who approve of the religion, do not adopt it.

Having been born as a man, having heard the law, believing in it, and fulfilling it strenuously, an ascetic should restrain and shake off sinfulness. The pious obtain purity, and the pure stand firmly in the Law; (the soul afterwards) reaches the highest *Nirvana*, being like unto a fire fed with *ghee*". Mahavira's fame as an omniscient seer began to spread fast and widely; and among others, eleven of the learned *Brahmin* teachers, who had come with a band of disciples to participate in the *Yajna*, felt persuaded to visit him.

The visit and conversion of these eleven Brahmin teachers has been described in some detail by the Jaina texts, both *Svetambara* and *Digambara*. *Digambara* accounts mention that *Indrabhuti*, who had become a very learned *pandit* and grown extremely vain of his learning, was once questioned by an old man and asked to explain the meaning of a verse. The verse had been repeated to him by Mahavira, who had immediately afterwards become so lost in meditation that he did not get an explanation of it from the saint. It contained references to *kala* and *dravya*, *pancastikaya dravya* and *lesya* not one of which terms did Gautama Indrabhuti really understand. Nor, being a true scholar, could he pretend to have a knowledge which he did not possess. So he sought our Mahavira for an explanation. In the presence of the great ascetic all his pride fell from him and he became a pupil of Mahavira along with his band of disciples and learned brothers. The Svetambara account ascribes the meeting between Mahavira and Gautama Indrabhuti and others to a denunciation on the part of Mahavira of the animal sacrifice at which they were assisting. They were naturally much enraged at his audacity and came forward to oppose him and expose the falseness of his teaching; but when they listened to Mahavira's discourses and heard the gentle and thoughtful answers he gave to all questioners, they became convinced of the truth of his way, decided to cast in their lot with his and became his chief disciples or Ganadharas. Under these Ganadharas were placed all the monks of the Order.

> "Why has it been said that the venerable Ascetic Mahavira had nine Ganas but eleven Ganadharas? The oldest monk of the Venerable Ascetic Mahavira was Indrabhuti of the *gotra,* who instructed five hundred sramanas; the middle aged monk was Agnibhuti of the Gautama *gotra,* who instructed five hundred *sramanas;* the youngest was Vayubhuti of the Gautama *gotra,* who instructed five hundred *sramanas.* The Sthavira Arya-Vyakta of the Bharadwaja *gotra* instructed five hundred *sramanas;* the Sthavira Arya-Sudharman of the Agnivaisyayana *gotra* instructed five hundred *sramanas;* the Sthavira Mandikaputra of the Vasisthagotra instructed two hundred and fifty *sramanas;* the Sthavira Mauryaputra of the Kasyapagotra instructed two hundred and fifty *sramanas;* the Sthavira Akampita of the Gautama *gotra* and Sthavira Acalabhrata of the Haritayana gotra, both Sthaviras instructed together three hundred *sramanas* each; the Sthaviras Metarya and Prabhasa, both of the Kaundinyagotra, instructed together three hundred *sramanas* each. Therefore it has been said that the venerable Ascetic Mahavira had nine *Ganas* but eleven *Ganadharas*".

These conversions gave to Mahavira a respectable community of 4,411 *Sramanas.* It is presumable that at this place not only *Sramanas* but also lay disciples joined Mahavira's order; in

Jaina texts there are references to the Lord having established a community of four orders, i.e. monks, nuns, laymen and laywomen at the same time. We have already mentioned that unlike Parsva, who seems to have grouped all the laymen and similarly laywomen together, Mahavira made a clear distinction between ordinary laymen who merely expressed their sympathy with the Jaina doctrine and faith as Jainas and the body of laymen who took a special type of *Diksa* and who clearly undertook to observe the twelve lay vows. As Mrs. Stevenson has said, the genius for organisation which Mahavira possessed is shown in nothing more clearly than in the formation of this and the order of lay women *Shramanro- pasika*. These two organisations gave the Jaina a root in India that the Buddhists and, the other systems of Parivrajaka orders, never obtained, and that root firmly planted amongst the laity enabled Jainism to withstand the storm that drove Buddhism out of India.

Influence at Royal Courts

Magadha: From the scene of *Somilacarya's Yajna* Mahavira proceeded to *Rajagrha*, old capital of Magadha, where *Srenika* (*Bimbisara*) was the ruling monarch. As we have stated before, Mahavira was a Jnatrka from his father's side, but his mother was sister to *Cetake*, the King of Vaisali, who belonged to the Licchavi sect of the *Ksatriyas*. *Cetaka* had seven daughters, out of whom one preferred to be a nun and the other six were married in one or the other royal family of Eastern India. *Srenika*, the ruler of *Magadha*, was the husband of the youngest of these princesses, *Cellana*, who became a lay follower of Mahavira, of the Sramanopasak variety.

It is possible that there had been some connection between *Magadha* and the Jaina Church of the age previous to that of *Mahavira*. The Jaina text *Uttaradhyayana* mentions two early Kings of Rajgrha named *Samudravijaya* and his son *Jaya*; of these *Jaya*, the eleventh *cakravartin*, "together with thousands of Kings, renouncing the world, practiced self-restraint and reached perfection which has been taught by the *Jinas*". But during the rule of the *Saisunagas*, right from the beginning there undoubtedly existed strong personal connections between Mahavira at *Rajgrha*, during the period of his preparation and after his attainment of the *Kevala*; and it is certain that at least during the later period he repaired to the city "not merely as an independent preacher but as one who had the State behind him to directly patronise and sympathise with him in his great mission".

Videha: As with the rulers of Magadha, so with the other ruling houses in Eastern India, Mahavira had personal connections; and these connections must have inevitably helped him to gain followers for his order. From *Rajgrha,* where he gained numerous, both monks and laymen, including the *Princes Megha Kumar, Abhaya Kumar* and others, the Lord proceeded towards Videha country. The capital of Videha was Mithila, which is identified by some scholars with the small town of *Janakapura* just within the Nepal border. The Videhans seem to have been an adventurous people, scattered as far as *Vaisali* itself. Mahavira's mother, who was a Princess of Vaisali, is spoken of in the Jaina texts as *Videhadatta*; and there is ample evidence to prove that Mahavira was closely connected with the Videhans. The Videhans has a living interest in the Jaina Church. Form *Kalpa-sutra* we know that Mahavira spent six rainy seasons at *Mithila,* the *Metropolis* of Videha.

Vatsa: The capital of *Vatsa, Kausambi,* was also visited by Mahavira several times both during the period of preparation and after the attainment of the *Kevala.* The ruler of Kausambi was King *Satanika, Mrgavati* the third daughter of Cetaka was married to him. Both the King and the Queen were devotees of Mahavira and followers of the Jaina order. The Jaina tradition also affirms that the King's *amatya* (minister) and his wife were Jaina by faith. *Satanika's* son and successor, *Udayana,* was a great King who made some conquests and contracted matrimonial alliance with the royal houses of *Avanti, Anga* and *Magadha.* The Jaina literature claims him as a follower of the Jaina order.

Avanti: *Canda Pradyota* the ruler of *Avanti* (Capital, *Ujjain*) had married the fourth daughter of Cetaka, by name Shiva. *Pradyota* was called "*Canda*" or fierce, for he was temperamentally very excitable and was also the possessor of a large army. There is a story which says that he was fond of *Mrgavati,* the elder sister of wife, who had been already married to King Satanika of Vatsa, that he asked for Queen Mrgavati from Satanika, and that on the refusal of the latter he declared a war against him. Satanika appears to have died before actual hostilities could start; and when Mahavira visited Kausambi a little later, he induced Canada Pradyota to give up his feeling of revenge and to allow Mrgavati to become a nun. Thereupon Satanika's son, Udayana, became the King of Kausambi. Between this Udayana and Pradyota's daughter, the peerless Vasavadatta, there developed a long romance, round which a large cycle of *Sanskrit* stories has been written. Udayana, as we mentioned above, is claimed by Jaina tradition as having had respect and sympathy for the Jaina church; but Pradyota also had undeniable sympathy for the Jaina faith. There is a mention that along with Mrgavati of Kausambi, eight of his own Queens, *Angaravati* and others, with his permission, joined the order.

Campa, capital of Anga: The ruler of Campa, which was always recognised to be a great centre of Jainism, was Dadhivahana, who married Padmavati, the second daughter of Cetaka. Dadhivahana's daughter, Candana or Candanabala, was the first woman who embraced Jainism shortly after Mahavira had attained the Kevala. Jaina literature described in great detail the story of Candana. During the invasion of Campa by King Satanika of Kausambi, Candana was caught hold of by one of the enemy's army and was sold in Kausambi to a banker named Dhanavaha. After a short time the banker's wife Mula, felt jealous of her and having cut her hair, put her into custody. In this condition she served a part of her food to Mahavira, and finally joined his ranks as a nun. She headed the order of nuns in Mahavira's sangha. Campa seems to have been situated at a distance of a few miles in the neighbourhood of modern *Bhagalpur*. Its importance as a centre of Jaina influence is evident from the fact that Mahavira spent three of his rainy seasons in Campa. After Mahavira's death Campa was visited by Sudharman, the head of the Jaina Sangha, at the time of Kunika or Ajatasatru. Ajatasatru seems to have transferred his capital from Rajgrha to Campa of the death of his father; and Jaina tradition mentions that the King "came bare-footed to see the *Ganadhara* outside the city where he had taken his adobe," Sudharman's successor, Jambu, and Jambu's successor, Svayambhava, lived at the city where he composed the *Dasavaikalikasutra*, containing in ten lectures all the essence of the sacred doctrines of Jainism.

Licchavis and other Republican Clans

From this brief account of the several ruling houses of Eastern India, it will be clear that Mahavira obtained good support everywhere. His personal connections with the various rulers reached through his mother Trisala, the Licchavi Princess, and his maternal uncle Cetaka, the King of Vaisali. The Licchavis were recognised all round as high born Ksatriyas, with whom the highest born Princes of Eastern India, and not only Eastern India but also as far west as Sindhu-Sauvira, considered it an honour to enter into matrimonial alliance. We have already seen that out of the seven daughters of Cetaka, Padmavati, Mrgavati, Shiva and Cellana were married respectively to the lords of Anga, Vatsa, Avanti and Magadha. The eldest Prabhavati was married to King Udayana of Vitabhaya, which has been identified at various places in the Jaina literature with a town of Sindhu-*Sauvira desa*. As to what part of the country is Sindhu-Sauvira-desa, whether it is "the province of Badari or Eder, at the head of the Gulf of Cambay Cunningham, or "to the north of Kathiawar and along the Gulf of Cutch" (Rhys Davids) or "the province of Multan and Jahravar" (Alberuni), or "in Sindhu or Sindh" (Satrunjaya-Mahatmya), historians are not quite in agreement about; but according to Jaina sources Udayana was the overlord of three hundred and sixty three other towns. Through his relationship Licchavis, Mahavira's religion was greatly helped in the course of its spread over Sauvira, Anga, Vatsa, Avanti, Videha and Magadha, all of which were the most powerful kingdoms of the time. It is significant that Buddhist books do not mention Cetaka at all, though they tell us about the constitutional government of Vaisali used to be a stronghold of Jainism, while being looked upon by the Buddhists as a seminary of heresies and dissent".

The Licchavis were naturally favourable to Mahavira's order. There are many stray references in the Jaina *Sutras* which confirm the fact that the Licchavis were followers of the Jaina faith. The capital of the Licchavis formed one of the headquarters of the Jaina community during the days of Mahavira. Out of forty-two rainy seasons spent as a missionary during his later ascetic life, twelve were passed at Vaisali. Like the Licchavis, the *Vajji*, who in fact cannot be strictly differentiated from the Licchavis, came under the influence of Lord Mahavira, for Vaisali seems to have been regarded also as the metropolis of the entire *Vajji* confederacy. These republics in Eastern India had a type of government which was senatorial, like the government in the city-state of Rome. The *Jnatrkas,* whose most noble scion was Mahavira, also formed one of the most important clans included in the *Vajjian* confederacy. The several clans of the Vajjian confederacy must have been naturally affected by the doctrines of the Nataputta. The canonical literature of his bitter antagonists, the Buddhists, does not fail to make this admission, and preached his faith of unbounded charity to all living beings, the number of his followers among the Licchavis appears to have been large and some men of the highest position appear to have been among them".

The Mallakins also seen to have cherished a feeling of respect and sympathy for the great prophet and his doctrines. Both the Buddhist and the Jaina texts agree that the country of the *Mallas* formed one of the sixteen *Mahajanapadas.* At the time of Mahavira the *Mallas* appear to have been divided into two confederacies one with its capital *Pava* and the other at *Kusinara* the two places being respectively the cities where the Jaina prophet Mahavira and the Buddha reached their final liberation. With the Mallas, Jainism seems to have established almost a good connections as with the Licchavis. According to Dr. BC Law, we get ample proof for this even from the Buddhist literature, Geographically *Kosala* roughly corresponds to modern *dern Oudh,* and it seems to have contained three great cities namely *Ayodhya, Saketa* and *Sravasti-* the first two sometimes being often supposed to be one and the same. When one remembers that Sravasti was visited by Mahavira more than once and that he was always well received there one cannot but admit that the *Kosalas* also came under the influence of Mahavira.

9

Mahavira's Teachings

The teachings of Mahavira have come down to us as a living tradition which grew up and took a complete literary form through ten centuries from his demise. The original doctrine was contained in the *Purvas* of which there were fourteen, which Mahavira himself taught to his disciples. The fourteen *Purvas* were presumably preceded by the existence of ten *Purvas*, which had embodied the religious traditions of Parsva and which formed, as we are led to believe by a legend mentioned in the *Bhagavati*, a common basis of the Jaina and *Ajivika* canons. The knowledge of the *Purvas* was gradually lost till it became totally extinct. Only one of the Mahavira's disciples, Arya Sudharma, handed them down, and they were preserved during six generations more. In the second century after Mahavira's death there was a horrible famine in the land of Magadha, which lasted for twelve years. Bhadrabahu was then the head of the Jaina *Sangha*.

There is a legend which connects this Bhadrabahu with the Emperor Chandra Gupta Maurya and says that owning to the famine Bhadrabahu emigrated with a host of his disciples including Chandragupta himself to Karnataka in South India. This is clearly unwarranted by the chronology of the event. When the famine took place, Bhadrabahu took recourse to the neighbouring Nepal hills and there started his *Sadhana*. During the absence of

Bhadrabahu it became evident that the knowledge of the sacred texts was threatening to lapse into oblivion; and so a Council was called at Pataliputra to compile a recession of the canon. The Jaina belief is that the Tirthankara himself taught the *Purvas* to his disciples, the *Ganadharas,* and the *Ganadharas* then composed the *Angas* . The Council performed its task successfully, although there was great difficulty in the compilation of the twelfth *Angas,* the *Drstivada,* which is believed to have incorporated the fourteen *Purvas* at the time when they ceased to exist independently of the *Angas* literature. The difficulty was that the head of the community in the Magadha did not have a complete knowledge of the *Purvas* and so was not able to proceed with the *business* without the guidance from a distance of *Bhadrabahu* himself.

It may be mentioned that the famous Hathigumpha inscription of Kharavela furnishes a confirmation of the Jaina tradition regarding the Council of Patalipurta and the compilation of a recession of Angas "in sixty-four section". "It is not by accident that the knowledge of the Purvas" says Jacobi, "is said to have commenced to fade away at the same time when the *Angas* were collected by the *Sangha* of Pataliputra". The loss of *Purvas* and later on of *Drstivada* was due largely to the rise of other books on their basis. The very name *Purva* (which means the former, the earlier) testifies to the fact that they were superseded by a new canon. It may be inferred that the Purvas were, like the *Upanishads,* a heterogeneous type of literature presenting a wide diversity of sometimes mutually conflicting views, and therefore extremely difficult to master, is of the opinion that they were devoted to the description of controversies held between Mahavira and rival teachers. It is true that the *Drstivada,* which is said to have included the fourteen *Purvas,* dealt chiefly with the *drstis* or philosophical opinions of the Jainas and other sects. The title which is added to the name of each *Purva,* would seem to support this view. When the opponents of Mahavira died and the sects headed by them became extinct, the controversies related in the Purvas evidently lost their interest and ceased to be of any practical significance. That reason may have been partly responsible for their neglect.

The *Angas* came in the course of time to be known and acknowledged as the only authoritative sacred books of Jainism.

They were expressly referred to in the *Sutrakrtanga* as the "Canon of the Jinas, which has been taught, produced and declared by the *Sramana,* the *Nirgrantha*". The *Digambara,* however, refuse to recognise the authenticity of the *Angas.* After the famine and the Council of Pataliputra which had compiled the recession of the *Angas,* the adherents of Bhadrabahu returned to Magadha but refused to consider the compilation satisfactory and so declared that the Purvas and the Angas had been irrecoverably lost.

This became the basis of the belief of the *Digambara* who hold that what exists as the *Siddhanta* is not in its original form at all. Such contention does not appear to be well grounded on the facts of history, although it is undoubtedly true that the works of *Siddhanta* are the product of a process of compilation which extended over a long period of at least one thousand years. After compilation by the Council of Pataliputra the Canon fell into a state of great disorder again and was on the verge of being lost, when it was ultimately reduced to writing at the Council of *Valabhi* under the presidency of Devardhi Ganin in the 5th century AD During the period between the two councils, that is to say between the Council of Pataliputra in the 4th century BC and the Council of Valabhi in the 5th Century AD, written copies of the *Siddhanta* were not easily extant.

Some privately owned copies must have existed, but it is certain that the teachers made no use of written books when teaching the *Siddhanta* to novices, as they undoubtedly began to do afterwards. What the Council of Valabhi presumably did was to issue a large edition of the *Siddhanta* so as to provide every teacher with copies of the sacred books. This edition of course was merely a redaction of the sacred books, which existed already. But in the course of ages, passages must have crept into the text at any time and additions must have been made to the several books, as is clear from the variety of language forms in which different parts of the canon are written. Arguing from the language of the composition, Jacobi is of the opinion that "the first book of the *Acaranga* and that of the *Sutrakrtanga sutra* may be reckoned among the most ancient parts of the *Siddhanta*". The earliest portions of the Canon do undoubtedly belong to the period of the first disciples of Mahavira himself, while the latest portions would presumably be nearer the time of Devardhi Ganin.

Notwithstanding occasional later accretions, however, the text of the *Angas* and of some at least of the *Upangas* offer a substantially correct description of the state of society, religion and thought in which Mahavira performed his *Sadhana* and attained omniscience and of the teachings of the Lord himself.

Universal View

Like Buddha, Lord Mahavira presented a gloomy picture of the world. "The (living) world is afflicted miserable, difficult to instruct and without discrimination".

Thus begins the second lecture of the first book of *Acaranga*. Quality is the seat of the root, and the seat of the root is quality. He who longs for the qualities, is overcome by great pains, and he is careless. (For he thinks) I have to provide for a mother, for a father, for a sister, for a wife, for sons, for daughters, for a daughter-in-law, for my friends, for near and remote relations, for my acquaintances, for different kinds of property, profit, meals, and clothes.

Longing for these objects, people are careless, suffer day and night, work in the right and wrong time, desire wealth and treasures, commit injuries and violent acts, direct the mind, again and again, upon those injurious things (described in the first lecture). (Doing so) the life of some mortals (which by destiny would have been long) is shortened. For when with the deterioration of the perceptions of the ear, eye, organs of smelling, tasting, touching, a man becomes aware of the decline of life, they (i.e. those failing perceptions) after a time produce dotage. Or his kinsmen with whom he lives together will, after a time, first grumble at him and he will afterwards grumble at them. He is not fit for hilarity, playing, pleasure, show. Therefore proceeding to pilgrimage, and thinking that the present moment is favourable (for such intentions), he should be steadfast and not, even for an hour, carelessly conduct himself. His youth, his age and his life fade away.

> "A man who carelessly conducts himself, who killing, cutting striking, destroying, chasing away, frightening (living beings) resolves to do what has not been done

> (by anyone)-him his relations with whom he lived together, will first cherish, and he will afterwards cherish them. But they cannot help the or protect them".

In bold relief against this gloomy view of the *Samsara*, there is presented the bright prospect of religious life as lived and taught by Lord Mahavira. Mahavira developed a systematic exposition of *Kriyavada* or *Karmavada* which he clearly distinguished from (1) the *Akriyavada* of Gosala, who was essentially fatalist, (2) *Ajnanavada*or agnosticism of *Sanjaya*, and (3) *Vinayavada* of the average ascetic, who believes that the goal of religious life is realised by conformation to the rules of discipline. He also distinguished it from the other brands of *Kviyavada*, by defining his own creed as follows. "The painful condition of the self is brought about by one's own action, it is not brought about by any other cause (fate, creator, chance or the like)". "Individually a man is born, individually he dies, individually he falls (from this state of existence), individually he rises (to another). His passions, consciousness, intellect, perceptions and impressions belong to the individual exclusively. Here, indeed, the bonds of relationship are *not* able to help or save one". "All living beings owe their present form of existence to their own *Karman*; timid, wicked, suffering latent misery, they err about (in the circle of births), subject to birth, old age and death". Mahavira declared that there are as many souls as living individuals, and that *Karman* consists of acts, intentional or unintentional, that produce effects on the nature of the soul.

The soul is not passive in the sense that it remains untouched or unaffected by what a person does for the sake of some interests. It is susceptible to the influences of Karma, and it possesses the capacity to actively annihilate Karma. By the practice of austerities and penance's the *jiva* can wear our, and ultimately destroy the effects of sinful karma committed in former existence's and by the practice of far-reaching self-restraint it can free itself from the production of new *karmas*. The result of this freedom from the bondage of Karma will be a non-guiding of the self in the course of *samsara* in future, and the attainment of the eternal and blissful condition of the soul in its perfection.

Realisation of the Soul

This condition of the soul is realisable in this very existence and solely by human efforts, if rightly directed. The life of the Master stood for all his disciples as a living example of such realisation. The development and manifestation of supreme personality, such as was attained by Lord Mahavira himself, was the visible fruition of religious effort and self-discipline; and this self-discipline was set out and preached by him for the adoption of all persons, male or female, irrespective of any class or caste distinctions. But, said Mahavira, there is no right conduct without right knowledge and no right knowledge without the right belief. It is therefore, desirable to first explain the fundamental ideas of Jaina Philosophy.

The foundation of true metaphysics, according to Jainism, consists of nine categories *Jiva, Ajiva, Punya, Papa, Asrava, Samvara, bandha, nirjara,* and *Moksa*. Sometimes the number of categories is reduced to seven by including two of them, *Punya* and *papa* under other heads.

Soul, a Substance

Jiva or soul, according to Jaina metaphysics, is a substance, its chief characteristic being *Caitanya* (consciousness); but as a substance it is absolute and permanent, unlike the Buddhist belief. The Jaina idea of the *jiva* differs from the *Brahminic* idea, in so far as it is the *Jiva* which, in consequence of the *karma* it has acquired, is believed to go through the succession of rebirths and finally, obtaining freedom through the destruction of its karmas, to soar upwards to moksa. "It performs different kinds of actions, it reaps the fruit of those actions, it circles round returning again; these and none other are the characteristics of the soul". The soul in its pure state is possessed of infinite perception (*Anantdarshen*), infinite knowledge (*Anantgyan*), infinite bliss (*Anantsukh*) and infinite power (Infinite *virya*). It is perfect. Ordinarily however, with the exception of a few released pure souls (*Sidh*) all the other *jives* have all their purity and power covered with a veil of karmic matter which has been accumulating in them from the beginning-less time. *Ajiva* is in all respects the opposite of *jiva*, it means things inanimate, matter. *Karma* is *Ajiva*, which comes into contact with the *jiva* and bedims its power; but the union of *jiva* with *ajiva* can never be so complete as to make their separation impossible. The *jiva*is a substance (*drvya*) in the sense that it occupies a space-point in our mundane world, has a limited size and is not all-persuasiveness. But the *jiva* is not matter, for it has consciousness which matter cannot have. Of the *jiva* the Jainas have made a fivefold classification according to the number of senses it possesses. The *sthaverjiva* possesses only one sense, the sense of touch, but has four *pranr*, touch, body, the power of exhaling and inhaling, and allotted term of life. Water, fire, wind, and all vegetables are supposed to have *Jives*. The *Dvindryajiva* possesses two senses, the sense of taste and the sense of touch, and has six *pranr*, taste and speech in addition to the four *pranr* of the *sthaver jiva*. Such *jives* are in worms, leeches, earth- worms, etc.

The *Trindriyajiva* similarly possesses three senses, the sense of smell in addition to those of taste and touch and seven *pranr* examples of such beings ants, bugs, moths, etc. The *chaturindriya jiva* possesses four senses, of touch, taste, smell and sight and eight *pranr*, the category including such beings as wasps, scorpions, mosquitoes, gnats, flies, locusts and butterflies. The *panchindriya jiva* possesses all five senses, of hearing, taste, touch, smell and sight and includes human beings as well as animals, besides hell-beings and demigods. But all these classes of *jiva* are to be clearly distinguished from Ajiva which is classified into *Roopee* and *aroopee*. *Roopee* division is *pudgel* or matter, which possesses colour, smell, taste and form and is perceptible to touch. Its *Aroopee* division is further subdivided into which helps the *jiva* associated with *Pudgala* to progress, *Adhermastikaye* which keeps it motionless, *akashastikaye* which gives it space and *kal* which gives it a continuity of changes.

As was said above, it is the union of *jiva* with matter, which causes and constitutes *samsara*. The form of this union is determined by the force of *Karma*. Karma is a substantive force a sort of infra-atomic particles of matter, which have the peculiar property of developing the effects of merit. Karma acts in such a way that every change which takes place leaves a mark, which is retained and built into the organism to serve as the foundation for future action. *Punya* is the name of those actions which lead to the good *karma*, which in its turn is productive of peace of mind; *Pap* is just the opposite of Punya, may be laid up in the following nine ways; by giving food to deserving people who are hungry, weak, destitute of help and needy (*anpunrya*), by giving water to the thirsty (*panpunrya*); by giving residence, by giving sleeping accommodation, by giving clothes, by thinking well of every one and wishing them well (*snkelp*); by exerting ourselves to render service to others or to save life; by speaking sweetly and so as to influence others towards religion and morality (*stevan*); and by reverent salutations (*Namaskar*). *Pap* may be earned in eighteen ways; by destroying life (*pranrtipat*) by speaking untruthfull (*mrishavad*); by acting dishonestly (*adetadan*); by unchaste conduct (*Methuen*); by excessive love of one's own possessions (*prigreh*); by getting angry without a cause (*krodh*); by conceited behaviour (*man*); by intrigue or cheating (*Maya*); by avarice (*lobh*); by over-foundness (*rag*) for a person or a thing; by hatred or envy (*dvaish*); by quarrelsomeness (*klah*); by slander of others (*abhyakhyan*); by telling stories to discredit any one (*peshunya*); by continually thinking of other's faults (*parprivad*); by excessive attachment to temporal and transitory objects of affection (*Rti*); by hypocrisy (*mayamrisha*); and by false faith (*mithyatv*). It is needless to labour the point that such detailed analysis of the acts of merit and demerit entitles Jainism to be considered as primarily an ethical philosophy.

Result of Action

Karma, the accumulated result of action, is one of the central ideas of Jaina philosophy, and *Asrava* deals with the way in which *karma* is acquired by the human soul. There are forty-two chief channels of *Asrava* through which *karma* affects a *jiva;* of these seventeen are regarded as major- the five senses, the four *kasayas* i.e. anger, conceit, intrigue and avarice, the five *avrt* or omission to take the vows, and the three yoga's, that is to say entanglement with a material object of the mind, speech and body. But there is a distinction between the channels and the *Karmas* which actually enter through these channels, the distinction is represented by two terms *Bhavasrava* and *Karmasrava*. *Bhavasrava* means the thought activities of the soul through which or on account of which the *Karma* particles affect the soul; *Bhavasrava* is that kind of change in the soul which enables the *karma* to affect the soul while *karmasrava* is the actual movement of contiguous *karma* matter towards the soul. *Bhavasrava* is of five kinds, namely *mithyatv* (delusion), *Avirti* (want of control), *Prmad* (inadvertence), *Yog* (activities of body, mind and speech) and *kshaye* (passions). *Karmasrava*, which means the actual movement of matter towards the soul, affects the soul in eight different ways, *gyanavaranr*, *drshanavaranr*, *vaidniya*, *mohniya*, *ayu*, *nam*, *gotr*, and *antraya* all of which have been explained in another connection before.

Opposed to *Asrava* is *Samvara*, which means the arrest of the inflow of *karmas* into the soul. The subject is of supreme importance in so far as it implies a discipline which every individual is expected to practice in his own life. There are fifty-seven ways of impeding *karmas*; the five *samitis* consisting of the use of trodden tracks in order to avoid injury to insects *Eeryasmriti*, gentle and holy talk (*Bhashase*), care in eating (*Aishanra*), cleanliness (*adan*) and the careful disposal of rubbish and refuse (*prishthapnika*); the three *guptis* or restraints of body, speech and mind; the twenty-two *parishes* or endurance of hardships, of hunger, thirst, cold, heat, cloth, lodging, etc. ten duties (*dharm*) particularly incumbent upon monks, like forgiveness, humility, straightforwardness, freedom from greed, fasting, control of mind, body and speech, truth, cleanliness, non-attachment, chastity; five *Caritra* or rules of conduct, twelve *bhavanas* or reflections about the transient character of the world, about our helplessness without the truth, about the cycles of world-existence, about our own responsibilities for our good and bad actions, about the difference between the soul and the non-soul; about the uncleanliness of our body and all that is associated with it, about the influx of *karmas* and its stoppage and destruction of those *karmas* which have already entered the soul, about soul, matter and the substance of the universe, about the difficulty of attaining true principles of the world. Corresponding to the two modes of inrush of karma into the soul. *Bhavasamvara* means thought modifications with a view to stop the inflow of karmas and *Karmasamvara* or *dravyasamvara* means the actual stoppage of the inflow of *karma*.

Bandha is the name of the stage after *Karmasrava* as *nirjara* is the name of the stage after *Karmasamvara*. *Bandha* means the *bondage* of the soul by *karma*, that is to say, subjection of soul to the laws of birth and death, old age and decay, pleasure and pain and other vicissitudes of life brought about by the effect of karma. The jaina view is that we are, by our actions of mind, speech and body, continually producing subtle *karma* matter, which in the first instance is called *bhavakarma* and later on transforms itself into *dravyakarma*, thus pouring into the soul and sticking there by coming into contact with the passions of the soul. The process of generation of *Karma* and its pouring into and sticking to the soul has been analysed into four stages, which can be clearly distinguished from each other but not described in the spoken language with sufficient lucidity, *Bhavasrava, karmasravava, bhavabandha and karmabandha.* Accordingly as good or bad *karma* matter sticks to the soul, the soul gets coloured respectively golden, lotus-pink, white, black, blue and gray; these are known as. Like *Asrava, bandha, karma* etc. also have been considered in two forms, as *bhavalesya* i.e. the feelings generated by the accumulation of the *karma* matter, and the *dravya- lesya* i.e. the actual coloration of the soul by it. *Bandha* or bondage of the soul by the *karma* is of four kinds according to its nature, (*prakriti*), duration (*sthiti*), essence (*anubhav*), and content (*Pradaish*). Man's passions are responsible for the nature and duration of *Karma* and intensity and mass of *Karma* is largely determined by his exertion.

After the effect (*vipak*) of a particular *karma* matter has been once produced, it is discharged and purged off the soul. The process of purging off of the *karma* is called *Nirjara*. *Nirjara* also is of two kinds, *bhavanirjara*, i.e. the change in the soul by virtue of which the karma particles are destroyed, and *dravya-nirjara* i.e. the actual destruction of the *karma* particles. Destruction of the *karma* is automatic after reaping its effects *vipak* but is possible by proper exertion even before its time of fruition (*Opkrmik*). The best way is by burning up *karma* in the glow of austerities (*tap*). These austerities are of two kinds, exterior or bodily and interior or spiritual. The six exterior austerities are *anshan* (fasting), *unreedree* (graduated decrease of the quantity of food), *Bhikshacharya* (begging), *Respritya*g (giving up dainty foods), *kayaklaish* (mortification of the flesh), and *Sanleenta* (avoidance of temptation by control of limbs, etc.); and the six interior austerities include *Prayshchit* (confession), *Vinay*(reverence and humility), *vyavrit* (service), (study), *Vinay* (Meditation), and *Kayotserg* (showing and feeling absolute indifference to the body and its needs).

Freedom for Soul

When the soul is freed from all bonds to *Karma*, it gets released from the circle of births. It then attains *Moksa*or complete deliverance. It becomes a *Siddha* or a perfect soul, there is no returning again to a worldly state. The *Siddha* has been defined as a being "without caste, unaffected by smell, without the sense of taste, without feeling, without form, without hunger, without pain, without sorrow, without joy, without birth, without old age, without death, without body, without karma, enjoying an endless and unbroken calm". The attainment of *Siddhahood* is by no means restricted to Jaina ascetics, it is equally possible for householders of eminent holiness (*Grihasthlingsidh*) and even for non-Jainas who live a perfectly holy life (*Anyalingsidh*). Jaina ascetics obtaining *Siddhahood* would be known *Svlingsidh*. It has sometimes been debated whether *Moksa* is a place situated somewhere in the Universe or merely a state or condition of freedom. In the *Moksa* state the soul has absolute knowledge and absolute perception so that it knows all things simultaneously: it also has infinite capacity or power for right action (*anantveerye*), so that *karma* can never subdue this freedom and absolute bliss (*Anantsukh*).

Ethical System

From the foregoing analysis of the fundamental truths of Jainism, it will be clear that Jainism may fairly be regarded as a system of ethics rather than a religion. Its extremely severe practical discipline is a special feature of Jainism. Not only for the ascetic but also for the householder does Jainism prescribe a highly rigorous discipline. Like many other Indian doctrines, it emphasises enlightenment and conduct, but to these it adds faith, and so insists upon right faith, right knowledge and right conduct as the three precious principles (*Gunrratntriya*) of life. Right conduct includes the five vows, which have been mentioned before, - viz. *Ahimsa, Satya, Astay, Brahmcharya, and aprigreh* and a long list of items of self-control and self-restraint. Practically each one of these vows was enjoined in some form or other by other faiths also, but they were quite distinctively interpreted by Jainism. The way in which the doctrine of *Ahimsa* is made to pervade the whole code of conduct is peculiarly Jaina. *Ahimsa* has been understood to comprehend *Ahimsa* in thought, by word or act. It is important to add that it has not been explained merely as negative principle, it has been taken to mean the rendering of active service to others, for we shall be really injuring a person when we can help him but do not. The social or objective side of ethics is not ignored; but in so far as the final aim of Jainism is the development of one's personality, it emphasises the individualistic aspect.

Purification of the mind is insisted upon as the starting point of all ethical life. No kind of asceticism can be of any good until the mind is purified, for with purification of the mind is the removal of attachment (*rag*) and antipathy (*dvaish*) really possible. Purification of the mind is achieved by continuous meditation and constant self-control. During his *sadhakas* life Mahavira devoted himself intently to meditation and the practice of the ten *dharmas* including *Senyem* (self-control or control of the senses), *Stya* (truthfulness), *Showch* (purity), *Brahmcharya* (chastity), *Akinrchanya* (absolute want of greed), *tep* (asceticism), *Kshma* (forbearance and patience), *Mardv* (mildness), *Arjv* (sincerity), and *Mukti* (freedom or emancipation from all sins). It was by that means that he ultimately obtained enlightenment and true self-knowledge. *Samtv* (the capacity to look on all beings with equality) and *Dhyan* (or meditation) are interdependent; there can be no *Dhyan* without *samatva*, nor can there be *samatva* without *Dhyan*. The Jaina *Dhyan*, consists in the concentration of the mind on the syllables of the prayer phrases, and is enjoined to be practiced as an aid to making the mind steady and perfectly equal and undisturbed towards all things. Further aids to making the mind steady have been mentioned in the Jaina texts. They comprehend *Metree* (universal friendship), *Prmad* (the habit of emphasising the good sides of men), *Krunra* (universal compassion) and *Madhysthya* (indifference to the wickedness of people, i.e. the habit of not taking any note of sinners).

Jaina texts give a very close description of the system of ethics in their analysis of *Bandh* and *Moksh*. Unlike Hinduism, Jainism has correlated ethical teaching with its metaphysical system. The four most important sins are the *kasayas*, anger, conceit, intrigue and greed. They are sister sins, that is to say, a person committing one of them invariably goes to the commission of others. *Krodha* or anger has been stressed first, for it is the source of all sins then there is *mana* or conceit, *Maya* or cheatıng and or avarice. Jainism argues that the length of time, a sin is indulged in, affects the nature of the sin. The worst degree to which any of these four sins may be indulged in is called *Anantanubandhi* when the sin is cherished as long as life lasts; while under the sway of sin to this degree it is impossible for a man to grasp any ideas of religion or to give his mind to study, The next, i.e. *Apratyakhyana* degree is when the sin, though nursed for a year, is confessed at the great annual confession. Under the influence of these degrees of sins a man might possess an intellectual grasp of religious principles, but cannot possibly carry them our into his daily life, for he cannot really give up attachment to the world.

The least harmful of the degrees of sins is *sanjvalana,* when they are renounced at the evening confession. The matter has been brought home to the disciple by means of a number of parables. In the case of anger the least harmful degree has been likened to a line drawn on water which soon passes away; the next to one drawn to the dust, which is stamped out and effected in a day, the third to a crack in the dried mud at the bottom of an empty village tank which will not disappear till the yearly rains fill the tank and cover it, and the worst of all to a fissure in a mountain side, which will remain till the end of the world.

In the case of *Maya* or deceit, which leads to crookedness, the last degree can be straightened as one can straighten a *bamboo* cane; the second degree has been likened to the crooked crack of moisture left in the dust by the dripping from the water carrier's leather bucket; the third degree to a ram's horn; and the worst degree to the knot in the root of a bamboo, the most crooked thing in the world. The result of any of these four sins, if indulged in the worst degree, is to condemn a man to rebirth in hell; the next worst forces him in his next life to become a bird or a beast, or an insect; it is only the less harmful degrees which would enable him to be reborn as a man or a god; and in order to become a *siddha* one must completely renounce all wrath, conceit, intrigue and greed.

It is important to point out that not only wrath, conceit, intrigue, greed, attachment and enmity are sins in the Jaina view, but also such personal characteristics as quarrelsomeness, slander, the telling of stories to discredit others, undue fault-finding, excessive attachment to worldly objects of affection, hypocrisy and false faith. The list is a comprehensive one, and when one remembers that the Lord enjoined upon every Jaina ascetic or householder, to make a daily confession of these sins, one cannot help being impressed by the significantly ethical character of the whole system. Jaina ethics is not simply negative as some critics have been often inclined to point out. The chapter on *Pun* gives a list of positive social duties, the performance of which is regarded as bringing peace of mind to the individual. These duties are the giving of food to the hungry, the weak and the needy, the giving of water to the thirsty, the giving of clothes to the destitute, the giving of shelter and lodging to the homeless. By thinking well of every one and by exerting ourselves to render them services also we accumulate merit. Sweet and fruitful speech, reverential behaviour and generally amiable disposition are among the other acts of *Punya*. All these are virtues which are the only firm basis of a truly civic and socially useful life; and even Mrs. Stevenson admits "not in vain are practical ethic wedded to philosophical speculation" in Jainism.

Jaina Belief

It is sometimes said that Jainism is atheistic *nastika*. If *nastika* means an unbeliever in a life beyond, i.e. "one who does not believe in a surviving self," then surely Jainism is not at all *nastika*. If *nastika*, means one who repudiates the authority of the *Veda*, then Jainism is certainly nastika. If nastika means one who does not believe in God, then a categorical answer is not possible to make, for although Jainism does not believe in a creative God, it does believe in godhead. Jainism deliberately rejects the conception of a supreme personality responsible for the creation of the world. The Nyaya philosopher says that the world is of the nature of an effect and that it must have been created by an intelligent agent, the agent being God (*Ishwar*); but the argument is conclusively controverted by the Jaina. (1) The cause of an effect need not necessarily be intelligent, and if God who is regarded as the cause of the creation be regarded as intelligent on the analogy of human causation, then he must be admitted to be imperfect like human beings. (2) Also God must be admitted to have a body, for we have never seen any intelligent creator without a body. (3) Even if it is admitted for the sake of argument that a bodiless God can create the world by his will and activity, did he take to creation through a personal whim and give high status to some and poverty to others quite arbitrarily? If the creation took place simply through his own nature, then what is the good of admitting him at all? Professor Dasgupta sums up the rest of the argument like this:

> "Assuming for the sake of argument that God exists you could never justify the adjectives with which you wish to qualify him. Thus you say that he is eternal. But since he has no body, he must be of the nature of intelligence and will. But this nature must have changed in diverse forms for the production of diverse kinds of worldly, things which are of so varied a nature. If there were no change in his knowledge and will then there could not have been diverse kinds of creation and destruction. Destruction and creation cannot be the result of one unchangeable will and knowledge. Moreover, it is the character, of knowledge to change, if the word is used in the sense in which knowledge is applied to human beings, and surely we are not aware of any other kind of knowledge. You say that God is omniscient but it is difficult to suppose how he can have any knowledge at all, for as he has no organs he cannot have any perception, and since he cannot have any perception, he cannot have any inference either. If it is said that without the supposition of a God the variety of the world be inexplicable, this also is not true for this implication would only by justified if there were no other hypothesis left. But there are other suppositions also. Even without an omniscient God you could explain all things merely by the doctrine of moral order or the law of "Karma".

Jainism rejects the conception of creative divinity as self-discrepant. Its belief is that there is no God and that the world was never created. In the view the Jaina is curiously enough in agreement with the Mimansaka, the upholder of strict orthodoxy. But as we mentioned above, although Jainism does not believe in a creative God, it does believe in godhead. Theistic systems are generally anthropomorphic, they bring down God to the level of man. Jainism, on the other hand, looks upon man himself as God when his inherent powers are fully in blossom. Every liberated soul is divine. God in Jaina theory being only another word for the soul at its best. In rejecting God who is so by his own right and with it also the belief that salvation may be attained through his mercy, Jainism recognises that karma by itself and without the intervention of any divine power is adequate to explain the whole world of experience and thus impress on the individual his complete responsibility for what he does. "Jainism more than any other creed gives absolute religious independence and freedom to man. Nothing can intervene between the actions which we do and the fruits thereof. Once done they become our masters and must fruitify".

God in Jainism is the ideal man, that is to say, the ideal of man; there is a way to achieve it and that is the Jaina ethical way. Others have striven in that way and achieved it in the past, and their example is a constant inspiration to us. "Such an ideal carries with it all necessary hope and encouragement, for what man has done, man can do".

10

Significance of Mahavira

Preaching the Principles

Tirthankara Mahavira, after the attainment of omniscience at the age of forty-two, toured different parts of the country for a continuous period of thirty years, met people from various urban, rural and tribal societies, and preached the principles and rules of conduct as laid down by Jainism. The personality and preachings of Tirthankara Mahavira created a tremendous impact on the minds of all sections of people and especially on the down-trodden sections of the population. He not only revealed to them the path of Liberation, i.e. the path to attain the eternal happiness, which was the main object of the people, but also showed the actual means through which all people, irrespective of any distinction of class or status, can achieve this objective.

His sincerity of purpose, way of approach, method of explanation, divine speech and philosophical and ethical doctrines appealed to the people to such an extent that with a firm conviction of mind they began to adopt Jaina religion as lay followers or as ascetics. The number of confirmed adherents to Jaina religion began to increase steadily. In this way Tirthankara Mahavira ushered in a new era of hope and aspirations for the common people and succeeded in considerably changing the life, outlook and values of the people. He introduced various new concepts and ideas which revolutionised the entire course of life of the people. The significance of Tirthankara Mahavira lies in successfully effecting a social change and in making institutional and other arrangements for the perpetuation of his new social order. In order to solve the pressing problems of the time, he made several important salient contributions from a social point of view which are briefly out-lined here.

Inculcation of Self-reliance

Tirthankara Mahavira's contribution of a revolutionary nature consisted in completely changing the attitude of the people towards God and thereby inculcating the spirit of self-reliance among the minds of the people. The common belief held by the people according to the Vedic ideology was that as this world has been created by the God and that the work of controlling the events in this world is also carried out by the God. This' popular belief engendered a feeling of divine dispensation in the minds of the people because it was firmly held by the people that God can do and undo anything in this world in accordance with his wishes. Naturally this feeling created a sense of complete dependence on the God by the people in the conduct of their daily activities and in securing happiness in this world as well as in the next world.

Obviously this sense of dependence on the God urged people to find out ways and means so as to obtain in abundant measure the favours of God in mundane and spiritual matters and also to avoid the displeasure or wrath of' God which, it was thought, would not only bring several difficulties in the normal course of life but also would lead to complete disaster. As a result of this attitude, people began to place entirely blind faith on the omnipotent God and to secure his favours by practising certain rites and rituals laid down for the purposes. These prescribed rituals were so elaborate that they did require the services of priests who were supposed to have the special knowledge about these rites and Who were also specifically authorised to perform these rituals in a proper manner.

In this way the entire code of conduct of the people was fully dominated by the practice of various rituals throughout the course of life and by the priests whose help and assistance were considered most essential to work as intermediary between people and God for securing desired favours from God.

Tirthankara Mahavira launched an intensive attack on this attitude of complete submission to God by the people for attaining their final objective in life, viz. liberation. In this regard Tirthankara Mahavira firmly asserted that this world is eternal and has not been created by any power like God and that the happenings in this world are not controlled by God. He clearly proclaimed that nothing here or elsewhere depends on the favours of God but everything depends on the actions of the people. He confidently stated that all persons, irrespective of their class, family or position, have got a right to achieve salvation, their ultimate objective in life, by relying on themselves and through the observance of an ethical code of conduct and not by merely performing some rituals with the help of others.

For this purpose he laid down a path to liberation which consisted Right Faith, Right Knowledge and Right Conduct and appealed to the people to follow this path on their individual initiative and efforts and not on the help of any intermediary. Further, he impressed on the people the Theory of Karma which is based on the principle of self-reliance. This doctrine explains the reasons lying behind or causes leading to effects. It maintains that every happening in this world is the result of some antecedent causes. Since the individual soul is the doer of actions, it must bear the consequences of these actions sooner or later. There is no way out of it. The responsibility of consequences cannot be shifted nor exemption from the consequences be given by anybody. The soul has to enjoy the fruits of the Karmas in this life or in subsequent lives. There is no salvation until the soul stops the influx of Karmas and gets rid of existing Karmas and this it will have to do by its own deliberate efforts without expecting any help from an outside agency like God. There is no use in asking the favour of God or his representative because Gods have not the power of determining the consequences of the Karmas and have no authority to forgive people from future consequences of past actions.

This theory of Karma has been an original and integral part of the Jaina ideology and Tirthankara Mahavira convinced the people of the necessity of adopting this doctrine and of moulding their entire life on the foundation of this theory. Naturally Tirthankara Mahavira laid full stress on individual action and completely denied the existence of divine dispensation. He emphasised that man is the architect of his destiny and that there is no external power which can come in the way of getting the fruits of one's actions, whether good or bad. He assured the people that the attainment of liberation, the ultimate objective in life, is within their reach and it depends entirely on one's, own efforts in the march on the path to liberation. In this; way Tirthankara Mahavira wanted every individual to become a true hero on the battle-field of self-conquest. Thus Tirthankara Mahavira inculcated a spirit of reliance among the people in place of the feelings of utter dependence on the God. This basic change in attitude brought an over-all change in the course of life of the people who began to lay stress more on the ethical aspects than on the ritualistic aspects of their conduct.

Emphasis on Non-violence

Tirthankara Mahavira's most distinctive contribution consists in his great emphasis on the observance of Ahimsa, i.e. non-injury to living beings, by all persons to the maximum extent possible. Ahinsa in its full significance was realised and preached by twenty-three Tirthankaras preceding Tirthankara Mahavira. In fact, the philosophy and rules of conduct laid down in Jaina religion have been based on the solid foundation of Ahimsa, which hats throughout and consistently, been followed to its logical conclusion. That is why Jainism has become synonymous with Ahimsa and Jaina religion is considered as the religion of Ahimsa. The significance of this basic principle of Ahimsa was very powerfully reiterated by Tirthankara Mahavira as the practices of committing violence in the different pretexts had become rampant at that time.

During the Vedic period utmost importance was attached to the performance of sacrifices with a view to secure the favours of God and to avert His anger. The sacrifices were very elaborate, complicated and hedged with various restrictions. The sacrifices became a regular feature of the religious life of the people. The peculiar characteristic of these sacrifices was that they were usually accompanied by the slaughter of animals. As the sacrifices were mainly animal sacrifices they involved the practice of Himsa to a considerable extent: Along with this practice, the flesh-eating or non-vegetarian diet was extremely popular among the different sections of the people. The Rigvedic people, including the Brahmins, were fond of meat-eating and practically all the important ceremonies were attended with the slaughter of animals. Offerings of flesh were frequently made to the Gods, and worshippers, including the priests, ate the offerings.

The meat of cows and bulls does not seem to have been excluded. It was a custom to entertain a distinguished guest with the meat of a bull or a barren cow. At the wedding ceremonies oxen were slain, evidently for the feeding of the invited guests. In fact, the sacrifice of cow and bulls was not only optional as in the case of the arrival of a guest and marriage but compulsory on certain occasions and ceremonies. At Shradhhas, or periodical oblations to the manes, the sacrifice of cows was recommended, as substances like rice, barley, sesamum, fruits, etc. keep the manes satisfied for a month, the flesh of goats for six months, while beef satisfied them for a year. Meat was almost compulsory at Annaprashana, i.e. the first feeding with solid food, ceremony of a child and from then till death and cremation, sacrificing of animals was necessary on most of the ceremonial occasions of life.

Tirthankara Mahavira launched a vigorous attack against meat-eating and the performance of sacrificial rites by propagating the principle of Ahimsa, i.e. non-injury to living beings. In fact in all his preachings Tirthankara Mahavira invariably laid great stress on the observance of Ahimsa because the principle of Ahimsa is the logical outcome of the basic Jaina metaphysical theory that all the souls are potentially equal. He therefore asserted that as no one likes pain, one should not do unto others what one does not want Others to do unto one.

Since all living beings possessed soul, the principle of non-injury was obviously extended to cover all living beings. He explained the doctrine of Ahimsa systematically and to the minutest detail. He considered injury or violence of three kinds: (i) physical violence, which covered killing, wounding and causing any physical pain, (ii) violence in words consisted in using harsh words, and (iii) mental violence; which implied bearing ill-feeling towards others. Further, he made it clear that violence or injury should be avoided in three ways, that is, it should not be committed, commissioned or consented to. Moreover, among the five main Vratas, i.e. vows, the first place was given to the observance of Ahimsa. In addition, Ahimsa was regarded as the principal vow, and the other four vows were considered to be merely details of the principal vow.

All these preachings of Tirthankara Mahavira regarding: the strict observance of the principle of Ahimsa to the maximum extent possible by every individual in society produced far reaching effects in social field. The practice of performing sacrificial rites and especially the slaughter of animals at the time of sacrifices considerably fell into disuse. Similarly, killing of animals for hunting, sports and decoration purposes was greatly reduced. Further, the slaughter of animals and birds with a view to use their flesh as a form of diet slowly became unpopular. Ahimsa and inefficacy of sacrificial rites way injury to living beings was greatly reduced and the practice of vegetarian diet was adopted by large sections of population in different regions of the country. In this connection Dr. N. K. Dutt (in his book "Origin and Growth of Caste in India") observes that "Animal sacrifice had been of so long standing among the Aryans and such was the respect for the authority of the Vedas which made it obligatory to sacrifice with flesh offerings, that the abolition of sacrifices, even of cows, became a very slow process, effecting only a very small minority, the intellectual section of the people, and Might not have succeeded at all if Jainism and Buddhism had not overwhelmed the country and the mass of the people with the teach-

Thus Tirthankara Mahavira emphasised the basic fact that every living being has a sanctity and a dignity of its own and therefore one must respect it as one expects one's own dignity to be respected by others. He also firmly emphasised that life is sacred irrespective of species, caste, colour, creed or nationality. On this basis he advocated the principle of "Live and let live; In this way Tirthankara Mahavira convinced the people that the practice of Ahimsa is both an individual and a collectvie virtue and showed that Ahimsa has a positive force and a universal appeal.

As the principle of Ahimsa permeates the life of the Jainas, the Jaina culture is referred to as Ahimsa culture. If the Jainas are known for anything it is far the evolution of Ahimsa culture since they practised and propagated that culture from ancient times. The antiquity and continuity of Ahimsa culture is mainly due to the incessant efforts of the Jaina Acharyas, i.e. saints. Naturally the Jainas were in great numbers and wielded some influence they tried to spread Ahimsa culture among the masses. That is why we find that the States of Gujarat and Karnataka, which were the strongholds of Jainas from the beginning, are largely vegetarian. In fact it is admitted that as a result of the activities of the Jainas for the last so many centuries Ahimsa still forms the substratum of Indian character as a whole.

Insistence on Tolerance

Advocacy of the principle of religious tolerance has been the characteristic contribution of Tirthankara Mahavira. When; the promulgated Jaina religion, he never deprecated other religions and never tried to prove that other religions are false. In fact he propounded the doctrines of Anekantavada, i.e. many-sidedness, and showed that a thing can be considered from many points of view. That is why he always advised the people to find out the truth in anything after taking into account several sides or aspects of that thing.

This obviously broadens the outlook of the persons as they are made to look at a thing from different angles. At the same time the principle of Anekantavada does not engender the feelings of enmity or hatred towards the, other, religionists because it believes that other religions also would be having some truths from their points of view. Hence by enunciating the principle of ekantavada, Tirthankara Mahavira advocated the principle of tolerance and asserted that it could be applied to intellectual, social, religious and other fields of activities. As a result we find that Anekantavada has definitely a bearing on man's psychological and spiritual life and that it is not confined to solve a mere ontological problem. It has supplied the philosopher with catholicity of thought, convincing him that Truth is not anybody's monopoly with tariff walls of denominational religion: It also furnishes the religious aspirant with the virtue of intellectual toleration which is a part of Ahimsa.

Human beings have limited knowledge and inadequate expression. That is why -different doctrines are inadequate; at the most they are one-sided views of the Truth which cannot be duly enclosed in words and concepts. Jainism has always held that it is wrong, if not dangerous, to presume that one's own creed alone represents the truth. Toleration is, therefore, the characteristic of Jaina ideology as propounded by Tirthankara Mahavira. Even the, Jaina monarchs and generals have a clean and commendable record to their credit in this regard. The political history of India knows no cases of persecution by Jaina Kings, even when Jaina monks and laymen have suffered at the hands of others religionists of fanatical temper. Dr. B. A. Salefore has rightly observed in this regard that "The principle of Ahimsa was partly responsible for the greatest contribution of the Jainas to Hindu culture-that relating to toleration. Whatever may he said concerning the rigidity with which they maintained their religious tenets and the tenacity and skill with which they met and defeated their opponent in religious disputations, yet it cannot be denied that the Jainas fostered the principle of toleration more sincerely and the same time more successfully than any other community in India".

Establishment of Social Equality

The most significant contribution in the social field made by Tirthankara Mahavira was the establishment of social equality among the four Varnas,' i.e. classes, prevalent in the society. Mahavira succeeded in organising his large number of followers into a compact social order quite distinct from that of the Brahminic social order of the Vedic period.

The Vedic society was composed of four classes, viz. Brahmin, Rajanya, Vaishya and Shudra. They were said to have come from the mouth, the arms, the thighs and the feet of the Creator, Brahmin. The particular limbs ascribed as the origins of these divisions and the order in which they were mentioned indicated their status in the society of the time. The fact that the four classes were described as of divine origin could be taken as a sufficient indication that they were of long duration and very well defined. Not only the four classes were distinct and separate, but they were also affected by the spirit of rivalry among themselves. Even in the early Rigvedic times the Brahminical profession had begun to set up claims of superiority or sacredness for itself and, accordingly we find that different rules were prescribed for different classes. Thus the Shatapatha Brahmin laid down different modes of address for the four classes, differing in degrees of politeness, agachchha, adrava and adhava.

The Taittiriya Brahmin recommended the spring season to the Brahmins for the performance of sacrifices, the Summer to the Kshatriyas, and the autumn to the Vaishyas. The Atharva Veda proclaimed in the strongest language sin, peril and ruinous consequences for insulting Brahmins and robbing them of their property. This inordinate extension of the pretensions and prerogatives of the sacerdotal class naturally created cleavages in the Society.

The Kshatriya were assigned a position next to Brahmins, and Vaishyas and Shudras were comparatively neglected. Thus the Vedic Societry was completely class-ridden in the sense that unusual importance was given to the Brahmin class to the detriment of other classes and that no body was allowed to change his class' which he had got on the basis of his birth it, that class.

Against these glaring practices based on the acceptance of social inequality and on the wide observance of social discrimination, Tirtharikara, Mahavira launched his attack. He recognised the division of society into four classes but based them on the nature of activities carried out by the people and not on the basis of their birth. He gave full freedom to one and all, including women and Shudras, to observe common religious practices prescribed for all and admitted them into his religious order: In this way Tirthankara Mahavira threw open the doors of Jainism to all and gave equal opportunity to everybody irrespectives of his class or birth, to practice religion according to his capacity.

Those who followed religion as householders were known as Shravakas and Shravikas and those who observed the religion fully by leaving their houses and becoming ascetics were called as Sadhus and Sadhvis.

After Mahavira, various Jaina Acharyas made no distinction whatsoever among people in the matter of following religion arid conceived that the Varna system, that is, the division of society into four Varnas or classes, is based upon differences in professions. In their view birth played no part in determining the Varna or class of a particular person.

The whole mankind came into existence due to the rise of Jati-nama-Karma; and the mankind was divided into four categories of Brahmin, Kshatriya, Vaishya and Shudra according to the differences in the vocations they followed for their livelihood. Those who observed Vratas, i.e. religious injunctions, to a greater degree were known as Brahminas, those who carried weapons as Kshatriyas, those who acquired wealth by just means as Vaishyas and those who maintained by resorting to low professions as Shudras.

The Brahminahood of best ascetics as well as of ordinary people is considered on their actions and not on their birth in the Brahmin class. No class has been despised. The actions alone lead to good prosperity. Gods regard a Chandala, i. e. an outcaste, as a Brahmin, if he follows religious mode of life. The epithets of classes and Chandala, which are applied to mankind are famous in this world due to differences in their ways of life.

The idea of differentiations of classes comes in only because of differences in the ways of life. No single class has been settled as that of the true or real Brahmin class. Really there is only one class of four divisions, viz. Brahminas, Kshatriyas, Vaashyas and Shudras, and that is the class of human beings. They have been divided because of differences in the ways of life.

People of good conduct had attained heaven even though they were born in low families and on the contrary men devoid of good conduct and restraint had gone to hell in spite of the fact that they had taken birth in high families. A class is formed by following a particular mode of life and it perishes when that mode is left and that is why wise people should respect ways of life only. The good people should not have pride in any class as it leads to degradation but they should observe good conduct which might give them high position.

It is clear that the society as envisaged by Tirthankara Mahavira and other Jalna Acharyas was a society where classes were not hereditary and like water-tight compartments and where complete freedom was granted to the people to change to the class of their own aptitude. The society was not divided into distinct separate sections and no differentiation was made in the status of the classes. All were considered as different ways of life and utmost importance was attached to individual character and mode of behaviour. There was no room for anybody to feel that he was neglected or degraded as he was free enough to follow any profession he liked and he could, observe, all religious rites and practices along with others.

Thus Mahavira's conception of Varna system produced social impact of great significance. The principle of social equality among-the classes was firmly established and the social mobility among the classes was considerably increased as the criterion of birth for the membership of a class was straightway removed. This had a very wholesome effect on the conditions of the Shudras which were very deplorable in the sense that the Shudras were deprived of education, denied all rights, subjected to inhuman treatment and assigned the lowest position in society Formerly, the Shudras were completely disregarded in religious matters and several binding restrictions were placed on their movements and ways of living. Tirthankara Mahavira's teachings proved a great solace to the Shudras as the practices of social discriminations against them were fully banned.

This resulted in the rise of social status of the down-trodden people. Obviously there was a distinct change in the social attitude towards the non-aryans and the common masses. Slowly there was a strong opposition to the continuation of the practice of slavery in any form. The feelings of contempt and reproach towards them also began to disappear. Naturally the general masses were tremendously benefited as the practices of social discriminations were completely banished and they were given opportunities to improve their lot.

At the same time Mahavira's teachings affected to a very great extent the privileged position enjoyed by the Brahminas belonging to the priestly professions. From the Vedic period such Brahmin priests enjoyed high social status, political facilities, economic concessions, educational opportunities, cultural dominance and religious privileges to the exclusion of other classes. In view of this monopolistic condition the Brahmin priests held the position of prominence in society and freely made use of that position for the exploitation of the masses in different fields and especially in religious matters which were of highest-importance to the people. Obviously, the Brahmin priests were extremely keen on the perpetuation of their domination on the common masses and hence they did not hesitate to employ any means to keep the masses in their despised conditions and to make the masses entirely dependent on their favours.

Naturally, the common masses were leading a very low life in an atmosphere of severe discontent and utter frustration. Tirthankara Mahavira launched an open and forceful attack on the Brahmin priestly class and on their ingenious practices used for the excessive exploitation of the common masses. At the same time Tirthankara Mahavira made his religion easily accessible to the common masses, gave equal opportunities in the practice of religion to one and all irrespective of their class affiliations, and held out a sure promise for all persons to achieve Liberation, the highest goal in their life, by observing the rules of conduct laid down by the religion and not by merely getting the different kinds of sacrifices performed by the priests.

This practical and ethical approach to religion vigorously and effectively enunciated by Tirthankara Mahavira made people independent of the priestly domination, created a feeling of self-reliance and appealed to the common masses. Thus Tirthankara Mahavira's opposition was to the priestly class of Brahminas and to the several tactics employed by them for the exploitation of the common masses by managing to keep the masses virtually ignorant and entirely dependent on the favours of the priests. This strong opposition considerably reduced the influence and domination wielded by the priestly class over the other people.

But it is obvious that the opposition or Tirthankara Mahavira was confined to the priestly class of the Brahminas and not to the Brahmin Varna as such. In fact, Tirthankara Mahavira always appreciated the intellectual capacities of the Brahminas, initiated many learned Brahminas to the Jaina religion, admitted several scholars among the Brahminas to his ascetic order and even appointed Indrabhuti Gautama, the most learned Brahmin teacher, as his first Ganadhara, i.e. the apostle or the Chief Disciple. It has already been mentioned that Tirthankara Mahavira delivered his first Sermon after 66 days of attainment of Omniscience, only when he got the services of the most talented Brahmin teacher, viz. Indrabhuti Gautama, for the proper interpretation of his preachings to the people: In this way Tirthankara Mahavira always showed regard to the learning and education of the Brahminas but invariably led a strong and consistent attack against the priestly class of the Brahminas.

Encouragement to Social Welfare

Along with the maximum emphasis on the actual observance of Ahimsa, Tirthankara Mahavira greatly extended the implications of Ahimsa. He invariably stressed both the negative and the positive aspects of Ahimsa. He strongly advocated that the concept of Ahimsa should not be confined only to the negative side of it, that is, the avoidance of injury to the living beings of different categories, but should' be consistently, applied in the positive way, that is, in the direction of increasing the welfare of all living beings. Healways appealed to' the people to bear good intentions about the prosperity of others, to show active interest in the welfare of the needy persons, and to take practical steps to ameliorate the miserable conditions of afflicted living beings including insects, birds, animals and men. This positive encouragements to social welfare activities has been the most useful and noteworthy contribution of Tirthankara Mahavira to Indian Culture.

This humanitarian approach to lessen the miseries of living beings was included in the Yrata, i.e. vow of Aparigraha, i.e. abstention from greed of worldly possessions. The vow of Aparigraha is the fifth of the five main vows which must be consistently followed by all persons. Aparigraha involves avoiding the fault of Parigraha which consists in desiring more than what is needed by an individual. Accumulating even necessary articles in large numbers, expressing wonder at the prosperity of others, excessive greed and changing the proportions of existing possessions are all forms of Parigraha i.e. worldly attachments. This vow aims at putting a limit on the worldly possessions by individuals according to their needs and desires. That is why this vow of Aparigraha is many times' termed as Parigraha-Parimana-Vrata, i.e. the vow to limit one's worldly possessions.

This vow of Parigraha-Parimana is very noteworthy as it indirectly aims at economic equalisation by peacefully preventing undue accumulation of capital in individual hands. It recommends that a householder should fix, beforehand, the limit of his maximum belongings, and should; in no case, exceed it. If he ever happens to earn more than that he must spend it away, i.e. charities. The best forms of charities prescribed Hyruligiun are "Ahara-abhaya-bhaishajya-Shastra-dana,' i.e. k:ivom; food to the hungry and the poor, saving the lives of people in danger, distribution of medicines and spreading knowledge. These charities are called the `Chaturoldha-Dana' i.e. the fourfold gifts, by Jatna religion and it has been enjoined on the housoltolders that they should make special efforts to give these charil.ics to the needy-irrespective of caste or crecd from the beginning the Jaina householders made it one principles to give these four gifts to all persons who are in need of such help. In fact this help was extended to the prutcclian and well-being of insects, birds and animals also.

For this the Jainas established alm-houses, rest-houses, dispensaries and educational institutions wherever they were concentrated in good numbers. The Anna-chhatralayas, i.e. alm-houses, were conducted at pilgrim and other centres for the benefit of poor-people. In the Dharrna-Shalas, i.e. rest-houses, lodging arrangements were provided without any charges or at nominal charges at important towns, cities and pilgrim places. The Aushadhalayas, i.e. dispensaries, provided free medicines to the afflicted persons. Along with the dispensaries for men, the Jainas conducted special institutions known as Pinjarapols for the protection and care of helpless and decrepit animals and birds. In unusual times of flood and famine these Pinjarapols carry out various activities for animal protection. There is hardly any town or village of Gujarat or Rajasthan, where Pinjarapol is not present in some form or other. In the spread of education the Jainas took a leading part in the education of the masses. Various relics show that formerly Jaina ascetics took a great share in teaching children in the southern countries, viz. Andhra, Tamilnadu, Karnatak and Maharashtra. In this connection Dr. A. S. Altekar rightly observes (in his book 'Rashtrakutas and their Times') that before the beginning of the alphabet proper the children should be required to pay homage to the deity Ganesha, by reciting the formula "Shri Ganeshaya Namah", is natural in Hindu society, but that in the Deccan even to-day it should be followed by the Jaina formula "Om Namah Siddham" shows that the Jain teachers of medieval age had so completely controlled the mass education that the Hindus continued to teach their children this originally Jaina formula even after the decline of Jainism.

Even now the Jaina have rigorously maintained the tradition by giving freely these Chaturvidha Dana, i.e. four types of gifts, in all parts of India. In this manner legacy of Mahavira has been continued to the present day.

Thus there is an immense value attached to this vow of aparigraha or Parigraha-Parimana from social point of view. At the same time this vow has got a great significance in preparing a proper mental attitude towards material possessions, in forming a true scale of values, and in developing a right sense of proportion for individual possessions. This vow emphasises that one should not feel too much attachment towards his own possessions and should resist all temptations. It teaches that one may keep wealth and commodities to satisfy one's requirements but one should not lose oneself in the pursuint it in the pursuit of an after all gain. In this manner it appeals that ones greed, vanity, lust, etc. Thus the vow of apart, inculcates a particular mental attitude of self-restraint in the face of pleasures, of stoicism before temptations and of detachment from superfluities and superabundances. This attitude of mind is perhaps more necessary today than ever before.

Emancipation of Women

Another contribution of a distinctive nature made by Tirthankara Mahavira in the social field was in the direction of raising the status of women. In the latter part of the Vedic period women had practically been reduced to the status of Shudras. Like the Shudras, women were debarred from the right of initiation and investment with the sacred thread. They were considered to have no business with the sacred religious texts. In many passages we find that women and Shudra were bracketed together. The very sight of woman was considered as inauspicious and people were asked to avoid seeing women, Shudras, dead bodies, etc. Thus women had practically no place in the religious life of the society and as such she was neglected and degraded by the people.

This low position of women was definitely changed by Tirthankara Mahavira in many ways. He removed various restrictions imposed on women especially in the practice of religion. In fact Tirthankara Mahavira did not make any distinction between the males and females in the observance of religion.

The rules of conduct prescribed for the males and females were exactly the same. Both the sexes were given equal opportunities in different matters of religion like the study of sacred texts, observance of necessary duties, practice of vratas, i.e. vows, entrance into the ascetic order, practice of penance, making spiritual progress, etc. In the religious order of Tirthankara Mahavira the male householders were called Shravakas and the female householders were termed Shravikas and both were quite free to observe their common religious duties and to prepare themselves for adopting ascetic life in due course. Similarly, complete freedom was given to women, like men, to enter the ascetic orders.

The female sex was no bar to the practice of asceticism. Tirthankara Mahavira always showed this attitude of equality towards women and admitted them freely into his ascetic order, no matter whether the candidates for admission were royal consorts, members of the aristocracy, and those belonging to the common run of society. Naturally many ladies availed themselves of this opportunity of achieving their salvation in due course by entering into the ascetic order.

That is why in Tirthankara Mahavira's religious organisation there were two orders of ascetics, like those of householders, namely, Sadhus, i.e. male ascetics and Sadhvis, i.e. female ascetics. It is stated that in Tirthankara Mahavira's fourfold religious order there were about 14000 Sadhus, 36000 Sadhvis, 1,00,000 Shravakas and 3,00,000 Shravikas. This show that the female members out numbered the male members in both the categories of householders and ascetics. It is a clear indication that the females were very eager to take full advantage of the opportunity offered to them by Tirthankara Mahavira.

In fact, many females from royal families and close relatives of Tirthankara Mahavira joined his ascetic order along with the other ordinary members. For example, Chandana and Jyeshtha, the two younger sisters of Queen Trishaladevi, the mother of Mahavira, and Yashasvati; the wife of their maternal uncle, entered the ascetic order of Tirthankara Mahavira; and eventually Chandana assumed the' position of the head of the Sadhvis, i.e. the female ascetics. In this way Tirthankara Mahavira effected emancipation of women by giving them similar opportunities like men to achieve their highest objective in life, viz. Liberation. Females made best of these opportunities and many of them distinguished themselves as teachers and preachers.

Further the religious independence given to women had its repercussions in other fields also. Equality of opportunity was accorded to women in several social spheres of action. In education they were given equal treatment with the males. The utmost importance of imparting education to females, along with males, was realised even in the ancient past by Rishabhadeva, the first Tirthankara, who bad advised his two young daughters, Brahmi and Sundari, that "only when you would adorn yourself with education your life would be fruitful because just as a learned man is held in high esteem by educated persons, a learned lady also occupies the highest position in the female world". According to Jaina tradition a woman is expected to know 64 arts like dancing, painting, music, aesthetics, medicine, domestic science, etc. As a result of this high type of education received by women, we find, in Jaina tradition, that many women used to enter the teaching profession and to remain unmarried throughout the life in order to carry on their spiritual experiments unhampered.

It is recorded in Jaina tradition that Jayanti, a daughter of King Saliasranika of Kaushambi` remained unmarried out of her love for religion and-philosophy.' When Mahavira-first visited several abstruse ineta-physical questions and eventually became a nun. Similarly, in later periods of history also Jaina women not only kept up the pace of female education but at times made original contributions to literature.

For example, along with men Jaina women also added to Kannada literature. The greatest name among them was Kanti, who, along with the great poet Abhinava Pampa, was one of the gems that adorned the court of Hoyasala King Ballal I in Karnatak. She was a redoubtable orator and poet who completed the unfinished poems of Abhinava Pampa in the open Court of that ruler. Similarly, a Jaina lady Avvaiyara, `the Venerable Matron', was one of the most admired amongst the poets in Tamil language. Kaushambi, she discussed with him.

11

Jaina Tradition upto Mahavira

Historicity of the Jaina Tradition

The Historicity of this Jaina tradition is amply borne one both by literary and archaeological evidences. By the beginning of the 20th century many writers were under the impression that Mahavira was an imaginary or a legendary figure. Soon they realised that Mahavira was a historical figure but they believed that Mahavira and Gautama Buddha are the two names of the same person, viz. Gautama Buddha. Early researches in the 20th century dispelled this confusion about Mahavira and Gautama Buddha and established a separate and different identity of Mahavira. In this way though Mahavira's real and independent existence was accepted, still he was regarded as the founder of Jaina religion and as the champion of non-violence who revolted against the violent practices of Brahminism.

The recent researches in historical and indological studies carried out by Western and Oriental Scholars have removed beyond doubt the ideas of former writers about the role of Mahavira and have now conclusively established the fact that Mahavira is not the founder of Jaina religion but the promulgator of Jaina religion which was in prevalence in India, especially in Eastern India from the ancient past. This view is clearly stated by P. C. Roy Chaudhury in his book 'Jainism in Bihar' in the following terms: "A common mistake has been made by some of the recent writers in holding that Jainism was born because of discontent against Brahminism. This wrong theory originates because these writers have taken Vardhamana Mahavira as the founder of Jainism. This is not a fact. The creed had already originated and spread and Mahavira propagated it within historic times".

Thus it is now an accepted fact that Mahavira is the Tirthankara or prophet of Jaina religion and that he preached the religion which was promulgated in the 8th Century BC by his predecessor Parshvanatha, the 23rd Tirthankara. The historicity of Parshvanatha (877-777 BC) has been clearly established. Parshvanatha, the son of King Vishvasena and Queen Vamadevi of Kingdom of Kashi, led the life of an ascetic, practised severe penance, obtained omniscience, became a Tirthankara, propagated Jaina religion and attained Nirvana or salvation when he was 100 years of age at Sammet Shikhara, i.e. Parasnatha hill in Hazaribag District of Bihar State. Parshavanatha often gets the epithet 'a lovable or genial personality'. His pupils like Kesikumara lived at the time of Mahavira and held minor differences in dogmatic details though the basic religious ideology was fundamentally the same as that of Mahavira. Eminent historians like Vincent Smith, R.C. Majumdar, and R.K. Mukherji regard Parshvanatha as a historical personage and a great preacher of Jaina religion.

The predecessor of Parshvanatha was Nemi-natha or Arishtanemi, the 22nd Tirthankara and the historicity of Nemi-natha like that of Parshvanatha, could be easily established. Nemx-natha was the real cousin of the famous Lord Krishna of Mahabharata as Samudravijaya, the father of Neini-natha, and Vasudeva, the father of Krishna, were brothers. Nemi-natha possessed a unique personality due to his great compassion towards animals. This is clearly revealed by a significant incident in his life. While Nemi-natha was proceeding at the head of his wedding procession to the house of his bride, Princess Rajulakumari, the daughter of King Ugrasena, he heard the moans and groans of animals placed in an enclosure for some meat-eaters and instantly decided not to marry at all as his marriage would involve such a slaughter of so many innocent animals.

Immediately Nemi-natha renounced his royal title and became an ascetic. Leaving this renunciation of Nemi-natha, the betrothed Princess Rajulakumari or Rajamati also became a nun and entered the ascetic order. Nemi-natha preached religion for several years and finally attained Nirvana on the Mount Girnar, in Junagadha District of Gujrat State. As Nemi-natha renounced the world, he did not take part in the fraternal struggle of Mahabharata like his cousin brother Lord Krishna. Since this Great War of Mahabharata has to be assumed as an historical event and Krishna to be an historical personage, then his cousin brother Nemi-natha is also entitled to have a place in this historical picture There is also an inscriptional evidence to prove the historicity of Nemi-natha. Dr. Pran Nath published in the "Times of India" (dated 19th March 1935) a copperplate grant of the Babylonian King Nebuchadnazzar I (1140 B. C.) found at Prabhaspattan in Gujrat State, which, according to his reading, refers to the Babylonian King having come to Mount Revet to pay homage to Lord Nemi-rlatha. Dr. Fuherer also declared on the basis of Mathura Jaina antiquities that Nemiriatha was an historical personage (vide Epigraphia Indica, I and II, 208-210). Further, we find Nemi-natha's images of the Indo-Scythian period bearing inscriptions mentioning his name. These and many other inscriptions corroborate the historicity of 22nd Tirthankara Nemi-natha.

Among the remaining 21 Tirthankaras of the Jaina tradition, there are several references from different sources to the first Tirthankara Rishabhanatha or Adinatha. Thus the tradition of twenty-four Tirthankaras is firmly established among the Jainas and what is really remarkable about this Jaina tradition is the confirmation of it from non-Jaina sources, especially Buddhist and Hindu sources.

Tradition of Tirthankaras

Jainism is the ancient religion of India and during its long and unbroken existence it is promulgated by 24 Great Preachers known as "Jinas", i.e. "Conquerors" or "Tirthankaras", i.e. "Fordmakers across the stream of existence". These 24 Tirthankaras are: 1. Rishabh-natha or Adinatha 2. Ajita-natha 3. Sambhava-natha 4. Abhinandana-natha 5. Sumati-natha 6. Padmaprabha 7.

Suparshva-natha 8. Chandraprabha 9. Pushpadanta or Suvidhi-natha 10. Shital-natha 11. Shreyamsa-natha 12. Vasupujya 13. Vimala-natha 14. Ananta natha 15. Dharma-natha 16. Shanti-natha 17. Kunthu-natha 18. Ara-natha 19. Malli-natha 20. Muni-suvrata 21. Nami-natha 22. Nemi-natha 23. Parshva-natha 24. Mahavira or Vardhamana.

Thus the tradition of Tirthankaras begins with Rishabha, the first Tirthankara, and ends with Mahavira, the twenty-fourth Tirthankara. Naturally, there is a continuous link among these twenty-four Tirthankaras who flourished in different periods of history in India. It therefore means that the religion first preached by Rishabha in the remote past was preached by the succession of remaining twenty-three Tirthankaras during their life-time for the benefit of living beings. In view of this succession of twenty-four Tirthankaras a well-knit continuity is maintained both in the tenets and practices of Jaina religion. Since Mahavira is the twenty-fourth Tirthankara in this line of Tirthankaras, he, by no means, could be considered as the founder of Jaina religion. Hence Mahavira is not the founder but the promulgator and great preacher of Jaina religion during the sixth century BC. As Mahavira happens to be the last Tirthankara, he is regarded by the common people as the founder of Jaina religion. It is obvious that this is a misconception. Now it has been an accepted fact by the historians that Mahavira did not found Jaina religion but he preached the religion which was in existence from the remote past.

Tirthankara Parsva

There is a Jaina tradition that Jainism is as old as the human race, that the religion shall remain in existence till eternity, and that it has been and will be revealed again and again in the endless succeeding periods of the world by innumerable Tirthankaras. In each of these periods there are twenty-four Tirthankaras, the first Tirthankara of present age being Rsabha and the last two being Parsva and Mahavira. Historical research in India was so crude and unorganised at one time that all these Tirthankaras, including Mahavira, were looked upon by the historians of ancient India as just mythical personages. The credit of recognising the historical existence of Mahavira goes surprisingly enough, to a German scholar in the field of Indology, Professor Herman Jacobi, who made an English translation of the first Jaina *Anga*: *Acaranga*, and published it with a masterly introduction in the series called the "Sacred Books of the East" in 1884. Ancient historical research has made some progress since then, and today Indian historians are prepared to freely recognise not only that Mahavira was a historic personage but also that the twenty-third Tirthankara, Parsva, and some at least of his predecessors had historical existence.

Parsva was the son of King Asvasena of Banaras, who belonged to the *Iksvaku* race of the *Ksatriya*. In his marital relations he was connected with the royal family of King Prasenajit, whose father Naravarman designated himself as the lord of the universe. It has not been possible so far to historically identify Asvasena of Benares or Prasenajit and his father Naravarman of Kusasthala; but in spite of that limitation historians have been willing to accept the historicity of Parsva because of certain other historical and geographical coincidences. The existence of the great *tirtha*, the hill of Samet-Sikhara (which is locally known as the Parsvanatha Hill), on the spot at which the twenty-third Tirthankara attained his final liberation (*Nirvana*) affords a monumental proof of his historicity. Jaina literature, of course, contains numerous references to Parsva and records the facts of his life, but even contemporary Buddhist and other literature affords striking evidence about the existence of *Nirgranthas* before the time of Mahavira.

These *Nirgranthas* or followers of Parsva were undoubtedly Jaina monks; Mahavira himself was referred to as such, and he insisted on calling his followers by the same name. This system preached by Parsva must have been philosophically founded upon the same presuppositions that mark the present-day Jaina *Siddhanta*, but it is presumable that it did not quite offer the same pattern of ethical conduct or moral discipline. First, the religion of Parsva laid down only four vows (*chaturiam*) for the observance of his followers: *ahinsa* (non-killing); *sunirij* (truthful speech), *astay* (non-stealing), and *aprigreh* (renouncing of all illusory objects); while Mahavira specified, and present day Jainism recognises, five great vows, the vow of chastity being given the same status as the vow of *ahimsa*. Jacobi is of the opinion that "the augmentation in the text presupposes a decay of the morals of the monastic order to have occurred between Parsva and Mahavira". It was possibly a reflection in the domain of social ethics of the newly growing ideas of sanctity of property which marked the rise of economic capitalism in Indian society. Secondly, although it is clear that Parsva's *sanha* as well as Mahavira's comprehended the monk and the nun, and the layman and the laywoman, the type of distinction between an ordinary layman (*shravak)* and a layman who took a special type of *diksha* and undertook to observe the twelve lay vows (*shramano pasak*), which undoubtedly formed a peculiar feature of Mahavira's *sangha*, did not seem to characterise Parsva's *sangha* at all. The difference between a *sravak* and *sramanopasek* in Mahavira, *sangha* consisted presumably in this, that a *Sravaka* took no definite vows but merely expressed sympathy and his faith as a Jaina while a *Sramanopasaka* took definite vows: Mahavira drew a distinction between the five great vows which laid down the practice of right conduct for the ascetic, and the five lesser vows which indicated the rules of discipline for the layman and were reinforced by seven more lay vows under which the layman imposed on himself voluntary limitations regarding the areas of his desires, his travel, the things of his daily use, the performance of meditation every day and every month, and the giving of alms to the ascetic. There is an occasional mention of the twelve vows of the *sravaka* in Parsva's *sangha* also, but that appears to be no more than a conventional way of writing for it is obvious that there could not be twelve-there could be at best only eleven-vows of Parsva's *sravakas*.

What is significant is that Parsv's *sravakas*. What is significant is that Parsva's system is invariably spoken of as *catuyram* in the Buddhist and the Jaina texts, and such invariable use of the term does not warrant the type of distinction which Mahavira felt impelled to draw between the great and the lesser vows.

Jaina Tradition and Buddhism

As Mahavira was the senior contemporary of Gautama Buddha, the founder of Buddhism, it is natural that in the Buddhist literature there are several references of a personal nature of Mahavira. But it is very significant to note that in Buddhist books Mahavira is always described as Nigantha Nataputta (Nirgrantha

Jnatriputra, i.e. the naked ascetic of the Jnatr clan) and never as the founder of Jainism. Further in the Buddhist literature Jainism is not shown as a new religion but is referred to as an ancient religion. There are ample references in Buddhist books to Jaina naked ascetics, to worship of Arhats in Jaina Chaityas or temples and to the Chaturyama Dharma (i.e. fourfold religion) of 23rd Tirthankara Parshvanatha.

Moreover it is very pertinent to find that the Buddhist literature refers to the Jaina tradition of Tirthankaras and specifically mentions the names of Jaina Tirthankaras like Rishabhadeva, Padmaprabha, Chandprabha, Pushpadanta, Vimala-natha, Dharma-natha and Nemi-natha. The "Dharmottarapradipa", the well-known Buddhist book, mentions Rishabhadeva along with the name of Mahavira or Vardhamana as an Apta or Tirthankara. The "Dhammikasutta" of the "Anguttra Nikaya" speaks of Arishtanemi or nemi-natha as one of the six Tirthankaras. The Buddhist book "Manoratha-Purani", mentions the names of many lay men and women as followers of Parshvanatha tradition and among them is the name of Vappa, the uncle of Tautama Buddha. In fact it is mentioned that Gautama Buddha himself practised penance according to the Jaina system before he propounded his new religion.

Further, it is significant to note that the names and numbers of Buddhas, Paccekabuddhas and Bodhisattvas in Buddhism appear to have been influenced by those of the Jaina Tirthankaras. For instance, Ajita, the name of the 2nd Jaina Tirthankaras, has been given to one Paccekabuddha. Padma, the 6th Jaina Tirthankara, is the name of the 8th of the 24 Buddhas. Vimala, a Paccekabuddha, has been named after Vimala-Natha, the 13th Jaina Tirtliankara.

Jaina Tradition and Hinduism

The Jaina tradition of 24 Tirthankaras seems to have been accepted by the Hindus, like the Buddhists, as could be seen from their ancient scriptures. The Hindus, indeed, never disputed the fact that Jainism was founded by Rishabhadeva and placed his time almost at what they conceived to be the commencement of the world. They acknowledged him as a divine person and counted him amongst their Avataras, i.e. various incarnations of Lord Vishnu. They give the same parentage (father Nabhiraja and mother Marudevi) of Rishabhadeva as the Jainas do and they even agree that after the name of Rishabhadeva's eldest son Bharata this country is known as Bharata-Varsha.

So far as the oldest Vedic literature is concerned we find that in the Rig-Veda there are clear references to Rishabha, the lst Tirthankara, and to Arishtanemi, the 22nd Tirthankara. The Yajur-Veda also mentions the names of three Tirthankaras, viz. Rishabha, Ajitanatha and Arishtanemi. Further, the Atharva Veda specifically mentions the sect of Vratyas and this sect signifies jainas on the ground that the term "Vratya" means the observer of vratas or vows as distinguished from the performer of sacrifices, which applied to the Hindus at the times. Similarly in the Atharva-Veda the term Maha-Vratya occurs and it is supposed that this term refers to Rishabhadeva, who could be considered as the great leader of the Vratyas.

In the later Puranic literature of the Hindus also there are ample references to Rishabhadeva. The story of Rishabha occurs in the Vishnupurana and Bhagavata-Purana, where he figures as an Avatara, i.e. incarnation of Narayana, in an age prior to that of ten avataras of Vishnu. The story is exactly identical with the life-history of Rishabha deva has given in the Jaina sacred literature. In this way Rishabhadeva's life and significant importance narrated in the Jaina literature get confirmed by the account of Rishabha given in the Hindu Puranas.

Thus from the fact that Hindu tradition regards Rishabha-devass-and not Mahavira-along with Gautama Buddha as-an incarnion of God, it can be said that the Hindu tradition also accepts Rishabhadeva as the founder of Jainism.

Jaina and Vedic Religions Traditions

The antiquity of Jaina religious tradition can thus be traced back to the earliest period of Indian history. This Jaina tradition is not only Pre-Vedic but non-Aryan also. It is obvious that the Jaina religion was flourishing in India, especially in the eastern regions of India, when the Aryans came and settled in India. Hence from the advent of Aryans in India, we find the prevalence of two distinct religious traditions in India, viz. the Vedic and the Jaina religious traditions. It is true that because of their basic differences in tenets and practices of religion, these, two traditions were opposed to each other and that each tradition did try to dominate the other. In spite of this struggle we notice that both the traditions did run parallel in India, sometimes one becoming dominent and sometimes the other.

In the Vedic tradition the priest had a pre-eminent position as he was the champion of ritualism. He vigorously claimed that the welfare and indeed the very existence of the world, including even the Gods, depended upon the maintenance of their systems of sacrifice, which grew to immense size and complexity. The cults popularised by him were polytheistic; the deities were very often the forces of nature; and man was put, at their utter mercy, the priest alone being capable of saving him by seeking the favour of the deities through sacrificial rites. This school of thought was more prominent first in North-West India as the Aryans coming from outside settled first in that region; but later on it did spread towards the Eastern and Southern regions of India.

On the other hand in the Jaina tradition prominent position was assigned to the ascetic. In the Eastern region of India, and especially along the fertile banks of the Ganges and the Jamuna, there flourished a succession of ascetic Teachers, who, hailing from rich families, had enough leisure for high thinking and religious meditation. For them, the spirit in man and also in all animate beings, was the focus of religious meditation as well as an object of investigation in relation to all that is inanimate in the universe. This brought them face to face with the problem of life here and elsewhere, since both spirit and matter were real for them-real, and therefore essentially eternal, though passing through the flux of change.

Life here and hereafter was the result of the beginningless connection between spirit and matter, which was the source of all the misery in this world; and the aim of religion was to separate matter from spirit, so that the latter might achieve a state of liberation in which it would exist in a plentitude of purity, bliss and knowledge. Man is his own master; his thoughts, words and the acts have made him, and continue to make him, what he is;

it is in his hands to make or mar his present or future; the great Teachers of the past are his ideals to inspire him along the path of religion; and he has to struggle with hope, on the well-trodden path of spiritual progress, following a code of moral and ascetic discipline, till he reaches the goal of spiritual emancipation or perfection.

In view of this ideology there is no place, in the Jaina religious thought, either for a Deity who shape the universe and meddles in its matters, or for a priest invested with mysterious powers to propitiate that Deity. This line of thought is continuosly and forcefully represented by Jaina Tirthankaras right from Rishabhadeva to Mahavira. Later on a similar line of thought was adopted by Ajivika Teachers like Gosala, by Sankhya Philosophers like Kapila and promulgators of Buddhism like Buddha. As these acetic Teachers of different religions and sects represent virtually the same line of thought; they are said to belong to one comprehensive tradition known as Shramana Tradition. Naturally the Jainas are the oldest representatives of Shramana tradition and Mahavira was the last among the Jaina Tirthankaras who expounded the tradition for the benefit of living beings.

Jaina Tradition and Archaeological Evidence

From some historical references it can be regarded that Rishabhadeva, must be the real founder of Jainism. In this connection Dr. Jacobi writes thus, "There is nothing to prove that Parshva was the founder of Jainism. Jaina tradition is unanimous in making Rishabla, as the first Tirthankara as its founder and there may be something historical in the tradition which makes him the first Tirthankara". There is evidence to show that so far back as the first century BC there were people who were worshipping Rishabhadeva.

It has been recorded that Kin of Kalinga in his second invasion of Magadha in 161 BC brought back treasures from Magadha and in these treasures there was the statue of the first Jaina (Rishabhadeva) which had been carried away from Kalinga three centuries earlier by King Nanda I. This means that in the 5th Century BC Rishabhadeva was worshipped and his statue was highly valued by his followers. From this it is argued that if Mahavira or Parshvanatha were the founders of Jainism, then their statues would have been worshipped by their followers in the 5th Century B.C, i.e. immediately after their time. But as we get in ancient inscriptions authentic historical references to the statues of Rishabhadeva it can be asserted that he must have been the founder of Jainism.

Other archaeological evidences belonging to the Indus Valley Civilisation of the Bronze Age in India also lend support to the hoary antiquity of the Jaina tradition and suggest the prevalence of the practice of worship of Rishabhadeva, the lst Tirthankara, along with the worship of other deities. The recent excavations at Mohenjo-Daro and Harappa have revealed the real existence of a very well developed Pre-Vedic and non-Aryan Civilisation known as the Indus Valley Civilisation. As a result, history of India can now be traced back to the Indus Valley Period (i.e. about 3500 to E.C.) and not upto the Vedic period (i.e. about 1500 to 1000 BC) only as was being done formerly. In fact the recent researches have shown that there is an organic relationship between the Indus.

Valley Culture and the Present Day Indian Culture: It is very pertinent to note that many relics from the Indus Valley excavations suggest the prevalence of Jaina religion in that most ancient period.

- It is observed that in the Indus Valley Civilisation there is a great preponderance of pottery figures of female deities over these of male deities and that the figures of male deities are shown naked. In this regard Dr. Earnest Mackay, the renowned Archaeologist intimately connected with the Indus Valley excavations, mentions that "For some reason which it is difficult to understand, figures of male deities in pottery are distinctly rare: They are entirely nude, in contrast with the female figures, which invariably wear a little clothing; necklaces and bangles, may be worn, but this is by no means always the case". `This fact clearly reveals the traces of Jaina religion among the Indus Valley people as the worship of nude male deities is a very well established practice in Jaina religion.
- Further, the figures engraved on the seals found in the excavations also suggest the same thing. For example, we find that the figures of six male deities in nude form, are engraved on one seal (Vide Sir John Marshall: Mohanjo-

Daro and the Indus Civilisation, Vol. I and that each figure is shown naked and standing erect in a contemplating mood with both the hands keeping close to the body. Since this 'Kayotsarga' way (i.e. in standing posture) practising penance is peculiar only to the Jainas and the figures are of naked ascetics, it can be maintained that these figures represent the Jaina Tirthankaras.

- Again, the figures of male deities in contemplating mood and in sitting pasture engraved on the seals (Vide Sir John Marshall: Mohanjo-Daro and the Indus Civilisation, Vol. III, (a), Plate No. 116, Picture No. 29 and (b) Plate No. 118, Picture No. 11) resemble the figures of Jaina Tirthankaras because in these, the male deities are depicted as having one face only while the figures of male deities, supposed to be the prototypes of Lord Shiva, are generally depicted as having three faces, three eyes and three horns (vide Sir John Marshall: Mohanjo-Daro and the Indus Civilisation, Vol. I, Plate No. 12, Picture No. 17).
- Moreover, on some seals we find the figure of a bull engraved below the figure of a nude male deity practising penance in the "Kayotsarga" way, i.e. in a standing posture. These figures appear to be the representations of Rishabhadeva, the 1st Jaina Tirthankara, because of the facts that among the 'Jainas there is an established practice of depicting the Lanchhana, i.e. the emblem of each Tirthankara below his idol and that the emblem of Rishabhadeva is bull.
- In addition, the sacred signs of Swastika are found engraved on a number of seals. It is pertinent to note that the Swastika signs engraved on Seals Nos. 502, 503, 506 and 514 exactly resemble the established Jaina practise of drawing Swastika signs.
- Further, there are some motifs on the seals found in Mohanjo-Daro and it is suggested that these motifs are identical with those found in the ancient Jaina art of Mathura.

From these archaeological evidence it can be stated that there are traces of worship of Jaina deities and that there was the prevalence of worship of Jaina Tirthankara Rishabhadeva along with the worship of Hindu God who is considered to be the prototype of Lord Shiva in the Indus Valley Civilisation. This presence of Jaina tradition in the most early period of Indian history is supported by many scholars like Dr. Radha Kumud Mukherji, Gustav Roth, Prof. A. Chakravarti, Prof. Ram Prasad Whanda, T.N. Ramchandran, Champat Rai Jain, Kamta Prasad Jain and Dr. Pran Nath.

Regarding the antiquity of Jaina tradition of Tirthankaras Major J.G.R. Forlong (in his books 'Short-studies in the Science of Comparative Religion') writes that from unknown times there existed in India a highly organised Jaina religion from which later on developed Brahminism and Buddhism and that Jainism was preached by twenty-two Tirthankaras before the Aryans reached the Ganges. Dr. Nmmerman also strongly supports the antiquity of Jaina tradition in the following terms. "There is truth in the Jaina idea that their religion goes back to remote antiquity, the antiquity in question being that of the Pre-Aryan".

Jaina Idea of Biography

It is amazing that historical scholars should have ever been inclined to doubt the existence of Mahavira. Jaina literature, particularly Jaina canonical literature, which is avowedly older than the classical Sanskrit literature and which vies in its antiquity with the oldest books of the northern Buddhists, is replete with the facts of Mahavira's life. Jacobi is of the view that European scholars were confounded by the similarities between Buddhism and Jainism and between Buddha's and Mahavira's life and that they came to this conclusion due to their lack of study on the subject. The numerous names and appellations by which these two prophets were called Jina, Arhat, Mahavira, Sugatta, Sarvajna, Tathagata, Siddha, Buddha, Sambuddha, Parinivrtta, Mukta, etc. and the fact that both of them were given the same titles and epithets further confused historical scholars. But, Jacobi has stated, with the exception of Jina and perhaps Sramana, which were quite commonly used by both the sects, the Buddhists and the Jainas made a preferential selection of certain titles only. Thus, Buddha, Tathagata, Sugata and Sambuddha are common titles of

Sakyamuni and are only occasionally used as epithets of Mahavira. On the other hand, Mahavira is often referred to in the Jaina Agama as Vardhamana, Because of the "increase that had taken place in the popularity of his parents ever since the moment he had been begotten", still more often as Jnatrputra. The Buddhist texts refer to him as Nataputta, and it was not until quite late that Jacobi identified the term Nataputta to be a variation of Janatrputra. He is also called Vira, Ativira, Sanmati and by a host of other names in the later literature of the Jainas.

These names are clearly qualitative names, that is to say, they are meant to draw attention to certain qualities possessed by Mahavira; and they are all indicative of a distinct point of view which underlay the Jaina idea of biography. The Jaina viewpoint while writing a biography is not that of the usual historical biographer. The Jaina interest is not diffused over the whole range of the subject's activities; it is all centred at one point, and that point is the attainment by his subject of salvation. The Jaina biographer writes about other things only in so far as they have to do with the attainment of his ultimate object.

Interest would be spread over the whole wide field of activity when a biography like that of Rama or Krishna, is written with a view to help the codification of the principles of *dharma*. The Brahminic view, which was based on a desire for success in the world as well as the next and which linked up, in the significant phrase of Sir S. Radha-Krishna, "the realm of desires with the prospective of the eternal", thought in terms of the *purusharth* or human values- *Dharma, artha, kama,* and *moksa* and considered the acquisition of wealth and the enjoyment of the present life as worthwhile as the ultimate attainment of the moksa. But to the Jaina there is no such thing as a real enjoyment of material things.

The Jaina *siddhanta* is based upon the presupposition that the whole universe can be classified into one or other of the two everlasting, uncreated, coexisting but independent categories, the *jiva* and the *ajiva*; and the Jaina metaphysics proceeds on the assumption that the *Jiva* (which corresponds in general to the *atman* of the other schools of Indian thought) not only exists but that it also acts and is acted upon. The intrinsic nature of the *Jiva* is one of perfection and is characterised by infinite intelligence (*anantgyan*), infinite perception (*anantdarshan*), infinite peace (*anantsukh*), and infinite power (*anantveeriya*). During the period of the union, however, of the *Jiva* with matter which constitutes *samsara*, the characteristic features of the Jiva's qualities are obscured, although not destroyed, and "the exterior semblance of the Jiva belies its innate glory"; and from this obscuration it becomes the duty of each individual soul to free itself.

Man's personality in this view consists of two elements, the spiritual and the material; and according to Jainism, the object of life is so to subdue the latter as to completely sake off its malignant influence and thereby enable the *Jiva* to all its inherent excellencies in their fullness. A man's action in life may be of two kinds, that which maintains, or even strengthens, the bond of union between Jiva and the matter, and thus-whether it brings pleasure or pain to the doer-effectually keeps the Jiva in a state of bondage, and that which tends to cut asunder the union between Jiva and matter and thus helps the Jiva to attain its freedom and ultimately perfection.

The first kind of action, and its is just this action which is germane to what we call worldly achievements, is from a spiritual point of view undeserving of very much attention; and so the Jaina biographer, whose main interest is centred on the attainment of the ultimate, has been on the whole inclined to omit it from his analysis. It is only the spiritual activity of the individual about which he has written.

Thus, there is no dearth of biographical material for Mahavira, who holds the honoured position of being the twenty-fourth and last in the galaxy of Tirthankaras of the present age and who is also the ruling personality of the present patriarchate; but this material is primarily and essentially concerned with the details of the spiritual activities of Mahavira. Of the purely material side of his life, the details provided are not many and not sufficiently lucid or specific.

Jacobi is of the opinion that the first book (*Shrutskandh*) of the *Acarangasutra* and of the *Sutrakrtanga sutra* may be reckoned among the most ancient parts of the Jaina *siddhanta*. Their style and metre prove the correctness of this opinion.

The date of these Sutras would be somewhere between the Pali literature and the composition of the Lalitavistara, and has been worried out by Jacobi to be in the 4th century BC. It is in the first book of the Acaranga that the outlines of Mahavira's life appear for the first time, but these outlines have been drawn in a rather rough and limited way.

There is no mention here of early or householder's life at all; the story begins with Mahavira's "entry into the order" and goes on to the narration of his daily habits of life as a monk and the numerous penance's he went through. The second book of the *Acranga,* which obviously is a later composition and which does not even fit in with the scheme of writing adopted in the first book, refers possibly, in point of time, to the first part of the 3rd century BC when the whole canon was brought together under the patriarchate of Sthulibhadra; and in this book we can obtain the first glimpse of the detailed account of Mahavira's birth and early life. Certain specific details mentioned here, like the change of embryo, the periodic attendance upon Mahavira of the four orders of Bhavanapati, Vyantara, Jyotiska and Vaimanika gods and goddesses, the enunciation of the five great vows, etc. were described more elaborately and certainly with an element of exaggeration by later writers on the life-history of Mahavira.

The *Kalpasutra,* written and composed by Bhandrabahu I, is elaborated upon these details with poetic imagery and ir picturesque style and further added to them the new element of the fourteen dreams according to*Svetamber* and 16 according to *Digambara* sect-the dreams of

- an elephant;
- a land;
- a lion;
- the anointing of the Goddess Sri;
- a garland;
- the moon;

- the Sun;
- a flag;
- a vase;
- a lotus lake;
- the ocean;
- a celestial abode;
- a heap of jewels; and
- a flame which a Tirthankara's mother was believed to have seen.

The final forms of Mahavira's life was attained in the Avasyaka-Niryukti of Bhadrabahu II, which may be ascribed to the 5th century AD and in an anonymously written commentary on it added some time in the 6th or 7th century AD. These books, however, represent the Svetambara version of Mahavira's life. At the hands of the Digambara acaryas a somewhat different version was prepared on the basis of *pumchriya* written by Vimala, whose date may be somewhere between the 1st and 3rd century AD, fist in the *Padmapurana*, which may be ascribed to the 8th century AD and later on by others in various Puananas. The Digambara version gave the facts of life with the usual and in certain ways with more than usual embellishment, but it differed from the prevailing Svetambara version in one or two major details.

12

Jainism, a Religion of Asceticism

Jainism, as a Religion

Jainism is a Dharma, synonymous with English word Religion. The translated term "Religion" has been derived from the Latin verb "Religare" meaning to bind together or from "Religere" meaning to execute" painstakingly, which suggest both groups identity and ritual. Its combined form connotes that religion is to impose binding duties and required observances on its adherents. On this basis, it can be defined expressing valuation or designations and certain kinds of beliefs and practices. The word Dharma in our Indian tradition is derived from the verb Dhr to bear that indicates that Dharma is a base of all entities (Dharanad dharma mityahurdharmao dharayate praja (Mahabharata, Karmaparva).

Hundreds of definitions of Dharma and Religion have been made in different perspectives. One needs not go into them. As regards the Jain tradition, it has two broad meanings: one is generic in usage and the other, technical and specific to the use of the term. Dharma in technical sense is the basis for dynamism in life that helps in our movement or motion. It is opposed to Adharma, stillness or rest. No other system of thought in India has conceived these two terms in such a fashion as in Jain system. It is possible that these two terms may signify the moral connotations of life with its movement and death.

The generic term Dharma has two levels of meaning: one is metaphysical and the other one is ethical and moral. Jain philosophers defined the Dharma as follows:

- that which saves the being from worldly sorrows (Sansaradukkhatah sattvan yo dharatyuttame sukhe-Ratnakatranda Sravakacara).
- To observe non-violence, compassion, restraint, right penance, brotherhood, forgiveness, truth and other human qualities (Dhammo dayavisuddho- Bodhapahud)
- Ratnatraya (Right faith, Right knowledge, and Right conduct) is Dharma (Sadrastijnanavrttani dharmam dharmesvara viduh - Ratnakaranda Sravakacara)
- Nature of the entity is Dharma or nature of purified soul is Dharma (Niscayadharma, Vatthusahavo dhammo, Pravacanasara.)
- Devotion, donation, worship, service, etc. are included into practical aspects of religion.

All these definitions are related to each other with different aspects. Acarya Kundakunda, for instance, defined the Dharma in several ways: Vatthusahavo dhammo, Rayannatayam ca dhammo, Carittam khalu dhammo, khamadidasaviho Bhavo dhammo and so on. These definitions are associated with right faith, right knowledge, and right conduct, which are called Ratnatraya. The Ratnatrayas constitute together the path of emancipation from all Karmas or Moksa. The religion cannot be observed without Ratnatraya. Here the observation of ten kinds of religion becomes essential in Jain tradition: Ksama (forbearance), Mardava (humility), Arjava (uprightness), Satya (truthfulness), Sauca (desirelessness), Samyama (self-discipline), Tapa (self-mortification), Tyaga (renunciation), Akincanya (poverty), and Brahmacarya (celibacy) (Tattvarthasutra, Thananga, etc.).

All these Dharmas in Jain tradition carry the adjective "Uttama" which indicates the right attitude of the follower towards all the aspects of religion with great spirituality and profundity (Sarvarthasiddhi, 9.6). They do not have any relation with wealth of fame (Rajavartika, 9.6.26; Caritrasara, 1.58). This tenfold ascetic

Dharma consists of four elements: Dana ((almsgiving), Sila (virtue), Tapas (ascetic practices), and Bhava (spiritual attitude).

This is the generic meaning of Dharma indicating the metaphysical, ethical and moral attitude to human values. It relates with the ultimate aim of life (liberation or Moksa). The traditional Jain view does not accept the grace of God or help from any external agency for achieving the final goal. The Bhakti element is of course there but it is from the conventional or practical point of view (Vyavaharanaya) and not from real standpoint (Niscayanaya). Any one could achieve this goal by one's own efforts. Non-possession, non-violence and vegetarianism have their roots in such efforts. This is the humanistic approach to the goal of life.

The religion in Jain Sramana cultural system is of two types: one is pertaining to individual, and the other one is concerned with the society. Individualistic religion is meant for spiritual aggrandisement and pleasure of temporal and next world of all beings whereas the other one confines to the prosperity of the society or community for mundane gratification and nation as well. It is of view that the caste system depends on one's deeds (Kammana jati) and not on birth. Maitri (friendship), Karuna (compassion), Mudita or Pramoda (sympathetic joy), and Madhyasthabhava (impartiality) are the cultivation of the social emotions.

An Antiquity of Jain Asceticism

The sources of Jain history and asceticism are Angas, Upangas, and other literary works, inscriptions, Pattavalis and antiquities of all types written in Prakrit, Sanskrit, Tamil, Kannad and other classical languages. The earlier literary works are more important but they are full of mythical legendary elements, which are mingled with historical facts. The Pattavalis are also not fully reliable as their authors added and omitted the mater according to their discretion. Secondly, the supernatural and egregious elements along with technical terms like Purva, Dhanusa, Raju, etc. are so much occurred that the historical facts are covered with their devotional impact of umbrella. The veil of historical darkness could be removed if the researcher strives to comprehend them through different developmental stages in the light of modern perspective. Researchers of east and west tried to determine the historical position of Jainism right from the beginning of 18th century and submitted their different speculations, which were simply fantastic and divergent. Some of them tried to establish that Jainism is the reformed religion of Brahminism while others are of view that either Buddhism emerged from Jainism or Jainism is the Buddhist schism. All these speculations were successfully and admirably criticised and refuted by Professor H. Jacobi in 1879 in his introductions to the volumes XXII and XLV of the sacred Books of the East Series who convincingly shown that Jainism and Buddhism are two completely different religions and they are not offshoots of Brahminism. He also proved through early Pali literature that Mahavira and Gautama Buddha were quite different historical contemporary personalities and Jainism was definitely in existence prior to Buddhism.

Gosalaka, the founder of Ajivika sect was the follower of Mahavira and the Buddha was the follower of Parsva tradition. The scholars now accept this theory. He further quotes the Uttaradhyanasutra which mentions an interview near Sravasti between Gautama Indrabhuti, the disciple of Mahavira and Kesi, the follower of Parsvanatha in which after the good conversion as to the number of vows and use or disuse of clothes, the twc leaders recognised that the doctrines of their respective teachers were essentially the same. This fact points out that an older faith prevailed before the advent of Lord Mahavira who reorganised the same faith on a former basis. Professor Jacobi thus established once forever the theory that Jainism is not an offshoot of Buddhism. Likewise, it is also established fact that Jainism is not an offshoot of Vedic religion. It also supports the Jain tradition that it is the ancient and pure Aryan culture of India.

Two types of Indian cultural systems are found in India, Brahminic and Sramanic or Non-Vedic. The early Brahminic system is the civilisation of those who subjugated the senses and established a materialistic empire. In later period, it sought the grace of God with violent approach and clashes started with each other. The Ksatriya class developed its earlier system bestowing the name of Sramanology in early days. During the Upanisdic period, even the well-versed Brahamnic sages went to Ksatriyas to acquire the spiritual knowledge. The Sramana tradition is therefore not an offshoot of Vedic or Brahminic cult, but it is quite an independent religion and philosophy based on equality and equanimity and self- efforts leading to salvation. According to Sramanas, the being is himself responsible for his/ her own deeds. Salvation (Moksa), therefore, can be attained by anyone. Jainism is thus a very democratic religion. Ritual, in its opinion, is not the only means of emancipation. The only means of escaping from the misery of Samsara, the cycle of birth and death, is the path of moral, mental and spiritual development based on complete ascetic non-violence and truth.

These characteristics of Sramana culture can be understood, as indicated earlier, by the word "Sramana (Prakrit Samana) itself which is derived from "Srama (Prakrit Sama) to exert, effort, labour or to perform austerity, but is mixed in meaning with "Sama" to emancipate from Karma with observing "Sama" equality and equanimity. One Sramana who performs acts of mortification (Sramati tapasyatiti Sramanah), which are very popular in both the Sramana traditions, Jainism and Buddhism.

According to this definition, as earlier told, the beings are he responsible for their own deeds. Salvation, therefore, can be achieved by any-body irrespective of caste, creed, colour, sex and culture. The cycle of rebirth to which every individual was subjected was viewed as the cause and substratum of misery. The goal of every person was to evolve the way to escape from the cycle of rebirth. Each school of Sramanas preached its own way of salvation. But they all agree in one respect, namely in discounting violent rituals as the means of the emancipation from misery of Samsara, and establish that only pious religious activities can lead the being to the eternal happiness.

Jainism is claimed to be one of the most ancient religious systems. According to its tradition, it is an eternal and imperishable religion, which is manifested heretically by all Tirthankaras and Jinas time to time from generation to generation in the same manner. It has no beginning and it will never cease to exist. In its tradition, as many as twenty-three more Jinas or Tirthankaras are recognised as heaving preached the doctrine of Jainism prior to Vardhamana Mahavira or Nigantha Nataputta, the contemporary of the Buddha who is very much known to us. They are so designated as they had conquered themselves through perfect knowledge and gained absolute freedom from the bondage of Karmas and as they had founded the four Tirthas or orders of ascetics monks, nuns, and male and female disciples to continue to do so for ever. They are human beings, born of human parents, renounced the world individually, initiated the spiritual life and became superhuman, Jina or Tirthankara the propagator of Truth and not the founder of a religion. After attaining perfect knowledge, Tirthankaras deliver sermons for well being of all. They preach universal love, compassion, harmony, equality and equanimity and way of life to all the human beings irrespective to caste, creed, colour and gender.

The Jain tradition is of view that the universe and its creation are eternal and infinite and are divided into two eras (Kalpas), viz.1) Avasarpini or descending era subdivided into six ages, (i) Susama-Susama (happy-happy), (ii) Susama (happy), (iii) Susama-Dusama (happy-unhappy), (iv) Dusama-Susama (unhappy-happy), (v) Dusama (unhappy), and (vi) Dusama-Dusama (Unhappy-unhappy), and 2) Utsarpini or ascending era sub-divided into six having the same names in reverse order. In the Avasarpini era we are passing through, the people attain all the pleasure and the happiness at the starting point, which reduce gradually up to the last era. The Utsarpini era commences with utmost sorrowful condition and ends with most pleasant age. The first three of the Avasarpini era and the last three of the Utsarpini era are collectively called the Bhogabhumi (happy and contended) where the people achieve and fulfill their requirements from Kalpavrksas (wish-fulfilling trees). They used to inhabitant in forest and lead their lives on fruits and trees. Art and industries were also not known to them. From historic viewpoint. This may be called the early and later Stone Age.

The remaining ages are called Karmabhumi (age of action where the people learn to work, toil, write, educate and express art, etc. The inventors of this age are called Kulakaras (legislators and founders of civilisation) who are said to have appeared in the first of these last three ages or in the fourth age of the era, the transitional period of the age. The result of the phenomenal change compelled the kulakaras to create the revolutionary Karmabhumi period for welfare of the society. The number of Kulakaras is varied in ancient Jain literature, but ordinarily the number is fourteen. Nabhiraya, the father of Rsabhadeva, the first Tirthankara of Jainism is said to be last one. These kulakaras changed the old order and invented the number of new methods for evolving the civilisation and educating the people in various ways. In those days the life was very easy and simple. It changed gradually and, as a result, the Kulakaras are said to have adopted three types of Dandaniti (punishment), viz. admonition (Hakara), warning (Makara), and the reprimand (Dhikkara). The first five Kulakara's found it enough to rebuke the wrongdoer with "Ha". The next five Kulakaras had the need of "Ma" to reinforce the effect of disapproved. "Ha" expressed the exclamation towards the misdoing while "Ma" signified regret, as if to say, "I regret that you should have done such a thing as this". This was enough to curb the offences to set right the way for the future. The remaining Kulakaras added "Dhik" to the existing code of penalties to express their abhorrence of the evil deed. The first Tirhtankara Rsabhadeva and his son Bharata laid down the regular laws. This may be said the starting point of Jain asceticism.

The human civilisations have been divided into three parts, viz. Paleolithic, Mesolithic and Neolithic. Human beings got real entry into civilisation in the third Neolithic age, which may be named as Fourth age is supposed to be the best in which the Tirthankaras Kulakara or Avasarpini period in the light of Jaina tradition. Accordingly, the and other great personages take birth and enlighten the human beings for their spiritual development. We are at present living in the Fifth age of the Avasarpini, which commenced the few years after Mahavira's Parinirvana (527 BC) and is of 21000 years duration. It may be mentioned here that the Kulakaras are also called Manu in the Adipurana of Jinasena (3.211-12). The fourteen Manvantaras in Vedic tradition also carry out the same activities. 6 The Visnupurana (3.2.45-47) describes the main functions of the Manvantaras.

After Kulakaras, the sixty-three Great Personalities or men of mark (Salakapurusas) appeared in the current Avasarpini period, viz. i) 24 Tirthankaras, ii) 12 Cakravartis, iii) 9 Balabhadras, iv) 9 Vasudevas or Narayanas, and v) 9 Prativasudevas or Pratinarayanas. Of these, Rama, the hero of the Ramayana and Padmapurana of Jainas flourished in the age of Tirthankara Munisubrata. The impact of Nami and Parsvanatha's philosophical conceptions can be perceived on the Upanisdic mysticism. Lord Krisna, the apostle of Non-violence was the cousin of Neminatha, the 22nd Tirthankara. Jacobin rightly pointed out that out of 63 Salakapurusas, 27 are related to krsna legend. It amounts to come to the conclusion that an attempt for reconciliation between Brahminical and Sramanic systems was made during this period.

There were three types of cultural groups in India: 1) the Northern group which was spiritual, non-violent, and who were idol worshippers is known as the "Aryans". 2) The Southern group which was well-versed in the arts and industries is called the "Dravidas" or "Vidyadharas", and 3) the North-western group which spread over Asia, Europe, Iran, etc. is known as the "Indo-Aryan. On the basis of new researches, scholars are of the view that the Aryan and Dravidian cultures originally belonged to Jainism. Dravidas were definitely not the Vedic Aryans and they are, therefore, called Anaryas. Dasas (slaves), Dasyus (thieves), Arhatas, Vratyas, Anaryas, and Asuras (demons) are referred to in Vedic literature as opponents of the Vedas. Jain culture has been refuting the idea that the Vedas were not composed by man (Apauruseyatva) since inception. Therefore, these ancient references must be connected with Jainism.

Jain Asceticism in Vedic Literature

Jainism stayed with Vedic religion since inception. It also co-existed with Buddhism and shared history in India. Its interaction between them finds ample reference to in the early literature like Rigveda, Atharvaveda, Samhitas, Upanisadas, Puranas and Pali literature. 24. Indus civilisation is related with pre-Aryan and pre-Vedic culture. The people were there polytheistic. The nude figures excavated in Indus Valley and Lohanipur may be identified as the Jain statues of Tirthankaras, most possibly of Rsabhadeva, the first Tirthankara of Jainas. Most of them are in yogic postures. The Vratyas were the followers of Vratas or vows. They used to stay in the group form 7 and were against the Brahamanas. The Vratyakanda of the Atrharvaveda describes the characteristics of Vratyas, the Non-Vedic Aryans who used to practice austerities. Acarya Sayana has appreciated the Vratyas by calling them the Vidvattama, Mahadhikara, Punyasila, Visvasammanya and Brahminavisista in the Sayanabhasya. The Rigveda refers to them as Vratasaha (5.53.ll), which is interpreted as Utsedhajivi. They were initiated by using the Bratyastoma for making them Aryans they are also called Anaryas and Magadhas. The subject of the Vratyakanda may be compared with the life of Rsabhadeva, the first Tirthankara who have been honoured by the Vedic Rsis in several verses. The Vratyass were definitely against the Vedic idealogy. According to the Pancavimsa Brahmin, they were divided into two classes, i.e. the Arhatas and Yaudhas, As we know, the Arhathood is very popular in the Sramana culture in the sense of Vitaragatva. The Buddhist monks were also called Arhatas and Ascetics. The word "Arhat" is used in the Rgveda in the sense of the leader of Sramanas.

The Munis of the Rigveda were the followers of Tirthankara Rsabhadeva. The famous Kesisukta of the Rigveda describes the Munis who bear long hair, clad in dirty, tawny coloured garments, and walks in the air of flies. He is delirious with the state of being a Muni. He enjoys friendship with Vayu and drinks poison with Rudra and follow the moving wind and attain the status of God. Mortal men could only see his body and no more. He treats the path of sylvan beasts, Gandharvas and Apasaras. Corresponding to these references, the references to Vatarasana Sramana Rsis and their leader Rsabhadeva occurred in the Bhagawat Purana may be compared and said that Rsabhadeva, the first Tirthankara of Jainism is well recognised by the Vedic sages. He was accepted as the incarnation of God Visnu even earlier to the incarnation of Rama and Krsna.

Like Munis, Yatis were also prevalent in the Vedic period. They were mediators belonged to Non-Aryan Group called Asuras. According to the Sayanabhasya, Indra killed Asuras. The war between Devas and Danavas or Devodasa and Purukutsa was the war held between Vedic Aryas and pre-Vedic Anaryas (Sramanas). Asuras were not defeated at once. The Vedic Aryans could conquer them only after the moment they become stack in following the right conduct as revealed by the dialogue held between Laxmi and Indra. Then the leadership went to the hands of Indra who ruled over the Northern India and the Asuras centred in Southern India. The Santiparva of the Mahabharata speaks of the spiritualism of the Asuras who were the followers of Sramana ideology.

Likewise, the Panis were also the followers of Sramana tradition. They are called Devas (7.6.2), Krpanas-misers (1.124.10; 4.51.3) who do not donate any thing to the Purohitas or Devas (1.33.3; 1.83.2; 6.13.3, etc.) in the Rgveda. Naga clans may also have been somehow connected with the Sramanism. The Asuras, Vratyas, Yatis, and Munis were also called Brahmacaris who used to control over sexual passions and followed Sramanology (Atharvaveda, 11.5). They were also worshiper of nude figures, which were not recognised by the Vedic Rises, who clearly prayed, "Let not Sisnadevah enter our sacrificial Pandala.

The words "Barhat" and "Arahat" are found used in the Rgveda. The followers of Barhat tradition accept the authority of the Vedas and were used to the practice of performing sacrifices (Yajnas) whereas those of the "Arhata" community, the upholder of the cult of non-violence (Ahimsa) and kindness (Karuna) did not accept the authority of the Vedas and were against performance of sacrifices since they involved in the killing of innocent animals (Visnupurana, 3.18.12; Padmapurana, 13.350).

These references compel us to be of view that the Sramana Jain system of Aryans was prevalent even before the Vedic age in India. These Aryans are called afterwards Anaryas. The Vedic Aryas were their opponent having eternal antagonism (Nakula-sarpavat sasvat- virodha) and therefore their antiquity goes definitely back to Indus civilisation and even earlier to that it was in existence. The cult of Rudra or Siva may be closely associated with the Sramana culture led by Jainism. The Buddhists joined this Sramana tradition afterwards in the 6th century BC. The findings of excavations at Mohan-jo-daro, Harappa and other sites also support this fact.

Rsabhadeva and other Tirthankaras

Rsabhadeva, the first Tirthankara of Jainism was the progenitor of the Iksvaku race from which the Surya and Candra Vamsas were branched off. He was himself belonged to the most primitive and indigenous race of India, the Manus. The other tribes like Rksa, Yaksa, Naga, Pani; Gandharva, etc. termed under the name of Vidyadharas were his followers. They are called Dravidians. According to Jain tradition, Prince Dravid was one of the sons of Rsabhadeva. He was the progenitor of the race who later on came to be called as Dravidians.

Rsabhadeva, was born from the womb of Maru-Devi in Ayodhya, the birth place of so many other Tirthankaras also, long ago in the fourth age of time-cycle, traditionally 84,00, 000 Purvas, may be about six to eight thousand years in Pre-Aryan period. His father was Nabhi Who had one hundred sons. After the name of his eldest son Bharata, the Great Emperor, our country is known as Bharatavarsa. He introduced the Karmabhumi to human civilisation and founded the social order, law and order and justice. He also taught the art of fighting (Asi), writing (Masi), cultivation of land (Krsi), trade (Vanijya), arts (Vidya), and crafts (Silpa).

After leading a domestic life for a quite long time, Rsabhadeva left the home, went to the forest to lead the life of penance and austerity, attained the Kevalajnana in Prayag and created a shore beyond the ocean of Sansara in the form of Dharma that requires the total renouncement of worldly attachment for achieving the spiritual excellence. He was the first preacher of Non-violence (Ahimsa) and asceticism and did excellent penance and followed the path of self- control, destroyed all the Karmas, became an omniscient and established the four-fold unity of the Sramanas, Sramanis, Sravakas and Sravikas in our era of present Avasarpini period. He was really a lord of Yogis (Yogesvara) (Srimad Bhagawatapurana, 1.3.13). He is also called Svayambhu and Mahadeva. Rsabhadeva attained Nirvana at Mount Kailasa in the fourth age of time-cycle.

Jainism does not believe in concept of incarnation (Avataravada) but in ascendance of man to Godhood (Uttaravada). According to its ideology, any one can become an omniscient, Tirthankara or Jina by way of developing one's own internal qualities and spiritual development through leading a path of purification (Asceticism). Tirthankara Rsabhadeva followed such pious path of asceticism and reached to the highest status of soul.

Tirthankara Rsabhadeva has been referenced in the Vedic literature as has already been mentioned. The Rigved (4.58.3; 10.136.1) clearly refers to his spiritual personality. The Vatarasanas people surviving on air and not eating must be related to Digambara Jainism (Munayo vatarasanah pisangah vasate malah—Rg.10.11.136.2). Sayana also mentioned them as Atindryarthadarsi (Sayanabhasya, 10.136.2). They are also referred to in the Taitriya Aranyayakas (1.23.2.1; 24.4.2.71). Keshi (Rg. 10.11.131.1) and Rsabhadeva (Rg.10.9.102-6.136) are one and the same personalities (Rg.10.136.1). So many other references to Rsabhadeva may be mentioned from the Rgveda (Rg.1.10.52.15; 1.15.103.6; 1.24.190.8, etc.) and other Vedas (Yajurveda, 20.46). The 15th Vratyakanda of the Atharvaveda is very important from standpoint of Jain Sramanic history and philosophy. Vratyas were Arhatas, the followers of Rsabhadeva. He is remembered as Bhagawan in the Chandogyopanisad (5.1).

All these references from Vedic literature submit a glimpse of Jain history. Vrsabha, Nabhi, Jatirupadhara, Vitaraga, Nagna, Digvasa, Vatarasana, Arhat, Jitendriaya, Kesi, Digamnbara, Sristanemi, Nirgrantha, Hiranyagarbha, Asura, Sisna, Dasyu, Paramesthi, Vratya, and such other words are closely related with Jain asceticism. The Bhagawat Purana submits Tirthankara Rsabhadeva's life in detail, which is followed by Vishnu, Siva, Agni, Kurma, Markandeya, Vayu, and other Puranas. He is mentioned there as Mahayogi and the 8th incarnation of Visnu (5.4.9; 5.3.20; 11.2.15-20, etc.). Considering all these references, one may come to the conclusion that Bhagavan Shiva and Tirthankara Rsabha are identical (10.9.102.6). The Sivapurana refers to Rsabhadeva as one of the twenty-eight incarnations of Siva (4.47-48; 7.2.9), even prier to Rama and Krsna. Jinasena supports the view by saying "Ime tapodhanah diptatapaso vatvalkalah (Adipurana, 2.18) and Munayo vatarasanah (ibid. 2.64).

The Rgveda is supposed to be the first and oldest book of world. The majority of scholars are of view that it was composed sometimes between 4500 BC and 2000 BC Rsabhadeva was much anterior to these times. Professor S. Srikantha Shastri takes back the antiquity of Jain tradition to at least 20,000 BC. The pre-historic Indus Valley civilisation of Mohenjodaro and Harrappa supports the antiquity of Jainism and establish its independent existence. Sir John Marshal also asserts that the Indus and Vedic cultures were unrelated. He is of view that nude figures discovered there on the Seals posture of Yoga are no other than Yogis or Jain Sramanas. These statues clearly indicate that the people of the Indus Valley, in the Chalcolothic period not only practiced Yoga but worshipped the images of the Yogis which are found in not of sitting, but of standing Kayotsarga posture and the Kayotsarga posture is the peculiarity of Jain asceticism as depicted in the Adipurana of Acarya Jinasena (18.75-90) in connection with the penances of Rsabhadeva or Vrsabhadeva. Professor R.P.Chanda (in the Modern Review for August, 1932, pp. 155-160) referring to the figures of standing deities on some six seals (Plate exviii, Sir John Marshall's work on Mohenjo-daro) especially numbered (f), (g), (h), of plate ii [Ib]) expressed his views that the standing deity with a bull as an emblem in the foreground can be the forerunner of Rsabhadeva.

If so, Jainism also, along with Saivism, must takes its place as one of the oldest religions of Chalcolithic origins. The reference has also already been made to the stone portrait head of a Yogi with the eyes fixed on the tip of the nose. Thus he pings over the status between the Indus and subsequent Indian civilisation as phases in the common cultural evolution in Sindh Five Thousand Years Age. Megasthenes mentions the traditional beginning of Indian history from 6,462 year before the time when the Great Indian Dionysus and his son Hercules, had been living.

This Megasthenes's description undoubtedly indicates that Adideva Rsabhadeva and his son Bharata are meant thereby. Rsabhadeva's another son Bahuvali, the Bharata's younger brother is remembered by erecting the monumental 57 feet high world famous statue at Sravanablagola in the Karanataka state of India. The ancient script Brahmi is named after the daughter Brahmi of Rsabhadeva.

The historicity from Second to the Twenty-first Tirthankaras is not much known to us, may be mythical till proved by historical and archaeological evidence, though they are somehow mentioned in the Pali literature. During this period, so many Great Risis and Munis in Vedic tradition have been referred to in the Vedic and

Puranic literature. It appears that the Indus valley civilisation had continued to flourish for quite a long time up to rise of Vedic Aryans and their Brahminic culture. Further the country got gradual Aryanisation and expansion of the power of Vedic Aryans to a great culmination point.

During the period of Munisuvrata, the twentieth Tirthankara of Jainism, Rama, a great hero of both the systems of Brahmin and Sramana (Vratya) may have tried to reconcile between Vedic and Jain schools of thoughts. The animal sacrifice of Vedic religion was also questioned for the first time in his times. The mystic-spiritualistic thought was initiated in the form of Upanishads, which opposed the sacrificial cult, during the period of Twenty-first Tirhtankar Nami.

The twenty-second Tirthankara, Aristanemi or Neminatha is referred to in the Rgveda (7.32.20) and the Yajurveda (25.28). He was the cousin of Lord Krisna, the great Revivalist and apostle of Ahimsa who preached against killing of animals and shattered the leadership of Vedic Brahamanism. This may have been happened in about the 15th century BC.

Tirthankara Parsvanatha

Tirthankara Parswanatha is undoubtedly a historic personage who flourished 250 years earlier than Mahavira (850 BC) at Varanasi to a non-Aryan Naga race of the Vratya-Ksatriyas. His father's name was King Asvasena and that of the mother was Vamadevi. He reached an age of 100 years and height was 7 ells. His concept of Caturyamadharma is clearly mentioned in the early Pali literature of Buddhism. Parsva tried throughout his life to purge the asceticism of corrupt practices such as Pancagnitapas and violent sacrifices and taught the real type of penance and religion. His conceptual impact can be observed on the Upanisadic speculations. After practicing severe austerities, he attained Keivalya in forest of Ahicchatra (Bareilly, U.P.) and then attained Nirvana at Mount Sammeda-sikhara in Bihar in 777 BC.

The Parsvanatha's asceticism is very important point from the view of history of Jain asceticism. It is related with the fundamental difference between Digambaras and Svetambaras. We can also observe some differences between Parsvanatha and Mahavira traditions some of them are as follows: 1) Caturyama-samvara (Dharma) has been mentioned in the early Pali literature. It involves restraint from four sorts of activities-i) injury, ii) non-truthfulness, iii) taking what is not given, and iv) possession. Here no possession includes celibacy, which was made the separate one by Mahavira. This Caturyama is not mentioned in Digambara literature. Likewise, the Kesi-Gautama dialogue of the Uttaradhyayanasutra is not available in Digambara Texts, which poses the question of principle of nudity.

Digambaras reject the authenticity of such dialogues and establishes nudity as the fundamental principle. This is even fully supported by Svetambara Agamas. Sthanangasutra (Sutra 916) shows Mahavira saying, "I uphold the practice of nudity (acelae dhamme pannatte). Digambaras are of view that all Tirthankaras from Rsabhadeva to Mahavira followed the nudity, the basic practice of the Jain mendicant. The Svetambara Texts have so many references where they made nudity as an original, main but an optional practice.

The Acarangasutra (Sutra 433) clearly says that weak men, who cannot tolerate going in nude form but wish to practice fasting and other virtuous activities should do so while continuing to wear clothing. They have traditionally accepted two sorts of monks, the Jinakalpins who follow complete nudity and the Sthavirakalpins who bear the clothes. Both these ways are considered equally valid for attainment of salvation. It may also be mentioned here that the word "eka- sataka" occurred in the Anguttaranikaya (111, 384) does not recognise the clothed state but it, in fact, indicates the eleventh stage of a Jain mendicant. Considering all these facts, Digambaras refused altogether the authenticity of Svetambaras Agamic Texts.

They are in favour of strict renunciation of all possessions, internal as well as external since inception. The Caturyama may be a part of Samayikacaritra or Samayika-samyama as indicated in the Mulacara (7.23). It is also said that the first and the last Tirthankara prescribed the Pancayamas while second to twenty-third Tirthankaras laid down the Caturyamasamvara.2) From Ajitanatha to Parsvanatha Tirthankaras prescribed four types of

Caritras, Samayika, Pariharavisuddhi, Suksmasamparaya and Yathakhyata, while Rsabhadeva and Mahavira laid down five types of Caritras, which include Chedopasthapana into the list.3) The religion of first and the last Tirthnkara was Acelatva (nudity) while the remaining Tirhtankaras allowed the Sacelata (clothing) simultaneously.4) The first and the last Tirthankaras included the renunciation of night- eating (Ratribhojanatyaga) into Vratas while other Tirthankaras made it as the part of Ahimsavrata.5) The Pratikramana was observed in Parsvanath tradition only on offences while Mahavira made it compulsory.

Tirthankara Mahavira or Vardhamana

Mahavira or Nigantha Nataputta, the Samana ascetic or Dighatapassi" of Pali literature is the 24th and last Tirthankara of the present evolutionary cycle. The last two Tirthankaras are more known historically to us naturally as they are immediately precede the present age. Almost all the Tirthankaras were born and actively engaged in their propagation in the middle part of India bounded by the Himalayas on the North, the Vindhya Mountains on the South, Allahabad on the East and Kuruksetra on the West, particularly the plain part of middle-Ganges and Bihar. Though the historicity of this region commences from 6th century BC but the human existence prior to 6000 years B.C is hereby proved through archaeological evidence. Therefore the mythological tradition cannot be altogether rejected.

Tirthankara Mahavira, the propagator and not the founder of Jainism were a great spiritual leader of India in sixth-fifth century BC. This was not his personal name. His contemporaries better knew him as Nigantha Nataputta. Nigantha is a religious epithet while the Nataputta epithet indicates that he belongs to Naya, Nata or Jnatri clan of the Ksatriyas just as the Buddha was called Sakyaputta because he was the young member of his clan. The term Nigantha or Nirgratha for a Jaina came to be used perhaps along with the origin of Jainism itself.

Mahavira or Vardhamana was born on the 13th day of the Caitra Sukla, corresponding to 30th March 599 BC at Kundalapur or Kuṅdagrama (Vaisali) from the womb of Trisala or Priyakarini or Videhadatta, the daughter of Licchavi King Cetaka of Videha.

His father King Siddhartha, belonged to Kasyapa Gotra and the clan of Jnatrika or Vratya Ksatriya. Jacobi identified Kottigama of the Mahavagga with Kundagama of the Jain Texts. Mahavira's parents Siddhartha and Trisala were the chief of Vaisali and followers of Parsvanatha tradition (Pasavaccijja- Ayaranga, 2.15-16). They named him "Vardhamana because with his birth, the wealth, fame, and merit of the family increased. So many legends tell about Vardhman's supreme velour as how easily he excelled all his companions in strength and physical endurance during boyhood. As he was in the midst of dangers and fears, patiently enduring all hardships and calamities, adhering to the chosen rules of penance and asceticism and as he was wise (Sanmati), indifferent to pleasure and pain alike, rich in self-control and gifted with fortitude, the name Mahavira was given to him.

Not much is found about his childhood and householder life in early Prakrit and Pali literature. Mahavira's paternal uncle was Suparsva. His elder brother was Nandivardhana and his elder sister Sudarsana. His parents died when he was thirty years old. There are some controversies and differences between Digambara and Svetambara traditions regarding his life and practices.

Regarding Mahavira's ascetic life, of course, we find some valuable references in the Acarangasutra, Kalpasutra, Adipurana and other literature. Accordingly, he renounced the worldly life at the age of thirty and gave up all possessions and became unclothed with the vow of asceticism. After devoting himself to self-discipline and self-purification, practicing the severest penance and austerities for twelve years, he attained Kevalajnana (Perfect knowledge) while sitting in transcendental spiritual concentration under the Sala tree at the age of forty-two in Jambhiyagrama (modern village Jamui) situated on the bank of quil (Rjukula) near Rajagraha.

During these years of his pursuit, a number of incidents occurred in his life, viz. Calamities of Gopalakas, Sulapani, Agni, Taptadhuli, Lohargala, Kataputana, Sangama, Candakausika, Karnasalaka-niskasana, Meetings with Makkhali Gosalaka, sages of Parsvanatha tradition, separation with Gosalaka, etc. which he bore with the greatest equanimity. He is said to have pursued the hardest austerity practices, which are described in the Acarangasutra.

After the attainment of Kevalajnana, he entered into new stage of life, the life of a religious teacher and head of the sect called the Nirgranthas. A Samavasarana (religious conference) was held on the bank of the river Ujjuvaliya, but it is said that the first discourse of Mahavira remained unsuccessful. He is said to have returned to Majjhima Pava and wandered continuously for sixty-six days in silence reached Rajagrah, the capital of Magadha. Outside the city of Rajagrah, at Vipulacala where he settled, a second Samavasarana was convened in the garden of Mahasena for his first sermon. Here first of all, after a long discussion on various religious and philosophical points, Mahavira converted the eleven Brahmin Vedic scholars headed by Indrabhuti Gautama to his fold who came to attend a sacrifice at Rajagrah where he preached before masses for the first time. They became his disciples and heads of monastic orders called Ganadharas. The eldest Indrabhuti became first and prominent Ganadhara. The name of his congregation was given Samavasarana where all beings had equal religious opportunities. All these Ganadharas except Indrabhuti and Sudharma, died during the lifetime of Mahavira.

He then travelled on foot from place to place, preaching his message of peace and goodwill for all the beings, without any distinction of race, caste, class, age or sex for about thirty years through Ardhamagadhi Prakrit language. We should bear in mind here in this context one fact that Mahavira's medium of preaching was spoken Ardhamagadhi consisting of so many dialects including Magadhi and Sauraseni, and the language of the canon is literary Ardhamagadhi which is also called Arsa Prakrit or old Ardhamagadhi. Another important feature of Mahavira's mode of teaching is his question-answer or dialogue method through illustrations keeping before his eyes the social grade and the receptive capacity of his listeners.

Tirthankara Mahavira camped these years in the rainy sessions and visited different places mostly in Bihar and some areas of Bengal and U.P. for the spiritual upliftment and betterment of the society. He added Chastity (Brahmacarya) as the fifth vow to the Caturyamadhamma of Parsva and made it Pancayamadhamma. Among the manifold contributions of Lord Mahavira to human life and wisdom, the most outstanding ones may be said to be his gospel of Ahimsa (Non-violence), Aparigraha (non-possession), Anekantavada (the multi- dimensional theory), Kriyavada (the doctrine of action), and Sakahara (vegetarianism). He tried to tackle the problems of slavery, status of women in family, society and religion, caste system, un-touchability, exploitation, economic inequality, violent sacrifices, desires and passions of the flesh, etc. All these concepts make man him responsible for all his deeds, physical, mental and verbal. The God is nothing to do with. His path may enlighten him to walk on the road of life safely and piously.

The great Kings like Prasenajit of Sravasti, Srenik Bimbisara of Magadh, Dadhivahana of Campa, Satanik of Kausambi; Jitasatru of Kalinga, etc. were the followers of Mahavira. It appears that Jainism had spread all over India. We do not know whether Mahavira ever visited South India. But Jain literature is of the view that Jainism was prevalent there even prior to Mahavira. The Pali sources inform that Jainism was the state religion of Sri Lanka well before Sanghabhadra and Sanghamitra reached there.

After passing twenty- ninth Varsavasa at Rajagraha, Mahavira reached to Apapuri or Pava (may be Majjhima), the capital of Mallas where he spent his last Caturmasa. At the morning of the fourth month Kartika Krisna Amavasya, he left the mundane world and entered into salvation at the age of 72 years at Pava in 527 BC. At that time the King of Kashi, Licchavis of Kausala, nine Mallas and eighteen Ganarajas were present who celebrated the Nirvana Mahotsava by lighting the lamps.

The Samannaphalasutta of the Dighanikaya (I, p.57) refers to this event. Mahavira achieved this highest religious status of Tirthankaratva after a long series of his rebirths, which started from Marici, the son of Rsabhadeva's Bharata. In the birth of lion, he got the opportunity to here the sermon of Ajitanjaya and changed his mind towards religious performances and asceticism and then finally became Mahavira.

Makkhali Gosala was originally a follower of Mahavira but due to personal enmity he founded his own sect called Ajivika. The Ajivikas used to practice nudity and other forms of Digambaras and hence they were absorbed into the Digambara community in medieval times.

The scripture whatever we have at present reached to us through Mahavira. It may be mentioned here that the Indrabhuti Gautam is quite deferent from the Gautama Buddha, the founder of Buddhism and contemporary of Mahavira.

Jain Ascetic Sects and Schools

Arising new sects and schools in religious and philosophical spheres is the natural phenomenon. They come out of the main stream by expressing unhappiness and unwillingness towards the existing norms and tenets of asceticism the schism usually occurs owing to social needs, personality cults, and differences on some points, which require the reconsideration over the dogmas in the light of social requirements.

Jainism is not an exception. The Majjhimanikaya (vol. 2,p.117) refers to an event taken place immediately after Mahavira's Parinirvana. But there was no split in Jain order. Later on, it is started with two divergent narratives of one event and caused to split into two traditions, Digambara and Svetambara. It is said that about a hundred years after Mahavira's Parinirvana, the terrible famine in the northern region took place for twelve years. Therefore, Bhadrabahu First sent the part of the Sangha (Order) to Southern India, particularly Karnataka where Jainas were very powerful under the leadership of Visakhacarya, the Maurya Emperor Candragupta who followed the severe conduct of asceticism of Mahavira in Toto. Another group of the Church went to the Sindh region under the leadership of Sthulabhadra who found the need to relax the traditional practices. Both the groups came back to Magadha as soon as the disastrous famine came to an end. Bhadrabahu himself passed away before any return of the Sanghas was possible. The former Sangha, who stuck strictly to the regulation of nudity and prescribed the methods of begging and eating food came to be known as "Digambara" (the sky-robbed) while the latter one, who continued to live under famine conditions and changed their ways accordingly became known as "Svetambara" (the white robbed). Thus the main cause for the schism in Jain order was the attitude to traditional norms of conduct. Thus Jainism was spreader slowly in South and the west from its original home Magadha region.

After Mahavira's Nirvana, According to Dhavala (pt. 1,p.66) and Tiloyapannatti (4.1482-84), Kevali Indrabhuti Gautama Ganadhara became the head of the Jain church for the next twelve years, followed by Sudharma or Loharya (11 years), Jambu (39 years), Srutakevalins - Visnukumara (Nandi)- (14 years), Nandimitra (16 years), Aparajita (22 years), Govardhana (19 years), and Bhadrabahu first (29 years). The total number of years comes to 162 (62 +100). But the Sthaviravali enumerates it as 215 years. The main reason behind this discrepancy is that Acarya Hemacandra slipped to add the 60 years administration period of King Palaka.

Then the difference becomes negligible. The Svetambara tradition submits the total period 580 years of Kevalis, Srutakevalis and Dasapurvadharis while the Digambara tradition in the Dhavala makes it 683 years. After this period, Ekangadhari Acaryas Gunadhara composed the Kasayapahuda on the basis of fifth Jnanapravada Purva and Puspadanta and Bhutavali on the basis of second Agrayaniya Purva composed the Satkhandagama. This was the migrated Jain ascetic order to Southern part of India called Digambara (naked or sky-clad) sect, which was afterwards claimed to be as belonging to the Mulasangha (the original order).

The other section of ascetics was named as Svetambara as they had started to cover their bodies partly with the piece of white cloth (Ardhaphalaka). This section stayed in Magadha even during the famine period. Afterwards they too had emigrated to Gujarat and Saurashtra in the third or second century BC. The schism in the Jain order was thus complete in first century AD Bhadrabahu First is only Aratiya Acarya who is regarded by both the traditions. But the Svetambara tradition is started with Sambhutivijaya Sthavira while the Digambara tradition is related with Bhadrabahu. Some more versions contrary to each other are available in Jain literature in this regard.

The Thanangasutta (Sutra 587) of Svetambara tradition termed Ninhava to such schism or difference of opinion occurred in the Jain order. It enumerates seven types of Ninhavas, which deal with Jain principles from one or other standpoint. But there was no schism taken place in Jainism due to such differences. Afterwards, Jinabhadragani Ksamasramana in his

Visesavasyakabhasya (Gatha, 2308- 32) added one more Ninhava and termed it as Botika (corrupted) originated from Sivabhuti event. This event is not in fact related with Digambaras but it is related with Yapaniya sect.

This third section of the Jain ascetic order named Yapaniya reached Southern part of India via Mathura of the Saurasena region and tried for centuries to reconcile between the two divergent sects together, though without success in about third century BC. They preached the conduct of Digambaras and favoured the progressive attitude of Svetambaras. They used to live naked, worship nude images, and adore Mayurapiccha, according to Digambara tradition, whereas they believed in Strimukti, Kevalikavalahara and Savastramukti, which resemble to the Svetambara tradition. During this period, Mathura became the prominent centre of Jainism where Jain Stupa was built in about first c. AD. The archaeologists through their excavations supported that all the three sects were in existence there up to about tenth c. AD. After that Yapaniya sect merged into Digambaras.

Digamma sect is said to have remained intact up to Lohacarya, 685 years after Mahavira's Nirvana and was not divided into Ganas and Gacchas. Thereafter came into existence the Aratiyas, the knower of part of Anga-Purvas. By that time some changes had naturally taken place in the order according to social needs and eventually these Sanghas arose up. Vanabasis became Caityavasi. The monks who were in favour of stern penance started new movements against the Caityavasis and other companions, the so- called Jainabhasas by Devasena. The Aratiya Acarya Sivagupta created Ganas and Sanghas at the time of monks' congregation held at Mahimanagari with the view to avoid relaxation of norms in conduct or asceticism.

The Digambara sect was afterwards divided into several Ganas and Gacchasa Like Nandisangha, Senasangha, Kundakundanvaya, Dravidasangha, Kasthasangha and Bhattarkas, etc. Vasatakirti started the Bhattarka (saffron-robed) tradition in the 13th century AD at Mandapadurga (Rajasthan) who preached to keep one garment and worship Ksetrapalas and Jinas with their follower deities. It made a remarkable contribution to the development of Jainism and its protection but a relaxation in conduct was not accepted by a section of order and ultimately Banarasidasa in the 17th century AD started the new sect called "Vidhimarga" or "Adhyatmi" around Agra and Jaipur. In spiritual language it is called "Terapantha" (thy way). The Bhattarakas accepted this nomenclature in the mocking spirit and called themselves "Visapanthi", the little higher than Terapanthi. These names may also be kept after some sort of code of conduct also. Terapanthis observed the thirteen types of Vratas, viz. five Anuvratas, five Samitis and three Guptis while the Visapanthis might have added seven types of Vinayas (Jnana, Darsana, Caritra, Mana, Vacana, Kaya, and Lokopacara) to the list. Taranaswami started another sect named "Taranapantha "in the 15th- 16th c. AD who advocated worshipping only the Agamas (scriptures), and not the idols.

The Svetambara sect too was divided into Ganas, Kulas, Gacchas and Sakhas. Caityavasi sect stood up in 355 AD against the Vanavasis and preached that one can stay in the temples and accept donations for his protection. They accept the validity of 45 Agamas. Haribhadrasuri criticised their conduct severely in the Sambodha Prakrana. Jinesvarasuri and Buddhisagarasuri debated with the Caityavasis in 10th century AD and defeated them in Anahilpur Patan and got the "Kharatara" name from Durlabhadeva. This was the background of establishment of the Kharataragaccha.

It was divided into nine types of Gacchas like Ancalagaccha, Purnimagaccha, and Agamikagaccha, etc. In 1228 AD, due to the observation of the Ayambila penance by Jagaccandrasuri, Jaitrasimha, the King of Mewar named the Sangha "Tapogaccha" which became the separate sect. Afterwards his pupil Vijayacandrasuri preached that the monk could accept the number of clothes, ghrta, milk, vegetable, fruits and meals brought by nuns.

Then Lokashah, the resident of Ahmedabad of Gujarat province started the Lokagaccha sect in 1451 AD against the Caityavasi tradition and recognised 32 Agamas as the main source of his sect. Then Labaji made an improvement in the Lokagaccha tradition and started the Dhundhiya Pantha in 1652 AD. The followers of Lokagaccha became the followers of this sect. They used to perform their all rites and rituals in the Sthanakas and Upashrayas and not in the temples. Therefore they were called

Sthanakawasi. The Terapantha sect is derived from the Sthanakavasi sect. Bhikkana founded it in 1760 AD. One who followed five Mahavratas, five Samitis and three Guptis is called Terapanthi. Acharya Tulsi's disciple Mahaprajnaji is at present Head of the Terapantha. There was another sect named Samvegi started in the same province by Vijayadevasuri in Sak. Sam. 1682.

There are so many controversial points between these two major sects of Jainism. For instance, 1) Digambaras recognise the practice of complete nudity and non-possession as an absolute prerequisite condition for achieving salvation while Svetambaras do not admit it as an obstacle to salvation, 2) An omniscient in Digambara tradition does not involve in worldly activities. He preaches by means of the magical divine sound (Divyadhvani) in Om form while the Svetambaras are of view that he can be engaged in normal human activities simultaneously enjoining omniscient cognition. 3) Digambara tradition does not find capacity and capability in women to attain salvation due to their physical weakness while Svetambaras oppose this view, 4) likewise, differences in begging and eating habits. 5) Svetambaras worship the naked Jina-images marking their lips, eyes, and torsos in decorated form while Digmbaras do not accept so.

Jain Scriptures

Scripture is the synonym of the holy text, which consists of religious dogmas, and assertions of an authentic authority (Apta Purusa). The Jainism has its own scriptures called Agamas or Srutas, which are directly derived from the Tirthankaras. The Agamas are divided into two Streams, viz. Sutragamas and Arthagamas. The sermons of the Tirthankaras are called Arthagamas and the Sutras written over them are named Sutragamas.

The Agamas compiled by Pratyekabuddhas or Sthaviras are also valid. Like the Buddhist Pitakas, they are called Ganipitakas. Agamas are the composed form of Angas and Purvas. Puravas are no longer in existence. They were based on spirituality and self-realisation consisting of esoteric methods of attaining emancipation form all Karmas (Moksa). They might have established their own tradition that would have been absorbed in the Angas. The knower of fourteen Purvas is called Srutakevali. The Scripture that we have at present is derived from Tirthankara Mahavira. The main teachings of Purvas are included into Drastivada, the twelfth Anga that is totally lost in the eyes of Svetambara tradition. But the Digambaras were able to preserve the few sections dealing with the Karma theory from the Agrayanipurva and Jnanapravada Purva. Drastivada is briefly divided into five parts, viz. Parikarma, Sutra, Purvagata, Anuyoga and Culika. The Kasayapahuda and Satkhandagama Texts are perhaps the earliest source of knowledge of the Purvagata Drastivada. In course of time it was lost with obliteration of Kevalajnana gradually as can be understood by the posthumous spiritual titles of Caudasa, Dasa and Nava Puvvis. The works of Kundakunda and other Acaryas are also recognised as the scriptures of Digambaras. Digambara Adhyatma Texts are based on the Purvas while the Svetambara Agamas are founded on Angas excluding Drastivada. The fourteen Purvas, which are all extinct, are as follows: 1) Utpada, 2) Agrayani, 3) Virya, 4) Astinastipravada, 5) Jnanapravada, 6) Satpravada, 7) Atmapravada, 8) Karmapravada, 9) Pratyakhyanapravada, l0) Vidyanuvada, 11) Kalyanavada, 12) Pranavada, 13) Kriyavisala, and 14) Lokavindusara.

The traditional way through hearsay (Evam maya suyam) has been the only means to preserve and protect the Anga Scriptures for sometimes. In due course, the addition and omission ought to take place in the Agamic Texts, which were used to examine by holding the Councils called Vacanas, like Buddhist Sangitis from time to time at Pataliputra, Mathura and Valabhi. The Third or Fourth Vacana was held at Valabhi 980 years after the Nirvana of Mahavira under the president ship of Devardhigani Ksamasramana who compiled and written down the available Scriptures. It may be mentioned here that no reference to these Councils is made in Digambara traditional literature.

In its view the original form of Agamas went into oblivion and alienation up to 683 years after Mahavira's Nirvana. The part of the Drastivada was of course remained which became the basis of the Sadkhandagama and Kasayapahuda. The Svetambara tradition does not refute the view but states that even if the original form of the Agamas is changed, its whole form cannot be completely rejected and ignored. Some cultural aspects and linguistic peculiarities prove its originality to a certain extent. Whatever the Agamas we have at present is belonging to Svetambara tradition. Digambaras are of view that they are lost and mingled with local elements.

The Jaina Scriptures are divided into several ways. Viz. i) Angapravista and Angabahya, ii) Kalika and Utkalika, iii) Anga, Upanga, Chedasutra, Mulasutra, Prakirnaka and Culika, iv) Krta and Niryuhana, v) Carananuyoga, Dharmakathanuyoga, Ganitanuyoga, and Dravyanuyoga, and vi) Prathamanuyoga, Karananuyoga, Carananuyoga, and Dravyanuyoga. The present Agamas are found in Prakrit. It was spoken in the part of Magadha and was mingled with other dialects. Therefore it is called Ardhamagadhi in which the Svetambara Agmas are written. The Digambara Agamic literature is found in Sauraseni Prakrit. The Agamas can also be, therefore, divided into two ways, viz. Ardhamagadhi and Sauraseni. The Murtipujaka Svetambaras recognise only 45 or 84 Agamas while the Sthanakavasis and Terapanthis accept 32 Agamas. On the other hand, the Digambaras are of view that the original Agamas became extinct. In their place they recognise the works of Pushapadanta, Bhutavali, Kundakunda, Vattakera, Sivarya, Umaswami, Samantabhadra, Akalanka and other Acaryas as the Agamas.

The fact that the Digambara and the Svetambara traditions agree on fundamental features of the structure of the Jaina Scriptures establishes beyond doubt, i) that the Jaina Scripture had been compiled, arranged and recognised before the schism and ii) that the traditional divisions were remembered even after the Digambaras rejected the Svetambara Scriptures as the later innovation. Thus there is no controversy between Digambara and Svetambara traditions about the twelve Angas, viz. Ayaranga, Suyagadanga Thananga, Samavayanga, Viyahapannatti, Nayadhammakahao, Uvasagadasao, Antagadadasao, Anuttarovavaiyadasao, Panhavanhagaranaim, Vivagasuyam and Ditthivaya. Due to lack of space, it is not possible to go through the Scriptures in detail, but it may be pointed out that they are full of linguistic, cultural, historical, philosophical and spiritual material. Likewise, the Kasayapahuda of Gunadhara, Sadkhandagama of Puspadanta and Bhutavali, Dhavalatika of Virasena, Samayasara, Pravacanasara, etc. of Kundakunda, Mulacara of Vattakera or Kundakunda, Bhagawatiaradhana of Sivarya, Kattigeyanuvekha of Kartikeya, Tattvarthasutra of Umasvami, Ratnakarandasravakacara, Aptamimamsa, etc. of Samantabhadra, Sanmatisutra, etc. of Siddhasena, Tattvartha-rajavartika of Akalanka and some more Texts are treated as the Scripture of Digambara tradition.

Jain literature is written in Prakrit, Sanskrit, Apabhramsa, Hindi, Gujarati, Marathi, Tamil, and Kannad languages. Prakrit and Sanskrit literature can be divided into Anga, Upanga, Mulasutras, Chedasutra, Culikasutras, Prakrinakas, Agamic Vyakhyas, Niryuktis, Bhasyas, Curnis, Tikas, Karma literature, Siddhanta, Acara, Vidhividhana, Bhaktimulaka, Pauranika-Aitihasika Kavyas, Kathatmaka, Laksanika (Jyotisa, Ganita, Vyakarana, Kosa, Chanda, Nimitta, Silpa, etc.) and Lalita literature. There is also the vast literature written in Apabhramsa.

Out of five epics in Tamil literature, three of them belong to Jainism. They are Silappadikaram, Valayapani, and Cintamani. Likewise, Pampas, Ponna, Ratna, Camundaraya and others are main Jain Kavis in Kannada literature. Similarly Hindi literature is enriched from its inception. Due to lack of space it is not possible to write on these types of volumes Jain literature.

Theory of Anekantavada

The Universe is the composite of groups consisting of adverse pairs like knowledge and ignorance, pleasure and sorrow, life and death and so on. Life depends on such adverse groups. All the groups have their own interests, which create clashes and conflicts in thinking among themselves. Religion is supposed to pacify these clashes through co- existence on socialistic pattern of society. The co-existence cannot be remained without relativity.

Jain philosophy is based on the nature of reality, which is considered through Non-absolutism or Many-fold Aspects (Anekantavada). According to this view, reality possesses infinite characteristics, which cannot be perceived or known at once by any ordinary man. Different people think about different aspects of the same reality and therefore their partial findings are contradictory to one another. Hence they indulge in debates claiming that each of them was completely true. The Jain philosophers thought over this conflict and tried to reveal the whole truth. They established the theory of Non-absolutistic standpoint (Anekantavada) with its two wings, Nayavada and Syadvada. Proper understanding of the co- existence of mutually opposing groups through these principles rescues one from conflicts. Mutual cooperation is the Law of Nature.

Things are visible and invisible as well. We stand by visible objects and accept them as they surely are but do not recognise their invisible characteristics. Until and unless one does not recognise both these characters of an object, he cannot reach to the truth and justice. None is absolutely similar or dissimilar, friend or enemy, good or bad. As a matter of fact, every entity hides in itself the innumerable possibilities. Coal can be converted into the state of the diamond or coal is the first stage of diamond. This is the conception of Anekantavada.

It should be remembered here that total impossibility of becoming is very rare. Rational cannot be irrational and irrational cannot be rational. On the contrary, it can be converted into some thing else. One becomes desperate, as he does not understand the theory of relativity. He forgets that the modes are not imperishable. They are to be changed. Sorrow can be converted into pleasure.

Absoluteness has no meaning in any field. Substance cannot be fully explained without the assistance of Anekantavada. Life itself cannot be properly understood without this philosophical notion. Pluralism, monotheism existence and non-existence, eternality and non-eternality and so on go together. These characters of an entity can be comprehended with the help of real standpoint (Niscayanaya) and Practical standpoint (Vyavaharanaya).

The Jainism believes, unlike Buddhism, that the substance is dynamic (Parinami) in character. It means the thing is eternal from real standpoint and momentary from practical standpoint. Causal efficiency, according to them, is possible neither in the thing which is of the static nature (Kutasthanitya) nor in the thing, that is incongruous with the doctrine of momentary (Ksanikavada), but it is possible only in the thing, which is permanent-in-change. (Parinamanasilata).

The controversial point in the philosophical system is mainly related with the nature of reality. Some systems of thought accept only the Universal (Samanya) character of reality. Advaitavadins and the Sankhyas are the typical representatives of this view. Some other schools led by the Buddhists recognise only particular (Visesa) character of reality. The third school of thought belongs to Nyaya-Vaisesikas, who treat Universal and Particular as absolutely distinctive entities.

According to Jainism, an entity has infinite characteristics, which are divided into two categories, viz. Universal and Particular. Just as different colours can exist in the lustrous gem without conflicting with each other, so the universal and particular elements could abide in the reality. Thus each and every reality in universalised- cum-particularised along with substance with modes (Dravyaparyayatmaka). Here Dravya represents the Universal character and Paryaya represents the particular character of the thing. For example, the jar is made of gold, which can be changed into several modes, while preserving gold as the permanent substance. They are mutually interdependent, identical and separate from each other.

The nature of reality, according to this theory, is permanent-in- change. It possesses three common characteristics, such as Utpada (origination), Vyaya (destruction) and Dhrauvya (permanence through birth and decay). It also possesses the attributes (Gunas) called Anvayi, which coexist with substance (Dravya) and modifications (Paryaya) called Vyatireki, which succeed each other. Productivity and destructivity constitute the dynamic aspect of an entity and permanence is its enduring factor.

Nayavada (the theory of partial truth) is an integral part of the conception of Anekantavada, which is essential to conceive the sole nature of reality. It provides the scope for acceptance of different viewpoints on the basis that each reveals the partial truth about and object. It is, as the matter of fact, the way of approach and observation which is an imperative necessity to understand of one's different interests and inclinations in different lights on the basis that there could be the valid truth in each of them, and therefore requires their proper value and impartial estimation. Naya investigates analytically the particular standpoint of the problem in all respects in the context of the entire reality. But if anything is treated as the complete truth, it is not Naya, but Durnaya or Nayabhasa or Kunaya. For instance, "It is" is Naya, and "It is and is only" is Durnaya, while "It is relatively (Syat)" is an example of Syadvada.

Syadvada investigates them into the constant and comprehensive synthesis. The prefix "Syat" in the Syadvada represents the existence of these characteristics, which, though not perceived at the moment, are present in reality. The word "Syat" (Siya in Prakrit) is an indeclinable and stands for multiplicity or multiple characters (Anekanta).

It reveals certainly regarding any problem and not merely the possibility or probability. It is unique contribution of Jainism to Indian philosophy. There is the word Kathancit in Sanskrit literature, which is used as the substitute for "Syat" by Jainism as well as non-Jain philosophers. In English it may be translated with the word "relatively".

Syat is connected with relative expression about the nature of reality. It makes an effort to respect other doctrines by warning us against allowing the use of "Eva" or "only" to proceed beyond its prescribed limits and penetrates the truth patiently and non-violently. It is a humble attitude of tolerance and justice and to pay respect for other's views. This view can be understood through the use of Saptabhangi or the theory of seven-fold prediction, which is the method of cognition to comprehend the correct nature of reality through the sevenfold relative dialectic method.

It is treated as complementary to the Syadvada doctrine. Akalanka thinks of it as the way, which considers reality in the positive (Vidhimukhena) and the negative (Nisedhamukhena) manner without incompatibility in the certain context. There is no violation of the Law of Contradiction here as dual character of entities exists in respect of its own individuality and does not exist apart from and outside this nature (Sarvamasti svarupena pararupena nasti ca). In relativistic standpoint, both being and non-being can exist together. The theory of Relativity, which is also supported by Einstein, is practically accepted by all as the perfect mathematical theory in the scientific world.

This Anekantavada guards us from holding opinions that are based on views that are one-sided and extreme and that under the cloak of Anekanta reality maintain one-sided views. Every person ventilates his views about the given object according to his attitude and capacity. His limited knowledge is inadequate to throw the flood of light on the entire object. Out of some many facts, he deals with only one or some.

This partial knowledge and partial success is dangerous especially when he feels that his knowledge is complete and correct. It is, therefore, imperative that we should study other's opinions logically and impartially, even though we belong to the certain brand of faith to try to understand others and accommodate other's views others. This is the real humanitarian outlook. Samantabhadra said it is the "Sarvodayatirtha". Haribhadra's quotation points out in the same direction. He means that we must think objectively irrespective of our religion and ideology: Agrahi vata ninisati yuktam, tatra yatra matires nivista. Paksapatarahitasya tu yuktir yatra tatra matiresa nivesam.

Acarya Hemacamndra also opines that we must not swallow uncritically any idea simply because it comes from the great man. The validity of that idea must be tested on the touchstone of logic. Paksapato na me Vire, na dvesah Kapiladisu.Yukti madvacanam yasya tasya karyah parigrahah.Dravyas or Tattvas.

Reality or substance in Jainism is distinguished from Dravya. Dravya means that which exists and possesses three fundamental characteristics, viz. i) origin (Utpada), ii) Destruction (Vyaya), and iii) permanence (Dhrauvya). It maintains its identity through its several qualities and modes. The Dravya in its reality can neither be created nor destroyed; it has only permanent substantiality. But through its modes, it secures the triple qualities. There is neither quality without substance nor substance without quality. Hence these two are not incompatible in their nature.

Dravya in Jainism is of six kinds, namely, Jiva (soul), Ajiva (non-soul), Dharma (principle of motion), Adharma (principle of rest), Akasa (space), and Kala (time). The first five types of Dravyas are called Astikayas (those exist and have different pradesas or areas like the body) and the last is named Anastikaya. According to another classification it is of three kinds, viz. Sakriya (active), Niskriya (inactive) and Sakriya-Niskriya. The Sakriya Dravya, which have the capacity of moving from place to place, are Pudgalas and Jivas. Contrary to this, the Niskriya Dravyas are space and Kala; Sakriya-Niskriya Dravyas are those realities, which move about without themselves undergoing changes or motion. Dharma and Adharma are Sakriya and Niskriya Dravyas respectively. Pudgala alone is Murta (having forms), which possesses the sense qualities of contact, taste, smell, sound and colour. In another classification, the Dravyas or Tattvas are divided into seven categories, Viz. Jiva (Soul) Ajiva (non soul) Asrava (inflow of Karmic matter) into the soul, Bandha (bondage of soul by Karmic matter), Samvara) stoppage of the inflow of the Karmic matter), Nirjara (shedding of Karmic matter), and Moksa (liberation of soul from Karmic matter).

Conception of Soul (Jiva)

As per Jain philosophy, soul is eternal and beginning-less. It has life, consciousness, Upayoga (knowledge and perception) and is potent. It performs actions and is affected by their results, is conditioned by its own body (characteristic of contraction and expansion), is incorporeal and is ordinarily found with Karma. In addition, it is capable of becoming free from the defect of Karma, gets to the highest point of the universe, knows all and perceives all and obtains the transcendental bliss ever-lasting The nature of soul is considered dual in character. According to the realistic standpoint, it remains the same under all states, while according to the practical standpoint, it is transformed into modes and this becomes different in number, place and form, etc.

The souls are of two types, namely 1) Samsaris (transmigrating beings) those who undergo or subjects to the cycle of wandering into births and experience the fruit of Karmas, and 2) Muktas, the emancipated souls. The transmigrating souls are of two kinds, Trasas (mobiles) and Sthavaras (immobile). The Sthavaras are further divided into five kinds, viz. earth, water, fire, air and plants possessing the touching sensation. The mobile beings are from two- sensed beings onwards. The senses are five, viz. touch, taste, smell, sight, and hearing. The senses are also of two kinds, the physical sense and psychic sense. Earth, water, plants, etc. have one sense of touch and the warm, the ant, the bee, and man, etc. have each one more sense than the preceding one. These living beings possess of some essential characteristics called Pranas, viz. Bala, Indriya, Ayu, and Ucchavasa (breathing). The means of birth of beings are also discussed. It is of three kinds, viz. i). Spontaneous generation (Sammurchhana), ii) birth from uterus (Garbhaja), and iii) Upapadajanma (that is the seat to which the soul goes and in which it is born).

The existence of soul is proved from the world "Soul" itself. The very thought whether the soul exists or not proves its existence, because man can think whether something is the pillar or the person while and inanimate substance cannot. No one except the soul can raise doubt. Modern scientists are also realising the existence of soul. For instance, it is said, "This world is not the machine without soul. It has not come into existence by accident. Behind the veil of matter, is working the mind and consciousness. This force may be given any nomenclature".

Ajiva Tattva

Ajiva Tattva is of five types, viz. Pudgala, Dharma, Adharma, Akasa and Kala. Pudgala has form and the qualities, Rupa, etc. while the rest are without form. Except Kala Dravya, all the Dravyas are called Pancastikayas. Functions of the media of motion and rest or steadiness are to assist motion and rest respectively, just as water facilitates the movement of fish and the earth gives support to object like the horse, are called Dharam and Adharma. Akasa (space) accommodates completely all Jivas and Pudgalas. Kala (time) denotes and existential fact.

Pudgala (Matter) connotes that which has accretion and depletion, addition and bifurcation, conjunction and reparation. It is characterised by touch, taste, smell and colour. Sound, union, fineness, grossness, shape, division, darkness, image, warmth, light, are also forms of matter. The divisions of matter are two, atoms and molecules. The atom is itself the beginning, the middle and the end. It cannot be perceived by the senses. Molecules are collections of atoms, which are characterised by sound, union, etc. Some of them are visible and some are invisible. Combination of atoms takes place by virtue of greasy (Snigdha), and dry (rough) properties associated with them in six ways- 1) Very Gross-land, mountain, etc. 2) Gross water, oil, ghee, etc. 3) Fine gross air and other gases, 4) Gross fine- light, shadows, etc. 5) Fine- matter of thought and speech, etc. and 6) Very fine. Skandhas composed of two, three, etc. Paramanus. Science gives three physical states of matter, viz. solid, liquid and gaseous, and these correspond with the first three divisions given above. Philosophers knew the existence of three more divisions, which can be compared with X-rays and Gamma rays. Jainism has also of the view that sound can reach the other end of the universe, if strongly produced. Radio, etc. have corroborated the statement.

The nature of universe is based on the nature of reality, which possesses triple characteristics, origin, destruction and permanence. The things that exist cannot be originated from the realistic standpoint, but they get transformed into their own attributes and modes from the practical point of view. This system of realities results in the universe being infinite as well as eternal in character. The entire universe, according to Jainism, is the compendium of the six Dravyas, which are the permutation and combination of atoms. God does not create it.

Theory of Karma

The theory of Karma is considered under the purview of Pudgala (matter). Karma in Jain philosophy emphasises that one has its pivotal stand for deciding the fruits of one's activities on an individual basis. No God can exercise its power as the middleman. One will have to bear the result of ones own deeds. The vibration (Yoga) and the passions (Kasaya) of soul attract Karmic matter and transform it into Karmic body. Yoga is the action of mind, speech and body due to desire, aversion and cognition. Soul is pure in its intrinsic nature. The relation of Karma is the cause that makes it the subject to the cycle of birth and death. There are two distinct causal agencies, viz. Nimittakaraṇa or Dravyakarma (remote or distant cause) and Upadanakarana or Bhavakarma (substantial cause). Soul is the substantial cause of the passions while Karmic matter is the remote cause. Acarya Kundakunda has discussed in detail about the interrelation between soul and body. That can be summed up with the words that the soul and body are capable of causal interrelation and the change in one always involves two antecedents, one physical and the other psychic. If causal interrelation is not admitted, certainly ethical values will remain unexplained and unintelligible.

On the basis of nature, the Karmas are of eight kinds, via. 1) Jnanavarana which conceals the light of knowledge, 2) Darsnavarana which obscures right intuition, 3) Vedaniya karma which obscures the pleasant feeling and unpleasant feeling, 4) Mohaniyakarma, the Karma which deludes faith, conduct, etc. This is the greatest powerful karma, which covers the powers of the soul like wine. As long as the Mohaniyakarma is powerful, all the karmas remain powerful and as soon as it gets weaker, all the Karmas lose their strength. 5) Ayukarma that which determines the quantum of life in the states of existence as internal beings, plants and animals, human beings and celestial beings, 6) Namakarma, the karma due to which the soul acquires Nama-rupa, etc. that is body, 7) Gotrakarma (status determining Karmas) are of two types, high and low, and 8) Antarayakarma that creates obstructions in making gifts, gain, enjoyment, effort, etc. Of these, Jnanavarana, Darsanavarana, Mohaniya and Antaraya Karmas i) Ghatiya Karmas which destroy the four main characteristics of soul- knowledge, perception, pleasure and effort, and ii) the remaining four Karmas are called Aghatiyakarmas which do not destroy the virtues of soul. On destruction of Ghatikarmas, one attains Kevalajnana and on destruction of remaining four Karmas he achieves salvation. Karmas are also divided into another two divisions, viz. Subha (virtuous), and Asubha (wicked activities). Just as water flows into the lake by means of streams, so also karmic matter flows into the soul through the channel or medium of activity. All the eight types of Karmas have the causes of the influx.

Theory of Karma, as in Buddhism, rejects the theory of God as creator, supporter or protector and destroyer of the world. Jainism does not believe in the principles of reward, judgement, incarnation and forgiveness. One will have to bear the result of one's own deeds. They cannot be extinguished simply by the mercy of God. Jainism, of course, unlike Buddhism, believes in Godhood, the Paramatman state of soul itself and in innumerable gods. Karma stands to reincarnate the soul as cause to effect. It can be purged through the trinity, right faith, right knowledge, and right conduct. Every soul is potentially divine and the manifestation of divinity is called Paramatman. It has three stages, 1) Bahiratman that engages itself in the external objects through the senses and is endowed with wrong views, 2) Antarataman, the stage which moves towards the real of soul, repents for indulging tendency of senses. 3) The third stage is the Paramatman, the Siddha, the soul that is freed itself from bondage of Karma and cycle of birth and death. This is the most purified stage of soul. Such the soul is bereft of the bodies produced by eight Kinds of Karmas, preserves infinite perception, infinite knowledge and infinite bliss and stays at the summit of the universe. This is called the stage of Nirvana (emancipation from all Karmas).

Classification of Knowledge

Jainism classified the knowledge in two ways; i) Canonical (Agamika), and ii) Philosophical (Darsanika). The five kinds of knowledge based on the former are- i) Matijnana (sensitive knowledge, ii) Srutajnana (Scriptural knowledge), iii) Avadhijnana (Visual knowledge), iv) Manahparyayajnana (mental knowledge), and v) Kevalajnana (perfect knowledge). The Pratyaksa (direct knowledge) and Paroksa (indirect knowledge) are developments of the latter. The Pratyaksa is defined as knowledge obtained by self without the assistance of an external instrument. It is only to the Jainas that "aksa" means "soul". Thus Pratyaksa in Jain Agamika tradition does not mean empirical perception, i.e. Knowledge obtained through sense organs. According to this definition, the Avadhijnana, Manahparyayajnana and Kevalajnana are comprised in Pratyaksa and Matijnana, and Srutajnana in Paroksa.

The Jain definition of Pratyaksa was quite different from those of other philosophical systems. According to the latter, Pratyaksa is an acknowledgement gained through sense organs. It created the serious difficulty for Jain philosophers. The rivals began to question their standpoint. Having examined their arguments, the later Jain philosophers accepted Pratyaksa as the knowledge produced by sense organs also. Jinabhadra and Akalanka however, analysed it as Samvyavaharika Pratyaksa (empirical perception), while the real Pratyaksa of Agamika tradition was called Paramarthika Pratyaksa (transcendental perception). Thus Matijnana, which was put under Paroksa in the Agamika tradition, came under the category of Pratyaksa in philosophical tradition.

Jain Ethics and Asceticism

Samyama or self-restraint is the basis of Jain asceticism. It is seen in the various vows, disciplines, codes of conduct and other doctrines propounded by Jainacaryas. The Maligns or basic virtues are nothing but regular practical exercise in self-control. Vinaya or humble attitude is the result of self-control. The commentator Aparajitasuri says in his Vijayodya Tika on the Mularadhana that which removes, keeps away or destroys inauspicious or sinful acts is Vinaya (Vinayati apanayati yatkarmasubham tad- vinayah). It is related with knowledge, faith, conduct and austerity.

Modesty, discipline, compassion, charity and other such good qualities are essence of Jainism and Jainism is to have a Right faith (Samyagdarsana) as its foundation. Right faith means right vision. Self-confidence, faith, trust and fidelity are its ingredients. Without realising the self, it is aimless wandering in the undiscovered caves of fallacious reasoning. Samvega (the fear of worldly bondage), Nirveda (detachment), and Astikya (theism, belief in the next life and in the next world) are other its remarkable characteristics. By this way, the ascetic becomes desire less, fearless, and doubtless in observing the religious vows. One attains more purity, peace, insight, conduct and attainments (Labdhis) through Samyakdarsana.

Spiritual disciplines and practices are representative wings of religion and philosophy. Spirituality is immanent in human nature; religion is the moral force and philosophy and asceticism are intellectual and practical instruments respectively for achieving the spiritual and religious goals. Under this perspective, Jainism originally preaches ideals for attaining spirituality. Its religious ascetic aspects enjoin discipline for social upliftment and enlistment and philosophy justifies them for exemplary behaviours. Spirituality relates to having belief in an independent existence of soul, its nature of innate purity, and the removal of ignorance through right means. To attain this spiritual goal the certain amount of disciplines and practices are prescribed by all the systems. Therefore there is no controversy over the spiritual goal but controversy lies in framing the disciplines and practices leading to the goal. Here we shall have the bird's view of the concept of Jainism in this regard.

Vows (Vratas) in Jain asceticism are the form of self- discipline. They should not be viewed superficially. A spiritual aspirant must observe vows both in theory and practice. Spirituality is the essence of spirit or self or ultimate reality in being which comprises its right knowledge and right conduct in its relation with the universe. It is beyond the physical or material world and therefore is immanent. It is called Adhyatma (pertaining to self) in Sanskrit. Spiritual knowledge of the self or Atman requires its realisation that one has capacity and aspiration to attain the highest and ultimate truth. Spirituality needs spirit in its purity, which can be achieved only by right conduct and inwardness, intuition and mysticism. Ultimate reality is related to world until one reaches ultimate spirit destiny. Therefore there is significant relationship between human and pure spiritual and natural and super- natural phenomena.

Soul or spirit is, according to Mahavira, the central point of spiritual discipline and practices. For spiritual realisation, he preached Right faith, right knowledge and right conduct which constitute all three together the path of spiritual salvation termed as triple jewel (Ratnatraya). The Uttaradhyayana clearly says that Nirvana cannot be attained without observing combined the Ratnatraya. Bhatta Akalanka explains the trinity with the help of medicine, which cures the diseases by following faith, knowledge and conduct accordingly this, is the abridged form of Astangikamarga or vice-verse.

Belief in the ascertainment of things in their true character is right faith. It can be achieved by avoiding doubts in the teaching of Jina, desire for worldly enjoyment, admiration for the knowledge and conduct of the wrong believers and so on. Anger, pride, deceitfulness and agreed are the passions which lead to endless worldly existences or transmigrations. Consequently on the fruition of Karmas, the soul wanders into different conditions of existence. When the infinite Karmas are completely destroyed, the perfect knowledge, perfect perception, fearlessness and infinite enjoyment are attained by the purified soul. This process comes under the Samvara and Nirjara Tattvas. Samvara means the obstruction of influx of Karmic matter and the Nirjara connotes the separation of part of Karmic matter from the soul. Stoppage and gradual dissociation of Karmas are the chief causes of liberation. Puiayapada defines state of the soul on the removal of all the impurities of Karmic matter and the body, characterised by the inherent qualities of the soul such as knowledge and bliss free from pain and suffering.

Categories of Jain Ascetics

There are two types of ascetics in Jainism: Sravakas and Munis. With the sole intention of achieving the purified state of soul, Jainism prescribes some fundamental spiritual disciplines and practices. They can be observed partially and totally. Partial observation is prescribed for the householder (Sravaka), as he is unable to desist from all sins completely whereas an ascetic Muni is expected to observe the code of conduct totally as he practically does not stay at tome. He observes vows completely (Mahavrati) and is free from sting, the main root of pain and emotion arising from Karmas. Sting is of three kinds, viz. i) Deceit termed as Maya, ii) desire for enjoyment termed as Nidana, and iii) perverse attitude termed as Mithyadarsana. The practice of asceticism with vigilance dispels sufferings and strings just as an excellent specific herb removes disease. Jainism lays greater emphasis on asceticism and so naturally there is more discussion on their conduct is found in literature.

The Householder (Sravaka)

The Householder (Sravaka or Sramanopasaka) is one who listens the Dharma with full faith from Acarayas and Paramesthis. He is one whose sins flow away from him (sravanti yasya papani). He is also called Agari or Sagari because he stays in the house. He prepares himself gradually and steadily to renounce the world with right faith by observing the rules prescribed and then fulfils the responsibilities for the welfare of the family, ascetics, society, nation and mankind. The Upasakadasanga, Sravakaprajnapti, Ratnakarandasravakacara, Vasunandi Sravakacara, Sagaradharmamrita, and so many other Jain Texts explained much on the characteristics of laity. Some of the important attributes of the householder may be mentioned as follows: - observation of non-violence, compassion, legitimate earning, hospitality, refraining from unnecessary criticism of government, keeping good accompany, paying respect to parents, service of people, observing religious preaching, firm in conduct, right character, gratefulness, generosity, being afraid of sin, meditation, celibacy, no food at night, refusal of food with life, giving up possessions, honesty, appreciating conduct, life and activities of spiritually advanced people, avoiding expenditures exceeding income and so on. Such rules make life pleasant. These attributes consider the ecology and indispensable part of spirituality and life as well. Possessed of such qualities the votary will reform not only himself but also his society. The spiritual status of the Householder is decided on his performance as Jaghanya, Madhyama, and Utkrasta or Paksika, Naisthika and Sadhaka. 1. Paksika Sravaka.

Paksika Sravaka is he who has an inclination (Paksa) towards Ahimsa. This is the first spiritual status of the Jain laity in which he first takes the vow with right faith not to eat meat, not to drink alcohol or wine and not to relish honey or any of the five kinds of figs containing souls. These are called Mulagunas. Then he desists from injury, falsehood, stealing, unchastely, and attachment to wealth. The Paksika Sravaka also takes the vow not to indulge in seven types of obnoxious habits (Vyasanas), which make the life disastrous. They are gambling and betting, meat-eating, alcoholic drink, prostitution, hunting, stealing, and sexual intercourse with another's wife or husband. These are the addictions, which make a hell of an addict's life. Addiction is the deep muddy pit overgrows with enticing vegetation and verdure.

He should also not be indulged in violence-carrying professions. Asadhara enumerated fifteen types of such professions (Karmadana) in the Sagaradharmamrta (v.21-23): 1) livelihood from charcoal (Angarakarman), 2) livelihood from destroying plants (Vana- karman), 3) livelihood from carts (Sakata-karman), 4) livelihood from transport fees (Bhataka-karman), 5) lovely hood from hewing and digging (Sphota-karman), 6) trade in animal by-products (Danta- vanijya), 7) trade in lakh and similar substances (Laksa-vanijya), 8) trade in alcohol and forbidden foodstuffs (Rasa-vanijya), 9) trade in men land animals (Klesa-vanijya), 10) trade in destructive articles (Visa-vanijya), 11) work involving milling (Yantra-pidana), 12) work involving mutilation (Nirlanchana), 13) work involving the use of fire (Davagni-dana), 14) work involving the use of water (Sarah-sosana), and 15) work involving breeding and rearing (Asati- posana).

The licit earning sources (Nyayoparjita), according to Jensen, are agriculture (Krsi), study, teaching and clerical occupation (Masi), art or craft profession (Silpa), trade (Vanijya), military occupation (Asi), practice of medicine (Vidya), of course, but the pursuit of the profession should be positively in the pure way. Along with these practices he should also practice some more activities called Avasyakas namely i) worship of the Tirthankaras, ii) Service to spiritual teacher iii) studying Spiritual texts every day (Svadhyaya), iv) practicing some form of self restraint every day, v) doing some form of penance daily, and vi) doing some kind of charitable act. This is an introduction to spiritual discipline of an ordinary householder. These observations create communal harmony and peace in society and in the nation.

Ecology and Spirituality in Jain Tradition

The global ecological crisis cannot be solved until spiritual relationship is established between humanity as the whole and its natural environment. Jainism has been staunch protector of nature since inception of the Jain faith. The religion of nature, Jainism paves the way to understanding nature's utility and the essential nature of plants, worms, animals, and all sorts of creatures that have their own importance for maintaining ecological balance. Jainism therefore says that the function of souls is to help one another (Parasparopagraho Jivanam-Tattvarthasutra, 5.21).

This principle is connected to the whole of life. It includes humans and other creatures. The plant, animal, and human populations are merely part of the landscape. For Jainism, the landscape is itself lives and breaths and merits protection.

Spirituality is essentially an individual endeavor. Individuals create collectivity on the basis of discipline and practice. Every basic reality of the universe is integral. Jainism reconciled the parts of reality with the whole by means of the relativistic approach. Spiritual relationships, from an ecological perspective, can be understood with the help of some of the basic tenets of Jainism; 1) injure no creatures (Savve pana na hantavva), 2) do not command any creature; 3) do not own any creature; and 4) do not employ one as the servant (save pana na pariggahetvva).

Jain ecology is based on spirituality and equality. Each life form, plant, or animal, has an inherent worth and each must be respected. Within Jainism, the term for ecology might be Sarvodayavada, or the concern for lifting up all life forms, as articulated by Samantabhadra (third c. A. D.), the prominent Jain philosopher. Acarya Jinasena explained the same view of social equality by saying that the entire human world is one because of the interconnectedness of different aspects of the human community. 26. Seeing other people as connected with oneself develops the spiritual perspective through which all life takes on sanctity that can and must be protected by observing the principles of ecology. The real task of religion consists in removing bitterness between people, between races, between religions, and between nations. That nature of religion has been discussed in Jain scriptures in various ways in the form of Non-violence (Ahimsa). That Ahimsa can be summarised: Aspire for yourself. Do not aspire for others. This is the fundamental principal of Jainism.

Jainism holds that the entire world, including plants, trees, birds, animals, water, and so forth, is possessed of life. It is our prime duty to protect all this. We are to treat others, as we want to be treated, and this refers not only to other people but also to the entirety of our planet. One is therefore expected to respect the land and its natural beauty. Jainism does so philosophically by accepting the principle of the interdependent existence of nature and animals.

Non-violence creates identity between self and self. Therefore Mahavira says, "Kill no creature", One has to experience personally the consequences of one's own Karmas. Through this unitised experience, the existence of souls is established. Mahavira goes on to say that one who is afflicted with lust is bereft of knowledge and perception. Truth will always baffle such a person. He indulges himself in action, causing violence to the beings of earth body, water body, fire body, vegetable body, and others. These beings have consciousness (Santi pana pudho siya).

The vivid description is found in Jain scripture as to how plants and other beings can and should be saved by a Jain. 32 These are very important principles laid down by Jainism to avoid harm to water, air, fire, and all forms of life and to minimise such evils as sound pollution, and thus to balance the community and ecosystem. To keep silence, to observe carefulness in speaking (Bhasasamiti), to protect the forest and plants- these are religious rules that apply even to the Jain laity. Jain cosmology gives paramount importance to mountains, rivers, trees, and other natural resources. In its opinion, non-violence should be observed strictly, at any cost to protect the ecological atmosphere.

Ecology sees the individual as interconnected with both nature and the fabric of society. Ecological theory considers the community the supra-organism, the complex social organism. Therefore, the Jain tradition instructs the Jain laity to keep the community very pure and pious. They are supposed not to indulge in obnoxious habits (Vyasanas), which make life disastrous. A Jain should be a strict vegetarian. He should not indulge in professions related to violence, such as dealing in weapons. Jain laymen also practice the twelve types of Vratas, which assist us in eliminating corruption from society and in purifying ourselves in the process.

Nonviolence, the humanistic element is based on the principles of equality and equanimity as applied in society. Non-violence still may allow for the theory of caste, but one based on one's own deeds and not on one's birth. Jainism tries to shape our attitude towards nature by prescribing humane and non-violent approaches to everyday behaviour. Jainism inspired its followers to safeguard what in contemporary discourse would be called the ecological perspective. Jainas even today practice these principles and religious traditions prescribed for the protection of nature. Through its philosophy, its ascetic practices, and in its narrative arts and architecture, Jainism and its leaders have made efforts to create the society dedicated to love for all creatures. Jain Philosophy and Psychology

Philosophy is the science of the general law of being and human thinking, which indicates the process of cognition and development led to the various aspects connected with ontology, epistemology, logic, ethics, aesthetics, psychology and sociology. It promotes man's self-awareness, his understanding of the nature of self or life and clarifies the content of problems that have been traditionally philosophical. It is also the speculum of life and thought, which deals with the psychology of beings' activities that become Karma.

Vegetarian Diet

Jainism stressed more and more on vegetarian diet since inception. According to it, the object of man's food is not just to fill his stomach, to maintain health or to satisfy his taste but to properly develop his mind, character and spirituality too. Our intake of food is closely related with our thinking, character and deeds. There is high truth in ancient saying that the kind of food you eat determines the kind of man you are. The taste of a mans indifferent types of food reflects his behaviour and character. In fact, it is an indicator of one's innermost self. Meat eating is totally against human nature. Jain thinkers discussed the subject at length in their works about its demerits. Modern physiologists also hold that human body and meat are contraries. The very Constitution of man does not warrant it. Man's habit of taking meat is not natural. It is the result of perverted taste, which becomes a sort of addiction. As such it should be completely discarded.

Our food should contain all those ingredients, which produce energy, health and heat. Our food should have proteins, sugar, vitamins, minerals and fats in adequate quantities and right proportions so that good quality of new cells and red blood corpuscles are produced continuously. It is misunderstanding that meat is invigorator. In fact it is medically proved that vegetarianism gives more lasting strength. Vasunandi and other Acharyas explained the fact in detail. Meat does not contain calcium, and carbohydrate with the result that meat-eaters are irritable, angry, and intolerant and pessimists. In vegetarian diets they are present in greater measure and so vegetarians are just the reverse in their nature. Animal proteins do not have additional value in the human nutrition rather it forms the potential risk for the development of the large number of serious meat borne diseases like cysticercus's, hydrated cuts, trichinosis which do not have any permanent treatment. Some of these diseases may be lethal.

It may be mentioned here that eggs are not included in vegetarian diet. The term vegetarian egg is the misnomer. Eggs are obtained from the birds whereas vegetables are obtained from plants. The question of unfertilized egg does not seem to have any clarification. Therefore, the eggs can never be vegetarian in origin. The term vegetarian egg is a misnomer and has misled the masses. The sperms cannot fertilize non-living material. Electrical activity has been recorded over unfertilized eggs, which clearly supports the life in them.

The Paksika Sravaka is also expected not to eat which is not fit to be eaten (Abhaksya). This is included into the Mulagunas. Asadhara gives the list of such Abhaksyas: i) four banned Vikrtis, ii) five Udambaras, iii) water, etc. in leather containers, iv) honey, v) flowers, vi) food eaten at night, vii) formented rice, etc. viii) Anantakayika Padarthas like Mulabija, Agrabija, Parvabija Kandbija, Bijaruha, Palandu (onion), ix) unknown fruits, x) curds kept for more than two days, xi) tainted food and so on. Such plants or food contain infinite number of living organisms. xii) Naisthika Sravaka (Allegiant Layman)

One who fulfils his religious duties with constant vigilance is the Naisthika Sravaka. He follows the twelve vows (five Anuvratas, three Gunavratas and four Siksavratas). First five Mahavratas are also called Silavratas, which are the fundamental basis of good conduct. They are: i) non-injury (Ahimsa) which forms the basis of Jainism. He avoids injury by mind, speech and body. He does not trade flesh and skin, nor does he incite others to do it. He avoids the prescribed limits to observe the Ahimsanuvrata. Its transgression may be as follows: i) Bandha or binding or to prevent one from going to the desired place. ii) Vadha or killing or torturing, iii) Chavicheda means to maim the person, iv) Atibhara or overloading, v) Bhaktapanaviccheda or carelessness in giving food and water. The second vow is Satyanuvrata, which means not to tell the lies. Under this vow, the householder is expected not to state the thing, which is not a fact, and not to twist facts. He should not transgress the vow by revealing the secrets of others, accusing somebody without any justification, writing counterfeit documents, playing tricks in weighing and measuring and so on. The third vow is Acauryanuvrata, which means not to appropriate to him what belongs to somebody else without his express permission. He should not purchase the stolen property, should not encourage and praise thieves, should not purchase the property in cheaper rates, should not indulge in illegal export and import business, should not adulterate at all and so on. The fourth vow is Svadarasantosavrata, which means to keep satisfaction with one's own wife or husband without any sexual craving for other women or men. Celibacy is the great force and potential aid to self-realisation. He is expected to avoid irrepressible yearning for sexual intercourse, etc. The fifth vow is Aparigrahanuvrata, which means to have the limited possessions, which are root cause of sins. Such passions are like territories, houses, ornaments, utensils, gold, silver coins, grains, animals, men, women, quadrupeds, clothes, conveyances, etc.

Gunavratas are intended to enhance the effect and value of the Anuvratas. They are for acquisition of religious merit. For instance Digvrata is the lifelong vow to limit one's worldly activities to fixed points in different directions. The Desavrata is to keep limit for a fixed period only. The Anarthadandavrata is not to commit unnecessary of purposeless moral offence, such as talking ill of others (Apadhyana), preaching evil (Papopadesa), facilitation of destruction (Himsa-pradana), purposeless mischief (Pramadacarita), and faulty reading (Duhsruti). In fact, it would include all acts which denigrate others or through which others are hurt or deprived of liberty.

The four Siksavratas are intended to prepare the aspirant gradually for the discipline of ascetic life. They are: i) Samayika (to contemplate of the self and attainment of equanimity), ii) Prosadhopavasa (to keep fast on the eighth and the fourteenth day of each fortnight of the month, iii) Bhogopabhoga-parimana (Putting the limit daily on enjoyment of consumable and non-consumable things for that day), and iv) Atithisamvibhagavrata (to entertain some ascetic or needy person with a portion of food who happens to come uninvited.). These Siksavratas are to practice the ascetic life. The Acaryas show their progressive trends in fixing them depending on the various regions, their needs, and times. Dana or gift is one of them. It has played the significant role all along the course of the history of Jainism Somadevasuri in his Yasastilakacampu (43.765-852) considered at length regarding Patra (the recipient), Datr (the giver), Datavya (the thing to given, Danavidhana (the method of giving), and Danaphala (the fruit of giving). All the Jain thinkers are of view that what is given should be for the pleasure of giving or for the spiritual rise and self-restraint of ascetics. The householders may also be considered for charity purpose on their genuine needs.

In order to prepare himself for the ascetic life, the householder goes further to observe the eleven spiritual stages (Pratimas). They are; i) Darsana Pratima; - it requires true and unshakable faith in Jainism with firm conviction in the reality of seven fundamental principles of Jainism and devotion to Pancaparameshthis. After the long practice he becomes Samyagdristi. He should also not be proud of knowledge, worship, family, caste, wealth, practices, and beauty. He will ponder daily over twelve points of meditation to realise self or deep-reflection Dvadasanupreksas as follows; - transitoriness, helplessness, transmigration, loneliness, distinctness, impurity, influx, stoppage, dissociation, universe, rarity of enlightenment and the truth. These reflections help the spiritual aspirants to practice ten moral virtues, such as forbearance, modesty, straightforwardness, purity, truthfulness, self-restraint, austerity, renunciation, non-attachment and celibacy. The realisation of self through these attributes generates tranquility, disenchantment with the materialistic world, prosperity and supreme perfection.

Vrata Pratima (the stage of observing vows); - In order to prepare himself for the ascetic life the householder goes ahead to observe the twelve vows for obtaining inner purity of the self. Firm conviction with right understanding in the reality of fundamental principles of Jainism generates benevolence towards all living beings (Maitri), joy at the sight of virtuous (Pramoda), compassion and sympathy for afflicted (Karuna), and tolerance towards the insolent and ill behaved (Madhyasthya). He who conducts himself in this manner is able to practice non-violence, truth, not stealing, refraining from all illicit sexual activities and non-possession to perfection. Non-violence is the fundamental principle of Jainism. Here violence means severance of vitalities out of passion. Negligence is the main cause of violence. Even violence in the thought in view of Jainism is the cause of injury. It is said that when the monk goes on foot with carefulness sometimes small insects get crushed under his feet and die. Still there is not the slightest bondage of sin in his cause.

From the spiritual standpoint, infatuation is called attachment. Violence is mainly of three-fold, i.e. i) committed by himself (Krta), ii) that which is committed by others (Karita), and iii) giving consent to violence done (Anumodana). This violence should be avoided by any of the three agencies of mind, speech and body. By this way the layman starts his steps towards equality and equanimity. The true householder should be kind enough to animals and others. He should not bind, beat and mutilate their limbs. He should not overload them and withhold food and drink. Another point should also be cleared in this respect. Jainism is very firm and says that one should not sacrifice animals for the adoration of gods, being dominated by the perverted notion of receiving benediction in return. It is inconceivable how the gods seek satisfaction and serenity from such in human deeds, which cause unbearable pain to the animals. It must not be obligatory to kill the animals for the entertainment of guests, the pious design by impious means.

All the other vows are intended to safeguard non-violence, speaking what is not commendable is falsehood. Preparing false records prompted by others in order to cheat others, misappropriation, proclaiming other's thoughts, etc. are included into the ambit of falsehood, which should be avoided in practice. Asteya means not taking the property of others whether pledged or dropped or forgotten unless it has been given. He again should not be indulged in activities like receiving stolen things, using false weights and measures, deceiving others with artificial or imitation goods. Unchastity and excess accumulation of wealth, etc. are also prohibited to the Jain householder. These observations should be in practice to make justice and create congenial atmosphere and relationship between fundamental rights and directive principles of state policy. Ordering someone to bring something illegally from outside the country is also prohibited for householders.

Rendering help to one another is the basis to the formula of Jain discipline. Some more supplementary vows are prescribed for householders, which pave the way for their spiritual elevation with the view to having socio-economic justice. For instance, to curb the mentality of masterminding operations aimed at enlarging one's wealth or concentrating their economic power to achieve greater exploitative capacity. Jainism directs the householder to fix boundaries for business, not to pursue commercial activities causing injury to living beings, to extend hospitality by offering food, implements, medicine and shelter and to bestow one's possessions upon one another for mutual benefit. He should also observe compassion towards living beings in general and towards the devout in particular. He should practice charity, contemplation, equanimity and freedom from greed.

Other Pratimas like meditation, fast, renouncing eating after sunset, etc. should also be observed, for attainment of gradual renunciation from worldly concern and becoming prone to monk hood. The spiritual aspirant who reaches the eleventh stage is called Kshullaka (junior) having three long pieces of clothes and the lion cover (Langota), the Kamandalu and the broom in Digambara tradition. In Svetambara tradition he is called Sramanabhuta possessing the begging bowl and whisk broom.

Sallekhana, the spiritual death in Jain tradition, is the third stage of the householder, which is very close to that of an ascetic where the subjugation of the senses is conducive to the removal of passions. He is, therefore, also called Maha-sravaka It is defined as making the physical body and the internal passions emaciated by abandoning their sources gradually at the approach of death with pleasure and not by force for various reasons one decides to perform Sallekhana. According to the Bhagawati Aradhana, the old age, physical weakness, famine, incurable disease, calamities, etc. are such reasons, which render the performance of Avasyakas impossible. It should be performed at the Jain temple or one's own house or in jungle at the eve of the death, so that one could achieve better prospects in the next birth. Sallekhana is also called Samadhimarana. It should be observed through Ayambils, Penances, Internal and external Tapas, renunciation of worldly affairs, forgiveness, Alocana, Pratikramana, Dhyana, etc. with the view to attain purification of mind. (Pravacanasaroddhara, 902-3; Bhagawati Aradhana, 253-4).

This is an important and interesting feature of the Jain householder and spiritual aspirants. Some scholars are of opinion that Sallekhana is a sort of suicide, since there is voluntary severance of life, etc. but this is not correct, as there is no passion. The person who kills himself by means of passion, weapon, etc. swayed by attachment, aversion or infatuation, etc. commits suicide. But he who practices holy death is free from desire, anger, and delusion. Hence, it is not suicide. This is called Sallekhana in Jain terminology, which means to make the body and the passion thin.

In modern days it is named "Euthanasia" or "Right to die" which is a sort of suicide and not the spiritual death. This has come into light the world over and became the subject of debate because of the revolutionary changes in medical knowledge and life- supporting systems, which could prolong human life even after the brain, stopped functioning. The practice, has, of course been accepted in countries like the United States, the United Kingdom and some other countries. But it should be treated as the case of suicide if it does not follow the line of spiritual death.

Thus the householder's stage is the pre-stage of the Jain ascetic. It is, therefore, simply natural for him to observe the ascetic practices to certain extent. The daily routine of the Jain lay disciple starts with reciting the Mahamantra *"Namo Arihantanam, Namo Siddhanam, Namo Airiyanam, Namo Uvajjhayanam, Namo Loe Sabbsahunam"*. In Brahmamuhurta (early morning) thinking" who am I? "What are my vows"? "What is my Dharma"?, etc. he observes Samayika, then mediates (Dhyana), studies the Scriptures (Svadhyaya), worships the Jinas Caityavandana or Jinapuja) and then takes the meals. Avasyakas, Alocana and Pratikramana, etc. are also to be observed by the householder.

Another type of division of spiritual stages is called Gunasthanas in the Jain scripture. They are fourteen in number stating the nature of the self in possession of the Ratnatraya on the path of purification. It starts with Mithyadrsti, the lowest one which involves gross ignorance where the self accepts wrong belief as the right, and therefore, the person cannot make the distinction between reality and unreality, and ends with Ayogakevali, the last one and most purified stage where all the passions and karmas are annihilated by the third and fourth stage of Sukladhyayana. This is called Siddhavastha. The spiritual development in fourteen steps can be comprehended by the three main divisions, viz. the external self (Bahiratman), internal self (Antaratman) and the transcendental self (Paramatman).

Jain Mendicant

Jain scripture prescribes the code of conduct for the spiritual aspirant (Mahavrati) who observes total renunciation. It is called Samacaro (Right conduct), which is formulated in consonance with the spiritual vigilance for the mendicant. The Elaka who is in the last of the eleven stages of monk hood and is virtually a recluse (Mahavrati), feels confident that he has had the requisite discipline and self-control over worldly things, gets initiation for Acelakatva from the Acarya into the Digambara order by pulling the hair out from his head with his own hands (Kesaluncana). He then becomes Panipatri in Digambara tradition that takes food placing it on the palm of their hands or Patradhari in Svetambara tradition that use some utensils while eating. He also keeps with him the small whisk broom (Rajoharana) made of peacock feathers for removing insects and a Kamandalu (water-pot) for sanitation purpose. The Svetambara Murtipujaka aspirant is provided three large pieces of cloth, a broom made of woolen tufts, a begging bowl, a blanket, a staff, and some scriptures. In addition to these articles, the Sthanakavasi and Terapanthi aspirant gets a small strip of cloth called Muhapatti for protecting the air bodies. A Jain ascetic will not stay alone, but he should join with two other ascetics to form the Gana. He will also not stay with nuns nor share alone with them at any occasion.

The ascetic observes first six essential duties (Avasyakas)- 1) Pratikramana (introspection, confession and repentance on sins, 2) Pratuyakhayana (to renounce thinking, speaking or doing all that is inconsistent with his code of conduct), 3) Stuti of Caturvimsati Tirthankaras, 4) Vandana (paying prostrating obeisance to the Arhats, Siddhas and other Parmesthis, 5) Samayika meditation upon one's own soul thrice in the day, and 6) Kayotsarga (to practice complete bodily abandonment for sometime daily, to relinquish all sense of attachment to the body and the things connected with it). Samayika is the foundation of all the Avasyakas. It gives tranquility of mind". It is to stay within "Sama" that means in the detached state with an excellent way and "Ayam" is conduct. So this is the right and faultless conduct. It is meditation regular and at fixed times. The Bhagawatisutra says that the soul itself is Samayika and that Samayika is the soul. Jainacaryas have considered it from different angles like name, time, place, etc.

The Pratikramana is to return from sin to virtue. It means retracing the step from wrong to right approach. Repentance is not only for misdeeds done in the past, but it refers to present and future as well. Not to let the influx of Karma enter the soul is present repentance and the resolve not to commit any sin necessarily refers to the future. Kayotsarga means renunciation of body that you are not the body but have your body must be contemplated every day so much so that it should become your second nature.

It is mostly done in a standing posture. It is not only the body that is straight, but also the mind, which is elevated side by side. It is concentration on prayer offered to twenty-four Tirthankaras. The Pratyakhyana is the renouncement of certain objects and acceptance of certain others to which also the aspirant is not in the least attached. He merely makes use of them. He thus becomes Samacari by observance of equality and right conduct.

Self- regulation and self- restraint are meant to stabilise and purify the five great vows. Uttaradhyana and some other Texts have called them Pravacanamata. Pravacana means right vision and right knowledge. To keep them intact there are five self-regulations (Samitis) and three restraints (Guptis), termed together Asta Pravacana Matrakas. Iryasamiti means carefulness in moving out. Bhasasamiti means anger, deceit pride, greed, fun, fear and irreligious things must be avoided in speaking. Esanasamiti is concerned with monk's diet, which should not suffer from 42 and

96 defects. Adananiksepanasamiti is to accept with circumspection cloth, utensils, book, etc. and place them on clean ground or floor. Nothing should be used without looking closely. Non-injury must never be lost sight of. The Utsargasamiti is to discharge the excreta and urine on the soulless ground. Gupti means self-control on mind, body, and speech. This is possible by taking the mind away from evil tendencies and fixing it on auspicious ones.

The mendicant stays in temples of woods with total renunciation and proper conduct. He must observe fully all the twelve vows prescribed to the householder. The ascetic cultivates and observes the ten noble virtues (Dharmas), viz. forgiveness, humility, simplicity of mind, body and speech, total abstinence from greed of life, sense-organs and pleasure, etc. truthfulness, self-control, penance, abstinence from the possession of things, etc. renunciation of attachment for body and like, and complete celibacy. He proceeds to arrest the karmic matter by controlling passions, careful movement, observing virtues, engaging himself in contemplation and conquering the suffering by endurance and conduct. For curbing the threefold activity of body, speech and mind an ascetic takes every care in walking, speaking, eating, lifting and lying down and depositing waste products for avoiding injury to organisms.

Besides, he has also to Endure twenty-two types of afflictions (Parisahas), such as hunger, thirst, Cold, heat, insect-bites, nakedness, abstinence of pleasures, women, pain, discomfort of postures, uncomfortable couch, scolding, injury, begging, lack of gain, illness, pain, inflicted by blades grass, dirt, reverence and honour, conceive of learning, despair or uneasiness arising from ignorance and lack of faith. These afflictions are to be endured so as not to swerve the path of stoppage of Karmas and for the sake of dissociation from Karma. He follows 28 Mulagunas completely.

Acelakatva or nakedness is the requisite characteristic of the ascetics. Mahavira is called Nigantha Nataputta in the Pali Literature. The term Nigantha reveals the qualities such as renunciation, purity, restraint, etc. As the result of the later development, the Scripture also allowed afterwards in the Svetambara tradition the mask for preventing the death of micro-organisms normally entering the mouth (Mukhavastrika), the piece of cloth

(Avamacela), blanket (Padakambala), broom (Rajoharana), pot (Patra), seat (Asana-peetha), phalaka, etc. Thus the ascetic constitutes the conduct by observing five causes of stoppage, namely control (Gupti), regulation (Samiti), moral virtues (Dharma), reflections or contemplations (Anupreksas) and conquest of afflictions (Parisahajaya) and conduct (Caritra).

In this context we should also understand the penance or religious austerity, which is the chief stoppage of influx and dissipation of Karmas. It is, of course, self-imposed. Penance purifies the body. It sets right blood circulation in the body and bestows the inner power to control the mind. There is no penance, of course, without the right knowledge and sense of discrimination. The first thing to comprehend is that the body is distinct from the soul and the aggregate of Karma particles that remain attached to the soul are separated by means of penances. The spiritual energy shines forth when the soul contains no impurities. The spotless soul then develops the latent energy and achieves so many miraculous powers like Sambhinnasrota (capable of seeing with his ears), Carana (going into sky), Kevalajnana (omniscience), etc. The penances are not leman to acquire miraculous powers. The aim is to achieve the purity of soul. Such powers may emanate from an immaculate soul, but they are not to be exhibited.

Penance (Tape) is of two types, namely external penance (Bahyatapa) and internal penance (Antarangatapa). The external penance is of six types, viz. fasting (Ansana), reduced diet (Avamaudaraya), special restrictions for getting food (Vrttiparisankhyana), giving up stimulating and delicious dishes (Rasaparityaga), and mortification of body (Kayaklesa). The main object behind the external austerity is to purify the mind and body, cultivate patient endurance of bodily pain and suffering in order to remove attachment to pleasure and to proclaim the glory of the teaching of the Jainism. They effect both external and internal purification. Only then their devotion becomes lustrous. Gold, in order to be purified, has first to be heated and then polished. External penance is a sort of naturopathy, which is beneficial to cure of all ills.

The internal austerities are also six types, viz. expiation over negligence of duties (Prayascitta), reverence to the holy personage

(Vinaya), services to the saints in difficulty (Vaiyavrtti), study of the Scriptures (Svadhyaya), and meditation for checking the mind. The auspicious meditations (Dharma and Sukla-Dhyana) became the cause for attainment of various types of transcendental powers (Riddhis). Eventually, the aspirant attains Kevalajnana (omniscience) as the result of destroying the Ghatiyakarmas and then finally reaches to the 14th Gunasthana, the highest stage of spiritual development where all the Karmas are destroyed. This is the most purified stage of soul, which is called Nirvana.

To attain this highest position in the spiritual sphere an aspirant undertakes daily Samayika and Caityavandana and then goes out to beg for food with the certain Aharamudra and eats in the standing posture from the hollow of his hands once in the day if he is the Digambara monk, while the Svetambara monks eat from their pot after returning to the monastery. Afterwards, they further engage themselves in studying the Scriptures, writing the books, preaching to the audience and performing penance. No female ascetic goes naked, but keeps herself covered from head to foot, except the face. The Taranapantha and the Bhattaraka-pantha of Digambaras and all the sects of Svetambaras do not observe the nudity. The Svetambara ascetics keep the long cotton-cum-woolen brush to dust the ground where they sit or lie down whereas the Digambara ascetics keep peacock-feather brush for the purpose and the Kamandalu for having water for cleanliness. The Sthanakavasi and Terapanthi monks and nuns also wear a small rectangular piece of cloth (Mukha-patti) over the mouth. There are some more minor differences in practice between Digambara and Svetambara ascetics, but all Jain ascetics go barefoot, and do not use vehicles. They do not stay in a place for more than a few days except during four months of the rainy season (Varshavasa).

Meditation (Dhyana)

Meditation (Dhyana) is to concentrate the mind on the nature of soul and substance. Umasvati says that the fixity of thought and perfect control over mind, body and speech is concentration Dhyana is classified into four types. It may be auspicious or inauspicious. Inauspicious meditation is on worldly things with revengeful and evil attitude. Such Dhyanas are called 1) Arta or unpleasant or sorrowful, and 2) Raudra Dhyana, cruel concentration. Both these concentrations are concerned with acquisition and possession of worldly objects, wealth, property, etc. These are Asubhadhyanas, which should be avoided by every one. The last two Dhyanas are considered the Subhadhyanas, which are useful for the attainment of Moksha.

The Dharmadhyana (virtuous concentration) is to concentrate on righteous and auspicious objects for the short period up to forty- eight minutes. It is of four types, i) Ajnavicaya which consists the intensive contemplating and meditating upon the Jina's teaching, ii) Apayavicaya which firmly believes that it is the true and right teaching which will emancipate the soul from Karmic bondage and misery of worldly existence, iii) Vipakavicaya, contemplating the outcome of the Karma, and iv) Samsthanavicaya, contemplation over the structure of the universe.

It is also classified into four types in later period: i) Pindasthadhyana which means to contemplate on the soul in the body. The only thing to be contemplated upon is the self and its nature. ii) The Padasthadhyana is to fix the mind on incant Tory letters Arihanta, etc. which may be adoration and devotion to the Istadeva Jina, iii) Rupastha-dhyana, concentration upon the form of the Jina, and iv) Rupatita-dhyana, concentration upon that which transcends form the nature of Siddha. The knowledge of scriptures is an essential qualification of the first two types of this Dhyana.

The Mahavrati is placed automatically in the sixth Gunasthana Pramatta-virata. One must be then at least in the seventh stage of spiritual development, the Apramattavirata where the Pramada is suppressed. Up to this stage, he prepares the ground for attainment of Moksa. He then overcomes the subtle passions and attains the eighth Gunasthan, the Apurvakarana, unprecedented spiritual progress that is the result of the practice of Sukladdhyana.

We may consider the meditation for solving the problems of day to today life. Present environment needs struggle for existence. Struggle develops tension. Tension is unavoidable. Dharma means inherent properties bestowed upon an individual. Water is cool.

Fire is hot. Wind is flow. Earth is to support. Vegetation is to build body. Baby has to smile. Mother is to feed. These are all basic Dharma. There is inherent flow of potential energy in all these Tattvas. Every thing goes on continuously without waiting for any command. Life is full of struggles. It starts with Want. This "want" is the main cause of changing natural potential energy into artificial kinetic energy.

Law of conservation of energy says, "Quantum of energy is constant and life span is fixed. Kinetic energy can get you the thing for the trim being but you have to come back to your normal position, i.e. Dharma where there is continuous flow of potential energy. You can- not avoid confrontation but soon come back to Dharma or you will go mad.

Psychiatrists give tranquilisers. Psychologists give suggestions. Doctors give medicines. Father gives consolation. Relatives give sympathy. Religious personalities show you the Multiage. And this "Autosuggestion" is meditation. Return to normal status is the Dharma. Kinetic energy can- not last long. They are to be changed into potential energy. It is Dharma. Do not come in the way of this natural change. Leave it to nature. This may be discussed in Photon Theory and behaviour of mind.

The fourth Dyane is the Sukladhyana (pure concentration) which is the highest type of contemplation when the heart is passionless and pure. It is of four types. The first two types concentrate upon the nature of the Tattvas as set forth in the Jain scripture. Even though living in the world, such monk is not of the world at all. This is possible only up to the twelfth stage of spiritual development. The last two types are possible only in the thirteenth and fourteenth stages. He then becomes omniscient and Arhat (Srutakevalajnani). Having destroyed the Mohaniyakarmas or Ghatyakarmas, he realises the state of perfect purity called Yathakhyatacaritra and rises spontaneously to the thirteenth Gunasthana, called Sayogakevali or Kevalajnani. Then he destroys the remaining four Karmas and attains the liberation or Nirvana Moksa, the last spiritual stage, fourteenth Gunasthana.

The difference between Siddhas and Tirthankaras is that the Tirthankaras possessed certain miraculous powers, like Divyadhvani. The Jain scriptures set forth sixteen forms of conduct (Purity of right faith, charity, etc.) cultivated in past lifetimes to attain such stage of Tirthankaratva.

Rites and Rituals

As we have seen, the rules of lay conduct are very strict. The rites and rituals make them charming and attractive. Jainism in the strictest terms does not prescribe invocation, propitiation, offerings, prayers and the like. But in popular practice a devotee expresses his or her devotional attachment to idols which symbolise the glorification of the spiritual state and he attributes manifested in the idol Jonahed itself.

There are six obligatory duties (Sadavasyakas) in Jain tradition, which are prescribed for both laity and mendicant order as well. They are: i) Samayika, the practice of equanimity or meditation, ii) Caturvimsaatistava, praise of the twenty-four Tirthankaras, iii) Vandana, veneration, iv) Pratikramana, expiation for transgressions, v) Kayotsarga, abandonment of the body in standing or sitting poses, and vi) Pratyakhyana, renunciation of certain foods or activities for certain times. Jinasena and Somadeva make them more popular for laities by replacing them with 1) Devapuja, 2) Guru- upasana, 3) Svadhyaya, 4) Samyama, 5) Tapas, and 6) Dana.

A Jain devotee worships the Jain image with two ways, the first is the abstract worship (Bhavapuja), which needs neither idol nor ritual, and the second one is formal worship (Dravyapuja), which needs the idol and some ritual performances. The mendicants usually perform the abstract worship. It is also performed by those laities who do not have the sufficient facilities for accomplishing formal worship. There is a certain method prescribed for formal worship. After taking a bath and wearing clean clothes, the devotee goes to the temple and recites Namokaramantra (the Mahamantra) with devotional songs and hymns, puts down a few grains of rice, bows and goes around a circumambulatory (Pradaksina) path three times, and repeats Arihanta-Siddha, etc. Then on a rosary of 108 beads, he starts performing Astadravyapuja, which is eight-fold worship. First of all, he bathes the image with pure water, which is a kind of reminiscence of the post-birth illustration of the bathing of the

Tirthankara by Indra, the Lord of Gods (not of Jinas). Then he recites the verses, drops one after another the water, sandal wood paste, cleaned rice-grains, flowers or saffron coloured Astadravyas (rice, coconut, lamp, incense, fruits like cloves and almonds and the last one mixed offerings Argha) in a platter placed on the table in front of him. This procedure of paying homage to the Jina or Tirthankara, the ideal Guru and the Sastras or Scriptures may be done individually or in a congregation. After this the devotee concludes his worships with the recitation of Santipatha expressing his wish for universal peace: "May Lord Jinendradeva, bestow peace on the land, the nation, the city and the state and welfare on all the citizens, may the rulers and the administrators be strong, law- abiding and righteous, the rains be timely and adequate, all the diseases and ailments disappear, no one in the world be afflicted with famine or scarcity because of theft, loot, plunder and devastation, nor with epidemics, even for a moment: Peace be to all".

Among other Jain rituals, idol installation includes Jinabimbapratistha or Pancakalyanakapratistha (five auspicious events) with devotional songs and hymns, which initiates the image for worship in a Jain temple. It is preformed with a great ceremony under the leadership of a learned priest through depicting the five auspicious events of a Tirthankara's life, namely, conception, birth, renunciation, enlightenment and Nirvana. The Pancakalyanaka Mahotsava continues for several days with great sprit and devotion.

There are some social ceremonies like Samskaras, which are somehow connected with spiritual and with physical purity. They are of three types, viz. i) 53 kriyas (rites) which cover the entire life of a person from conception to death (Garbhanvayakriyas), ii) 48 rites which are related to new converts and their spiritual development (Diksanvayakriyas), and iii) 7 rites which are meant for personality development of meritorious souls (Kartranvyayakriyas). It may be noted here that prior to Acarya Jinasena, the lay conduct was dealt only with the Vratas and Pratimas. Jinasena then borrowed the Sanskaras from Vedic sides and introduced them into Jain society. Jinasena adopted this policy to protect Jain society from outside dangers. This was the need of the day to avoid the dangerous situation from Brahminical society. The history confirms the successful endeavour of Jinasena to reduce intercommunity friction and raise the status of Jain society in the eyes of Brahminical counterparts. Looking to the surface similarity over rites and rituals between Jainas and Hindus, some scholars express the view that Jainas are indistinguishable from Hindus and should not be considered an independent group at all. But this is not correct. As has already been discussed and explained earlier, Jainsim is an independent religion. It is not and has never been the branch of Hindus.

Among festivals celebrated by Jainas are: Paryusana, or Dasalaksana Parva held during the rainy season for eight or ten days in Jain temples where the sermons on the Dasadharmas, which are the ten virtues of the soul described in the Tattvarthsutra and Kalpasutra Scriptures are regularly read to an audience. At its end, Ksamavaniparva or Samvatsariparva is celebrated, which is the day of universal forgiveness, when every Jain asks for forgiveness from everyone else and he himself forgives others for wrongs done towards him during the past year. Other festivals such as Raksabandhana, Sodasakaranvrata, Aksayatrtiya, Mastakabhiseka, Srutapancami, Dipavali, Mahaviranirvana Jayanti, Siddhacakravidhana, Astanhikaparva, Nandisvaravidhana, etc. should also be mentioned which are social festivals of the community. Worship is the form of Dharmadhyana. It is an act of selfless devotion done with joy, cheerfulness and due humanity and as the result, the worshipper earns Punya (merit) and destroys demerit. It is transcendent attachment (Prasastaraga) and devotion to the Vitaragi Jina with the view to get inspiration and guidance from him for achieving purified stage of mind and soul. In the eye of Jainism, the Paramatman or Vitaragi God cannot be an instrument for construction, destruction and protection of the universe.

Every morning the lay aspirant is expected after taking bath and donning the clean dress to pay homage to the Jina to temple for his Darsana and devotion. He usually takes with him the few grains of rice or coconut, etc. by way of token offering. On entering temple, he recites Nisei, Panca namokaramanta and some verses from scripture in praise of the Jina.

There are some other rituals also to be observed by the householder, which are known as Siddhacakra Vidhana, Indradhvaja and other

Vidhanas, Jinabimbapratistha, Pancakalyanaka Mahotsava, Vedipratistha, Mahavira Jayanti, Rsabhadeva Jayanti, Dipavali, Raksabandhana, Samadhimarana, etc. which are celebrated with the great zeal.

There are some Samskaras or ceremonies, which cover the entire life of a person from conception to Nirvana. But these rites do not include the offering of the funeral cake (Mratyubhoja) and propitiation (Tarpana) to the spirit of the departed. Likewise, to take the bath in the sacred water of the Ganga is not treated as the merit or Punya.

There is also an importance given to the Mantras in Jainism. But these Mantras are prescribed only for spiritual attainment and not for worldly affairs. Jainism does not believe in violent sacrifices. It also does not worship to such Gods and Goddesses who are violent. Om, Sri, Svastika, Triratna, Mangala Kalasa, etc. are the important mystic symbols and signs, which are used at the auspicious times. Fasting is also a sort of rite and ritual. It is of two types: 1) Itvarika - to give up food for the specified period up to six months, and 2) Yavatkathika- fasting till death. It is called Santhara or Smadhimarana or Sallekhana, which has already been discussed earlier. The second fast is Unodary, which means to eat less than usually required. Rasaparityaga (abstinence from delicacies), Bhiksacarita (to take alms through begging with its code of conduct), Kayaklesa (enduring physical hardships) are other types of penances prescribed for householders and mendicants.

Spiritual pilgrimage to places is also associated with the rites. It is the pious longing which one tries to accomplish in the span of life. It is called Tirthayatra. There are numerous places of Jain pilgrimage throughout India. Vaisali, Rajagrah, Varanasi, Ayodhya, Sravasti, Kausambi, Prayag, Sammeda Sikhara, Pavapur, Girinar, Nakodha, Satrunjaya, Resandigiri, Dronagiri, Ahicchatra, Kesariya, Kunthalagiri, Kakandi, Bhadravati, Campapur, Kampilya, Hastinapur, Mathura, Sauripur, Kundalapur, Gunava, Udayagiri, - Khandagiri, Sonagiri, and so on. There are so many Atisayaksetras, Siddhaksetras, kalaksetras and Sastrabhandaras for taking the pilgrimage.

Despite the attitude of peaceful coexistence, Jainism could not have continued its existence without struggle. Right from seventh to thirteenth century and onwards, the Jain community had to face so many violent opposition from Brahminic and Muslim societies. They destructed their thousands of temples and converted them into Hindu temples and mosques. Likewise, the rich Shastrabhandaras were also perished and reduced to ashes. For instance, the mosque *Adhai dina ka jhopada* of Ajmer and the *Kutub Minar* of Delhi were originally Jain temples, which were converted into Mosques by Muslims. Likewise, the Saiva Lingayatas and Alavarapanthis committed mass killing of Jain community in South and converted Jain temples into Saiva temples. However, Jainism could survive through its non-violent approach, moral and spiritual attitude and compromising policy with Hindu society. The internal reform movements in Jain community, though not much like Buddhism, have also assisted in keeping cohesive atmosphere in the societies.

Spread of Jainism

Jainism had already been established as an important religion in various provinces of India before Mahavira and the Buddha began their missionary activities. During their period, Magadha, Kausala, Kapilavastu, Vaisali, Pava, Mithila, Varanasi, Simhabhumi, Kausambi, Avanti, etc. were prominent Jain Centres. After Mahavira's Parinirvana, the Sisunagas, Nandas, Kharavela, Mauryas, Satavahanas, Guptas, Paramaras, Candelas, Kalacuris, and others, who provided all possible facilities to develop its literature and cultural activities patronised Jainism. The Southern part of India was also a great centre of Jainism.

Bhadrabahu and Visakhacarya with their disciples migrated to the South and propagated Jainism very much. Andhra, Satavahanas, Pallavas, Pandyas, Colas, Calukyas, Rastrakutas, Gangas, and others were main dynasties, which rendered sufficient royal patronage and benefits to Jainism and its followers through the spirit of religious toleration, which existed in this region. The Jainas were given magnificent grants for their spiritual purpose. Kings erected numerous Jain temples and sculptures throughout the ages and many facilities were provided for literary services throughout India. As a result the Jana Acaryas wrote their ample works in Sanskrit, Prakrit, Apabhramsa, Tamil, Kannada, Telagu, Marathi, Hindi, Gujrati and other modern Indian languages.

Jainism crossed India from South India at about eighth century BC, if not earlier, and become one of the most important religions of Ceylon, which was known in those days by the name of Lanka, Ratnadvipa or Simhala. The Mahavamsa (10.65-70; 33. 43-79) refers to the existence of Jainism in Ceylon even before the arrival of Buddhism. According to it, Pandukabhaya built a house at Anuradhapur for the Nigantha Jotiya and Giri and some more Niganthas, Jain tradition takes the history of Jainism in Ceylon even prior to its Aryanisation, or the Arrival of the Aryans. Ravana, a King of Lanka long ago is said to have erected a Jain temple there at Trikutagiri. Another statue of Parsvanatha, the 23rd Jina found in the caves of Terapur is also said to be from Srilanka. Jainism was a living religion of Srilanka up to the 10th AD.

Kalakacarya, another Jain monk, is said to have visited Burma or Svarnabhumi (Uttaradhyayana Niryukti, 120). Rsabhadeva is said to have traveled to Bali (Bacteria), Greece, Svarnabhumi, Panhave (Iran), etc. (Avasyaka Niryukti, 336-37). Tirthankara Parsvnatha also went to Nepal. The existence of Jainism can also be proved in Afghanistan. Tirthankara images in the Kayotsarga, or meditating pose have been found in Vahakaraj Emir (Afghanistan). Digambara Jain monks have been in Iran, Siam, and Philistia. Greek writers also mention their existence in Egypt, Abyssinia and Ethyopia. It had also propagated in Kabul, Campa, Bulgaria and some other foreign countries.

Jains as a Community

In light of modern definitions and speculations, the Jain society may be termed as "Jain Community" which states a particular form of social life, its cultural and ethnic ideas and values. It is originally based on the Jain principle of equality and equanimity, which stresses on the social and spiritual individual, and rejects the idea of God as mediator, and replaces it with the theory of Karma. It stresses on individual purification, which leads the society in peace and order. It regulates not only the present life, but also the future. Unlike the Vedic religion, the Jain Scriptures set forth the responsibility of one's deeds for deciding his caste. Jainism does not hold caste as a way of people being judged. In other words, caste cannot be decided by birth but it is one's own action or conduct, which decides the caste. It is said that by simply shaving the head, one cannot be a Muni (monk) and by only adhering to Kasayacivar (saffron clothing) one cannot claim to be a Tapasvi, a person who resides in a jungle cannot be called a Sramana. As a matter of fact, they should possess the attributes like Samata (equality and equanimity), Brahmacarya (celibacy), Jnana (knowledge), Tapa (penance) and Caritra (conduct) with the right attitude. This was the Varna system developed on the Rsabhadeva and his son Bharata legend. They have their own system for marriage and other celebrations.

The great devotional movement made an intensive impact on Jain society and made it changed to the great extent. The great Heros Rama, Krsna, Pandavas and others are accepted by Jainas as Salaka Mahapurusas and composed a large quantity of literature on their life and works. Jain Community in its historical and social perspective is a quite distinct, independent and new society with its Congregationalist nature. It has never abandoned the original spirit of Jainism. Therefore, the Jain community cannot be said to be the part of the Vedic or Hindu community, though it carries deep impact of it in the code of conduct of householders in the later period. Like-wise, in spite of occupying a large portion of business and industry it would not be a true speculation of the Jain community to be recognised only as the business community.

Numerically, Jainas form a very small segment of the Indian population. Approximately, 3.19 million followers, or may be a little more near about 12 millions according to the calculation of Jain society, of this religion account for 0.48 per cent of the total population as of 1981 census and thus ranked the sixth largest religious group. However, Jainas are spread over all parts of India and have contributed a lot in spite of being a small community in the economic, political, cultural, social, and literal, art, architecture and spiritual fields. They also never indulged in vicious and revengeful activities. Therefore the Jain community has its own distinctive place in the religious and human society.

Status of Women

As regards the status of women in the Jain community, we will have to go back to the period of Mahavira who made then a crucial revolt against the existing tradition and extended his solid support to uplift this very important but most neglected organ of the family where they became least powerful and most disregarded and controlled bitterly by men in each and every sphere. Considering all these nefarious practices and alimentative attitude of men towards women, Mahavira stood against these pernicious social elements and freed them from indignation for their own progress in all walks of life. Some reservations had, of course to be observed due to the slight physical incapability of women. Hence, some special rules were prescribed for nuns. Though they used to be heads of their units as Pravartini and Ganavacchedini, similar to Acarya and Upadhyaya, they were entirely responsible to the Acaryas. Candana, Puspacula, Subrata, and other well-known nuns of long ago, are referred to in this context. Even the, the patriarchal form of the society was developed and nuns were treated as slightly inferior to monks in certain respects. This however, does not hold women as anything less than human beings who, like all souls, have the right and capability to attain salvation.

Art and Architecture

The Jainas have been amongst the foremost in contributing to the field of art and architecture since early days. The images of Tirthankara Risabhadeva and the figures of standing or sealed nude Yogins found inscribed on some terracotta seats, relics of the pre-historic Indus Valley Civilisation, discovered at Mohenjodaro, as well as nude Harrappan red stone statue are almost equally old. The latter is remarkably akin to the polished stone torso of a Jana image from Lohanipur (Patna), which is ascribed to the Mauryan times (4th c. BC) King Kharavel of Kalinga, as the Hathigumpha inscriptions speaks, reinstalled the Jain image which had been taken away by Nanda to Magadha in (4th c. BC) During the Satavahana period (60 BC to 225 AD) Mathura and Saurastra were the main centres. The earliest Mathura sculpture represented by Kankalitila where from Ayagaptta, Stupa, images, and other Jain cultural material are recovered. Gandhara art and Mathura art belong to Kusana period (First BC to 2nd AD) in which Jainism flourished to Mathura and the Ardhaphalaka sect, Yapaniya Sangha and Nagara art came into existence.

Gupta period (4th to 7th C.A.D.) is said to be the golden period of ancient Indian Culture. Harigupta, Siddhasena, Harisena, Ravikirti, Pujyapada, Patrakesari, Udyotanasuri and other Jainacaryas have been in existence during the period. Karnataka, Mathura, Hastinapur, Saurastra, Avanti, Ahicchatra, Bhinnamala, Kausambi, Devagumpha, Vidisa, Sravasti, Varanasi, Vaisali, Pataliputra, Rajagraha, Campa, etc. were the main Jain centres of art and architecture. After the Gupta period, Kakkula, Vatsaraja, and Mahendrapala were the Jain Kings in the Pratihara dynasty. King Mona, Navasahasanka and Bhoja were followers of Jainism. Dhanapala, Amitagati, Manikyanandi, Prabhacandra, Asadhara, Dhananjaya, etc. had contributed to the literary field during the same period. Chittod was the capital of Paramaras where Kalakacarya and Haribhadra devoted their lives for he development of Jain art and architecture. During Candela dynasty, Khajuraho, Devagadh, Mahoba, Madanapur, Canderi, Ahar, Papora, and Gwaliar became famous for their Jain art. Some important inscriptions, Toranas, images and other sculptural material are found in Tripuri.

As mentioned earlier, Bihar has been a prominent state since very early days with regard to Jain culture. It is the Parinirvanabhumi of so many Tirthankaras and is enriched through Jain statues, relics, sculpture, etc. at Radiograph, Melinda, Parsvanatha hill, Simbhabhumi, Barabar hill, Patna, Pavapuri, etc. The earliest Jain images are recovered in Bengal from Surohar and Mandoil of Mathura style. The images of Jain Tirthankaras found in Udisa at Udaigiri-Khandagiri, and some other places such as Keonjhar, Mayurabhanja, Jaipur, Cuttack are very beautiful from artistic point or view.

Gujarat and Rajasthan have been strongholds of Jainism since an early time. Satrunjaya, Girinar, are Siddhaksetras of Jainism. Rastrakutas and Calukyas, Pratiharas, Paramaras, Cauhan and other dynasties patronised Jainism and its art and architecture. Hemacandracarya was a court poet of Jayasimha and Kumarapala. Vastupala and Tejapala who were ministers of Baghelas of Solanki branch built a large number of Jain temples at Girinar, Abu, Satrunjaya, etc. They are also found in large number at Ranakapur, Udaipur, Sirohi, Jaisalmer, Jodhpur, Jaipur, Alwar and so many places. The existence of Jainism in Punjab and Sindh can traced out long before the Christian era, from the sites of Mohanjodaro, Harappa, Taksasila, Simhapur, Sindhudesh, Lahore, etc.

The inscriptional history of Jainism in Maharashtra starts with the Parle inscription of first c. AD that commences with "Namo Arihantanam". Keljher, Pavanar, Nagpur, Bhandara, Remtek, Akola, Karanja, Achalpur, Latur, Bhadravati, etc. are main Jain ancient sites with archaeological remains. Sirpur is famous for its artistic decoration. Malakhed was found inhabitant when Padaliptacarya visited in about 1st c. AD, Jain caves are found at Ellora, Nasik, Dhaṙasiva, (Osmanabad), etc. Pratishthanpur, Belgaon, Kolhapur, Ehol, Alaktakanagara, Kunthalgiri, Ardhapur, Kandhar Karanataka (Karad), Mahimagiri, Vatapi, Meghuni, etc. have been main centres of Jainism where huge and magnificent Jain temples idols and inscriptions are found. Mrgesavarvarman's in inscription (450-478 AD) states that a huge donation was made to Digambaras, Svetambaras, Kurcakas and Yapaniyas. Belagaon and Kolhapur were also ruled over by Silaharas of Konkana who built their huge Jain temples like Adataraditya, Satyavakya, Candraprabha, Ratta, etc. Vatapi, Ehol, Meguli were also Jain centres of this period when Pulakesi First, Kirtivarman, and Ravikirti constructed Jain temples.

Andhra Pradesa has been a stronghold centre of Jainism. Acarya Kundakunda (1st c. AD), the spiritual leader of the time hails from Kondakunda situated on the boarder of Andhrapradesha. King Vishnuvardhan of Calukyas, Akalavarsa, Amoghavarsa, and Krashnaraja of Rashtrakutas, Bhima, Ganga Vijayaditya, Durgaraj, etc. of Vengis, Tailapa, Vikramaditya of Badami Calukyas, some Kings of Velanatichoda period patronised Jainism by way of constructing temples, Vasadis and Vidyapeethas. Some of them, afterwards, were occupied by Virasaivaitas and Lingayatas, who have been great destructors of Jain monuments and the community as well. Jainism in Karnataka goes back at least to Bhadrabahu and Candragupta Maurya who migrated to South India via Ujjain with twelve thousand disciples due to severe calamity and famine into he North. Simhanandin, the Jainacarya, established Gangavadi dynasty. Jainism was its state religion for about seven hundred years during which hundreds of Jain monuments were erected by the Kings. Pujyapada, Prabhacandra, Jinasena, Gunanandi, Patrakesari, Puspadanta, Vidyanada, Anantavirya, Joindu, etc. get the patronage of the dynasty. Of the Kings the name of Racamalla Satyavakya may be specially mentioned under whose reign Camundaraya, his great minister erected the colossal statue of Gomatesvara Bahubali, the unparallel statue in the world. After Rashtrakutas Jainism got set back. One Vasava murdered his master Vijjala, the Kalacuri Jain King and perished Jainism and its adherents. He established an independent sect named Lingayata and persecuted the Jainas. From Jain archaeological standpoint, the main sites are Mangal, Nandidurga, panditarahalli, Candrasala vasadi, Aarapur, Arkettar, Sarangipattam, Halebid, Kelasaur, Aihole, Marol, Honwad, Honnur, Kalholi, Mulguna, Lakkundi, Nagire, Billigi are the main places where the Jain monuments are richly available.

Jainism entered in Tamilnadu most probably from Kalinga in about 4th c. BC Visakhacarya proceeds to Cola and Pandya countries with the entire Munisangha. It can be supported by the caverns containing beds carved out in the rock found in hills and mountains around the Pudukottai, Madura and Tinnevelly and rock-cut sculptures and inscriptions in the hills of the north Arcot district which indicate the existence of Jainism in Tamil Nadu in 3rd c. BC Kanci was one of the important seat of learning in South India. It was the capital of Pallvas who were mostly Jainas in early centuries. The inscriptions of Jinakanchi refers to some prominent Jainacaryas of the city like Kundakunda, Samantabhadra, Jinacandra, Pujyapada, Akalanka, Anantavirya, Bhavanand, mallisena, etc. The North and South Arcot region is very rich from Jain archaeological standpoint. Pancapandava, Trirumalai, Vallimalai, Vidal, Villipuram, Chinglaput may be specially mentioned. Sittanavasal, Narttamalai, Tenimalai, Bommamalai, Malamala, Samanar Kudagu, etc. have been the Jain centres since last two thousand years. Most of these places have paintings, and sculptures of Sittanavasala tradition, which may be compared with Ajanta and Sigirya. Some of the rock-cut temples like Samanar Kudagu have been converted into Visnu temples.

Madura was the capital of Pandyas who took their favourable attitude towards Jainism. Its neighbouring hills Annaimalai,

Nagamalai, Alagarmalai, Muttupatti, Eruvadi, etc. are very rich from Jain sculptural and painting standpoint. It is a land of origin of Samgama literature. Tirukurala, Tolkappiyam, Naladiyara, Cintamani, Silakppadikaram, Nilakesi, Manimekhalai, Kurala, etc. are the Jain epics of early period. Pujyapada, Vajranandi, Aryanandi, Patrakesari, etc. were the prominent Jainacaryas of the period. Afterwards Jainism was patronised by the Kadamba Kings. In Tinnevelly region the Kalugumallai, Tiruchcharanattumalai, Nagarajaswami temple belonged to Jainas but they are under the control of Vedicas.

Thus the survey of Jainism in South India gives and apparent picture of its position that it was there popular during the period of Tirthankara Mahavira or even earlier to him. The popularity augmented gradually and Digambara sect became the prominent one. During about 11th c. AD, Vaisnavism, Alawara and Lingayatas came into existence and stood against Jainism that caused a serious blow to its propagation. The devotees of Sambandara, Tirunavukkarasata, Appara, Mukkanti, Tirumalasai, Tirumangai Vira-Saivas committed heavy atrocities on Jain society, temples, sculptures and Vasadis. Their massacres took place and the Jain centres were converted into Saiva or Vaisnava temples. Some places like Pillaiyarapatti and Kunnakkundi, Arittayatti, Nartamallai, and Kulugamalai, Tiruccirapalli, Virasikhamani, Kudumiyamalai, Dalavaura, Siyamangalam and Mamamdura can be cited in this respect. All this can be evaluated as follows.

Jain images, Ayagapttas, Stambhas, Toranas, Vedicas, etc. were excavatd from Kankalitila in Mathura belonging to Kusana period. The Stupa made of bricks is called Devanirmita Stupa. The symbols are not traceable on these images, the Sarvatobhadra Pratimas. The names of Kaniska, Ruviska and Vasudeva are inscribed on these images. The unique Jain image of Sarasvati may also be mentioned in this context. The Chausa bronzes, in some Jain images in Lucknow and Patana museums, the Jain remains at Vaibhara hill Rajagiri and the bronzes of the Akota hoard are also belonging to this period. Some auspicious symbols like Phana, Srivats, a Purnaganata, Svastika, Vardhmanaka, Matsya, Nandyavarta, etc. are also inscribed on one of the Parsva images. The image of Jivantasvami may also be referred to the period. Then the crystallised forms of the iconography were transferred to rocks on hills like Vaibhara hill, Udaigiri hills in Sanchi and Udaigiri, Kalagumalai in South. Afterwards, the iconography became fixed.

In other words it can be said that the Jain iconography was developed during the Gupta period in 4th century AD Decoration on Padpitha, Dharmacakera, Paramesthis, Gandharva Yugala, Navagrahs, Triratnas, Bhamandala, and Astapratiharys were included as the symbols of Jain images. However, all the symbols could not be decided in the early Gupta period. The images of the period can be viewed in Mathura museum, Vesanagar, Budhicanderi, Deogarha, Rajagiri, Kumarahara, Vaisali and other places. Some more images of the Gupta period are found in Udaigiri, Vesanagara, Nacana (Patana), etc. with somewhat more decorated forms. Some of the bronzes of the Akota hoara, particularly the image of Jivantasvami in Kayotsarga pose bearing a crown, Bhujabandha, Kundala, Kangana, and the image of Ambika decorated with ornaments and Yaksa-Yaksis are the representative images of the period. Sasanadevatas, Drum-player, a pair of elephants, etc. were also included in the symbols.

In late Gupta period these symbols were more developed and in about 8th-9th c. AD all the symbols, Yaksa-Yaksis, Sasnadevidevatas, were fixed. Afterwards, Ksetrapalas, Dikpalas, Navgrahas, and Vidyadharas were also placed around the Jana images. Tantrism entered into Jain iconography in about tenth century AD and as a result, the Yaksa-Yaksis, etc. got their due place on the pedestal or around the Jain images with more decorative sculptural surroundings. Sandy stone is widely used in about twelfth century along with black and white marble. The bronze images are also popularly available of the period. In the fourteenth century the development of Jain iconography stagnated and the decline started. This can be understood through perspective of iconographical peculiarities of Tirthankaras and their associates.

Temple art is of three types, Nagara, Vesara and Dravid. In Niagara style, the Garvagraha is quadrangular and its summit (Sikhara) is circular with Kalasa. It is used in Punjab, Himalaya, Rajasthan, Madhyapradesa, Udisa and Bengal. The Sikhara becomes flat in Vesar style, which is found in Madhyabharat, and the temple gets the form of pillar in Dravidian style. The earliest Jain temple is found at Lohanipur (Patna) of Maurya period. Then the temple art is available from the seventh century onwards. Painting has also been one of the best methods for expressing the ideas.

Jainism and Science

Jainism is perhaps one of the most scientific religions in the world and therefore it is still relivant to the society and the world. I do not find any contradiction between Jainism and science. It throws ample light on the real nature of substance or matter as propounded by Jain thinkers. Jain metaphysics approves of the scientific axiom that nothing is destructible. That means nothing can be created out of nothing, or out of something, which does not at all exist in one form or the other. The Jain doctrine is pertinent when it advocates that the universe is uncreated, real, eternal, and infinite with no beginning and end. The modern science has confirmed that this universe has automatic working process and the matter is never destroyed; it only undergoes changes into different states or modes. This is the law of nature.

The Jain thinkers expressed their views that plants and vegetables, earth, water, fire and air have souls and are endowed with only one sense organ of touch. Sir Jagdish Chand Basu had clearly proved in early 19th century in "Private life of Plant" through his scientific experiments beyond doubt that plants and all green vegetation also have life like human beings, and also experience feelings of joy, sorrow, anger, and fear like us. Webster and other scientists have already supported this view. Later on, Basu also proved the view of Jainism that there is life and growth in stones, which is also approved by scientists. The Sammurchana Jivas of Jainism are called abiogenists in science.

The Jain doctrine of Karma is fully substantiated by the obvious disparities among living creatures. This doctrine makes the transmigration of souls a proven fact, and establishes their continuity and immortality. The Karma doctrine of Jainism also does away with the necessity of any outside agency, an invisible all pervading, omnipotent and omniscient supreme being, creator, destroyer, preserver and dispenser of justice, for the purpose of punishing or rewarding living beings. Scientists also feel no need of any unknown hand to interfere with the automatic working of the universe.

The world-renowned great scientist Einstein in his work "The Theory of Relativity" has already supported the Anekantavada theory of Jainism. Scientists also support the theory of Lokakasa and Alokakasa of Jainism. Likewise, scientists on the basis of sound implements like gramophone, Radio and T.V. Casettes etc, prove its theory of sound or word as concrete. Like the Jainism, the European mathematicians Cantor Piano and Frege have accepted the reality of space and time.

Modern scientists had to assume an invisible element called "Ether" as the medium to transmit sounds and words across thousands of miles. This is the theory of Dharma and Adharma in Jainism, which has been propounded by Jain thinkers long ago.

The most remarkable contribution of Jainism relates to their analysis of atomic linking or the mutual attraction of atoms in the formation of molecules.

The principle of vegetarian diet (Sakahara) and vegetables and food habits is also totally supported by medical doctors. Jainism ordains its followers to drink water after proper distillation with the view to avoid the killing of germs of water. Through microscopes scientists have found innumerous tiny germs invisible to the naked eye moving to and fro in water. Jainism lays stress on taking meals before sunset in defence of the vow of non-violence. The modern science also tells that after sunset many tiny living beings come into existence in the atmosphere. These beings enter our food and drinks, and thereby enter our digestive systems. The physicians and Ayurvedic literature also supported Jain's viewpoint on day dining.

Likewise, the principles of psychology, sociology, anthropology, biology, chemistry, mathematics and other branches of science may also be supported by Jain theories.

13

Golden Words of Mahavira

- Non-violence is the highest religion.
- Respect for all living beings is non-violence.
- Have compassion towards all living beings. Hatred leads destruction.
- The greatest mistake of a soul is non-recognition of its real self and can only be corrected by recognising itself.
- Silence and Self-control is non-violence.
- Every soul is independent. None depends on another
- There is no separate existence of God. Everybody can attain God-hood by making supreme efforts in the right direction.
- Every soul is in itself absolutely omniscient and blissful. The bliss does not come from outside.
- All human beings are miserable due to their own faults, and they themselves can be happy by correcting these faults.
- A man is seated on top of a tree in the midst of a burning forest. He sees all living beings perish. But he doesn't realise that the same fate is soon to overtake him also. That man is fool.

- Fight with yourself, why fight with external foes? He, who conquers himself through himself, will obtain happiness.
- There is no enemy out of your soul. The real enemies live inside you; they are anger, proud, greed, attachments and hate.
- "Can you hold a red-hot iron rod in your hand merely because some one wants you to do so?" "Then, will it be right on your part to ask others to do the same thing just to satisfy your desire? If you cannot tolerate infliction of pain on your body or mind by others' words and actions, what right have you to do the same to others through your words and deeds?" "Do unto others as you would like to be done by".
- There is no separate existence of God. Everybody can attain God-hood by making supreme efforts in the right direction.
- Know thyself, recognise thyself, be immersed by thyself - you will attain God-hood.
- God is neither the creator nor the destroyer of the universe. He is merely a silent observer and omniscient.
- One who, even after knowing the whole universe, can remain unaffected and unattached is God.
- Every soul is independent. None depends on another.
- Fight with yourself, why fight with external foes? He, who conquers himself through himself, will obtain happiness.
- A man is seated on top of a tree in the midst of a burning forest. He sees all living beings perish. But he doesn't realise that the same fate is soon to overtake him also. That man is fool.
- Live and let live. Love all - Serve all.
- Where there is Love there is Life. Violence is Suicide.
- All living beings long to live. No one wants to die.

- Have compassion towards all living beings. Hatred leads destruction.
- Silence and Self-control is non-violence.
- Just I dislike pain, so all other beings dislike pain.
- A wise person does not kill, nor cause others to kill, nor consent to the killings by others.
- Respect for all living beings is non-violence.
- Non-violence is the highest religion.
- All human beings are miserable because of their own ignorance, and they themselves can be happy by acquiring proper knowledge.
- The greatest mistake of a soul is non-recognition of its real self and can only be corrected by recognising itself.
- Every soul is in itself absolutely omniscient and blissful. The bliss does not come from outside.
- All Souls are alike and potentially divine. None is Superior or Inferior.

14

Great Life at a Glance

599 BC: Lord Mahavira, who was born at Kshatriyakund near modern Patna in Bihar in *599 BC*. According to the Gregorian calendar, the Mahavir Jayanti festival falls during the period between March and April. As a part of Mahavir Jayanthi celebrations, the Jain temples are beautifully adorned with flags.

569 BC: Mahavira renowned the world.

527 BC: Bhagavan Mahavira attained nirvan in *527 BC* He had eleven ganadharas (disciples). Nine ganadharas attained liberation (salvation) during the lifetime of *Lord Mahavira*, while another two Gautamswami and Sudharmaswämi survived him. Gautamswämi attained perfect knowledge and perfect perception and became Arihant the very night of Bhagwan Mahavira's nirvän. The remaining ganadhar, Sudharmaswami, was the next to attain perfect knowledge and perfect perception and became Arihant ...

526 BC: Mahavira took his last breath.

500 BC: Mahavira's cremation was done.

Appendix

The Holy books of the Jainas abound in examples of great, heroic souls; but there are twenty-four stars shining above all, who go by the name of the Tirthankaras or the Arhatas; and in this book an attempt is made to familiarise the reader with an account of the worldly career of Lord Mahavira, the last of them. The noble appellation, Arhat, is applied to a soul, who has a perfect knowledge of all things, who has conquered the worldly passions; who is worshipped by all; who has preached the truth; and who is himself the Supreme Being in his perfect state. Vardhamana or Mahavira, as he was commonly known, was the last or the twenty-fourth of these Arhatas.

For a long time Mahavira was looked upon as a sort of mythical personage, brought into sacred existence by the imagination of some seceders from or opponents of Buddhist faith on the analogy of its well-known founder, Gautama, until 1884, when that German scholar of wide views and cautious judgement, Professor Hermann Jacobi, after removing the accumulated froth of myths and miracles, and sceptic misrepresentation of the Jaina Granthas with which the early life of Mahavira was covered and which had led M. Barth to call into question the intrinsic value of his tradition, came to the conclusion that ' enough is known of him to invalidate the suspicion that he is a sort of mystical person, invented or set up by a younger sect some centuries after the pretended age of their assumed founder'.

During the last many decades much more is known about him; and a careful study of the Pali and the Prakrit works of the

Jainas and the Buddhist writers has established the historicity of Mahavira as an universal truth. What chiefly led the scholars to suspect his historicity for so long a time were the different names by which he is known in different works. Thus in Digambara Shastras, besides Mahavira, he is also called Vardhamana, Vira, Sanmati, and Ativira. In Shvetambara Jaina works like the Kalpasutra, the Acharanga-sutra, the Uttaradhyayana, the Sutra-Kratanga, and other works, he is spoken of as a Gnatriputra. They further tell us that he was called Vardhamana, because from the moment the boy had been begotten, the silver and gold, the intensity of liberality and the popularity of his parents had increased.' "Nor are we by any means," says Professor Jacobi, "forced to rely on the tradition of the Jainas only, since for some particulars we have the testimony of the Buddhists also in whose writings Mahavira is mentioned under his well-known name Nataputta, as the head of the Niganthas or Jaina monks, and a rival of Buddha".

There is no difference between Nataputta and Gnatriputra by which the Shvetambara Shastras call him except that the former comes from Prakrit and the latter from Sanskrit. He was so called because he belonged to that clan of the Kshatriyas who were known as the Gnatrikas. In Buddhist works these Gnatrikas are known as the Natikas.

Thus we see that he is sometimes named after his country, sometimes after his Gotra, sometimes after his birth place, and sometimes after his meritorious qualities. It was this variety of names which led to the confusion, but it has been now removed and Mahavira has been recognised as a historical religious and spiritual hero who lived and preached in tie sixth century BC.

Stories behind Mahavira

It has been stated repeatedly that the greater part of the life of Mahavira as described in the Jaina Granthas is imbued with myths which mar the real value of these works. Some of these myths are rather curious, and a few of them are given below as typical of the rest.

The first of them relates to his previous births. The Mahavira Purana gives a long and a cumbrous list of his innumerable previous births with a detailed description of some of them. The value of this description is incomprehensible unless it be only to illustrate the Karma philosophy of the Tainas, or it only shows the bitter hatred of Jaina writers towards Brahmins. He is said to have existed even before Swami Adinath. He had the fortune of being the son of Bharata Chakravarti and grandson of Swami Adinath. This made him proud.

Through pride he began to preach and consequently had to undergo several existences. This myth shows how one is rewarded for the good or the bad acts of his previous births. It may be only to this end that this myth has been connected with the life of so great a personage as Mahavira. The Kalpasutra on the other hand, says nothing about this. It only asserts that Mahavira, leaving his long and happy divine life, only for the good of the world and the attainment of Nirvana, came to this world as a Tirthankara, descending from the great Vimana, the all-victorious and all-prosperous Pushpottara, to take the form of an embryo in the womb of his mother. Both the above quoted Granthas state the date of his entering the womb of his mother as the sixth day of the latter half of Ashadha.

The second myth of the transfer of embryo is also connected with this. It runs thus both in the Acharanga-sutra and the Kalpasutra. "Here, forsooth, in the continent of Jambudvipa, in Bharatvarsha, in the southern part of it, in the southern Brahminical part of the place Kundapura, he took the form of an embryo in the womb of Devananda, of the Jalandharayana Gotra, wife of the Brahmin Rishabhadatta, of the Grotra of Kodala

"Then in the third month of the rainy season, the fifth fortnight, the dark (fortnight) of Ashwin, on its thirteenth day, while the moon was in conjunction with Uttaraphalguni, after the lapse of eighty-two days, on the eighty-third day current, the compassionate god (Indra) reflecting on what was the established custom (with regard to the birth of the Tirthankaras), removed the embryo from the southern Brahminical part of the place Kundapura to the northern Kshatriya part of the same place, rejecting the unclean matter, lodged the foetus in the womb of Trisala of the Vasishtha Golra, wife of the Kshatriya Sidhartha, of the Kashyapa gotra, of the clan of Gnatris, and lodged the foetus of the Elshatriyani Trisala in the womb of Devananda, of the Jalandharay ana gotra.

Now it is certain that this legend is the invention of the author of the Kalpasutra, but the assumption made by Jacobi to give an explanation of it does not seem to be founded upon sound reason. To assume that Siddhartha had two wives, a Brahmini and a Kshatriyani, and to say that Mahavira was the son of the former is itself incorrect; for a Brahmin girl was not allowed to marry a Kshatriya Jaina. If it had been so, the Jaina law-givers, who have so closely followed the carrier of Mahavira in giving social laws, would not have prohibited intermarriage between a Brahmin girl and a Kshatriya boy. On the other hand, Mahavira Purana clearly says that Mahavira was the son of Trisala.

One may attribute the invention of the legend to the bitter hatred of the Brahminas by the Jainas of those times and to the preference that the Kshatriyas were given over the Brahminas by the Jaina Acharyas. We have the testimony of a tradition also. It runs thus:

> "Bhadrabahu", the author of the Kalpasutras, and his brother Varahamihira, the author of Brihat-samhita, were living together in the court of the King Dhruvasena of Gujrat. Both of them were great astrologers. On the birth of a child the King consulted Varahamihira as to the age of the child, and on learning from him that it would live for a long time, he held a Darbar in order to celebrate the birth of his child. On seeing that Bhadrabahu was not present in the assembly of his courtiers, he called him and asked to explain the cause of his absence. Bhadrabahu told that he did not like to rejoice for he shall soon have to lament the death of the child after ten days. The King, being very much annoyed with this unexpected reply, sent him to jail, but after ten days the King lost his child, and admiring the foresight of Bhadrabahu, not only liberated him, but gave him a seat near his throne, and turned out Varahamihira".

How far this tradition is true cannot be said, but it shows that Bhadrabaliu and Varahamihira were not on good terms and one hated the religion of the other. Now can it not be that Bhadrabahu, out of his hatred for the Brahminas, might have invented this story of the transfer of embryos?

Whatever it may be, it can be safely asserted on the authority of Mahavira Purana that Mahavira was the son of Trisala and not of Devananda as Professor Jacobi has assumed. As to his assumption that the story was borrowed from the Puranic story of the transfer of the embryos of Krishna from the womb of Devaki to that of Rohini, it cannot be said whether it were the Jainas or the Brahminas who borrowed it from the other.

Another myth is that of the sixteen dreams. It is stated that the mother of Mahavira like those of every Tirthankara saw sixteen dreams on the night on which Mahavira is believed to have entered the womb of his mother. These dreams were: —

- A fine, enormous elephant, possessing all lucky marks, with strong thighs and four mighty tusks. This was supposed to foretell the birth of a Tirthankara.
- A tame, lucky bull, of a whiter hue than that of the mass of petals of the white lotus illumining all around by the diffusion of a glory of light. This was supposed to foretell the birth of a great religious preacher.
- A handsome, handsomely shaped, playful lion, jumping from the sky towards her face. This was supposed to foretell the birth of a child who will be a destroyer of his karmaa (the enemies) and a possessor of limitless Veerya.
- Shree, or Lakshmi, the goddess of wealth, of famous beauty, with the face of the full moon, on the top of Mount Himavati, reposing on a lotus in the lotus-lake, anointed with the water from the strong and large trunks of the guardian elephants. This was believed to indicate that the child will be an anointed King.
- A garland charmingly interwoven with fresh Mandara flowers coming down from the firmament. This meant that the body of the child will be a fragrant one.
- The bright sun radiating his golden rays in all directions and shedding his lustre all round Mount Meru. This indicated that the child will be a dispeller of the mass of darkness which is the symbol of ignorance.

- The cow-milk-white full moon, the lover of Rohini, rising in the heavens and raising the waters of the ocean below. This portended the birth of a great religious preacher.
- Two fishes, which meant that the child will be a happy one.
- Two golden and costly vases, filled with pure water and indicating the birth of a child who will be constantly immersed in spiritual meditation.
- A great lotus lake adorned with water lilies round which the black bees and the mad drones were hovering. This was supposed to foretell that the body of the child will possess all the marks of a perfect being.
- The milk-ocean, white like the breast of Lakshmi, indicating that the child will be a Kevalin.
- A costly throne of diamonds and rubies which meant that the child will be a master of the three lokas.
- An excellent celestial abode shining like the disk of the morning sun.
- The great King of the gods residing below this earth.
- An enormous heap of jewels resembling Mount Meru and illuminating even the sphere of the sky. This was supposed to foretell the birth of a child who will be a possessor of right knowledge, right intuition and right conduct.
- A great fire fed with much shining and honey-coloured ghee and in vehement motion.

The Kalpasutra says that a large meeting was convened by the King on this occasion, and learned men were asked to interpret the dreams. But from Mahavira Purana we learn that in the morning the Queen herself came to the council of the King with all her maids. The King affectionately asked her to take her seat near him on the throne; and then he himself interpreted the dreams.

From these mythical descriptions we proceed to real facts in the life of our Lord Mahavira whose ideal and sublime life is to be written, as far as possible, in the life of each individual.

Bibliography

A. C. Mittal: *Economic Aspects of Jainism*, Vista International Publication, 2006.

Acharya, Shri Nagrajji: *Agama and Tripitaka : A Comparative Study of Lord Mahavira and Lord Buddha*, Concept, 2003.

Asim, Kumar Chatterjee: *A Comprehensive History of Jainism*, Munshiram Manoharlal, 2000.

B.R. Verma and S.R. Bakshi: *Hinduism, Buddhism and Jainism in Ancient India*, Commonwealth, 2005.

Babb, Lawrence A.: *Absent Lord: Ascetics and Kings in a Jain Ritual Culture,* University of California Press, Berkeley, 1996.

Banks, Marcus: *Organizing Jainism in India and England,* Clarendon, Oxford, 1992.

Bhargava, D. N.: *In Medieval Jainism: Culture and Environment,* Ashish Publishing House, New Delhi, 1990.

Bhatt, Sonali Marwaha: *Colors of Truth : Religion, Self and Emotions : Perspectives of Hinduism, Buddhism, Jainism, Zoroastrianism, Islam, Sikhism and Contemporary Psychology*, Concept, 2006.

Bool, Chand: *Lord Mahavira*, Banaras, 1948.

Buddhadev, Bhattacharya and Ramaranjan Mukherji: *Dimensions of Buddhism and Jainism*, Sanskrit Book Depot, 2009.

Caillat, Colette: *The Jain Cosmology*, Jaico Publishing House, Bombay, 1981.

Carrithers, Michael and Caroline Humphrey: *The Assembly of Listeners: Jains in Society*, Cambridge University Press, Cambridge, 1991.

Carrithers, Michael and Caroline Humphrey: *The Assembly of Listeners: Jains in Society*, Cambridge University Press, Cambridge, 1991.

Chakrabongse, Chula: *Lords of Life: A History of the Kings of Thailand*, London, 1967.

Chapple, Christopher Key: *Contemporary Jain and Hindu Responses to the Ecological Crisis*, University Press of America, Maryland, 1994.

————: *Jainism and Buddhism*, Blackwell Publishers, Oxford, 2001.

————: *Jainism and Ecology*, Mary Evelyn Tucker and Philip Hefner, Chicago, 2002.

————: *Jainism and Ecology: Nonviolence and the Web of Life*, Harvard Center for the Study of World Religions, Harvard, 2002.

————: *Nonviolence to Animals in Buddhism and Jainism*, State University of New York Press, Albany, 1992.

————: *The Living Cosmos of Jainism: A Traditional Science Grounded in Environmental Ethics*, Blackwell Publishers, Oxford, 2003.

Chimanlal, J. Shah: *Jainism in North India : 800 BC - AD 526*, D. K. Printworld, 2007.

Cort, John E.: *Models of and for the Study of the Jains*, In Method and Theory in the Study of Religion Oxford, 1990.

————: *Jains in the World: Religious Values and Ideology in India*, Oxford University Press, New York, 2001.

————: *Open Boundaries: Jain Communities and Cultures in Indian History*, State University of New York Press, New York, 1998.

Debajani, Mitra Dutta: *A Survey of Jainism and Jaina Art of Eastern India : With Special Emphasis on Bengal from the Earliest Period to the Thirteenth Century A.D.*, R.N. Bhattacharya, 2004.

Dibakar, Mohanty: *Jainism in Indian Philosophy*, Bharatiya Kala Prakashan, 2006.

Dundas, Paul. *In Jain Doctrine and Practice: Academic Perspectives*, Centre for South Asian Studies of the University of Toronto, Toronto, 2000.

Dundas, Paul: *The Jains,* Routledge, New York, 1992.

Dwivedi, O. P.: *World Religions and the Environment*, Gilanjal Publishing House, New Delhi, 1989.

Edward, Thomas: *Jainism or the Early Faith of Asoka : With Illustrations of the Ancient Religions of the East : From the Pantheon of the Indo-Scythians : With a Notice on Bactrian Coins and Indian Dates*, Asian Educational Services, 1995.

Fischer, Eberhard and Jyotindra Jain: *Art and Rituals: 2500 Years of Jainism in India,* Sterling, New Delhi, 1977.

Glasnap, Helmuth von: *The Doctrine of Karma in Jain Philosophy,* Bai Vijibhai Jivanlal Pannalal Charity Fund, Bombay, 1992.

Gopal, S.: *Outlines of Jainism*, New Delhi, 1973.

Haripriya, Rangarajan: *Jainism : Art, Architecture, Literature and Philosophy*, Sharada, 2001.

Hermann, Jacobi: *Jainism : Humanity's Oldest Religion of Non-Violence*, Lotus Press, 2006.

Huntington, Susan L.: *The Arts of Ancient India: Buddhist, Hindu, and Jain*, Weatherhill, New York, 1985.

Jacobsen, Knut A.: *Prakrti in Samkhya-Yoga: Material Principle, Religious Experience, Ethical Implications*, Peter Lang Publishing, New York, 1999.

Jagdish, Prasad Jain: *Fundamentals of Jainism*, Radiant Pub, 2005.

Jagdishchandra, Jain: *Studies in Early Jainism : Selected Research Articles*, Navrang, 1992.

Jain, Duli Chandra: *Studies in Jainism,* Flushing, NewYork, 1990.

Jain, Kailash Chand: *Lord Mahavira and His Times*, Delhi, 1974.

Jain, Prem Suman: *Essentials of Jainism,* Jain Center of Greater Boston, Boston, 1984.

Jaini, Padmanabh S.: *The Jaina Path of Purification*, University of California Press, Berkeley, 1979.

————: *Gender and Salvation: Jaina Debates on the Spiritual Liberation of Women*, University of California Press, Berkeley, Calif.,1991.

————: *The Jaina Path of Purification*, University of California Press, Berkeley, Calif., 1979.

Jussawala, J. M.: *Vegetarianism: A Way of Life, In Medieval Jainism: Culture and Environment*, Ashish Publishing House, New Delhi, 1990.

Jyotindra, J.: *Lessons for Jain Pathshala*, Cypress, California, 1988.

K.L. Chanchreek and Mahesh K. Jain: *Jainism : Rishabha Deva to Mahavira*, Shree Pub, 2003.

K.L. Chanchreek and Mahesh K. Jain: *Jainism and Western Thinkers*, Shree Pub, 2004.

K.V. Mardia: *The Scientific Foundations of Jainism*, Motilal Banarsidass, 2007.

Kumar, Sehdev: *A Thousand-Petalled Lotus: Jain Temples of Rajasthan – Architecture and Iconography*, Indira Gandhi National Centre for the Art and Abhinav, New Delhi, 2001.

Kurt, Titze: *Jainism : A Pictorial Guide to the Religion of Non-Violence*, Motilal Banarsidass, 1998.

Laidlaw, James: *Riches and Renunciation: Religion, Economy and Society among the Jains*, Oxford University Press, Oxford, 1995.

Lishk, S.S.: *Jaina Astronomy (Post-Vedic Indian Astronomy): A Challenge to Western Influences*, Arihant International, Delhi, 2000.

Lodrick, Deryck O.: *Sacred Cows, Sacred Places: Origins and Survivals of Animal Homes in India*, University of California Press, Berkeley, Calif., 1981.

Mardia, K. V.: *The Scientific Foundations of Jainism*, Motilal Banarsidass, Delhi, 1996.

Mrinal Joshi: *Women in Jainism : A Case Study of Gujarat Inscriptions*, Rawat Pub, 2009.

Muni, Shivkumar: *The Doctrine of Liberation in Indian Religion With Special Reference to Jainism*, Munshiram Manoharlal, 2000.

N.N. Bhattacharyya: *Jainism : A Concise Encyclopaedia*, Manohar Pub, 2009.

Nagraj, Muni: *Agama and Tripitaka: A Comparative Study of Lord Mahavira and Lord Buddha*, Today and Tomorrow's Printers and Publishers, New Delhi, 2003.

Naravan, Raideva and Janardan Kumar: *Ecology and Religion: Ecological Concepts in Hinduism, Buddhism, Jainism, Islam, Christianity and Sikhism*, Deep & Deep Publications Pvt. Ltd., New Delhi, 2003.

Natubhai, Shah: *Jainism : The World of Conquerors*, Motilal Banarsidass Pub, 2004.

Norman, K. R.: *The Role of the Layman According to the Jain Canon*, Cambridge University Press, Cambridge, 1991.

P.C. Nahar and K.C. Ghosh: *An Encyclopaedia of Jainism*, Sri Satguru, 1996.

R.K. Pruthi: *Jainism and Indian Civilization*, Discovery, 2004.

Rajdeva, Narayan and Janardan Kumar: *Ecology and Religion : Ecological Concepts in Hinduism, Buddhism, Jainism, Islam, Christianity and Sikhism*, Deep & Deep, 2003.

Rajjan, Kumar: *Different Aspects of Jainism*, Sunrise, 2006.

S. C. Jain: *Introducing Jainism*, B. R. Pub, 2006.

S. K. Ramachandra Rao: *Encyclopaedia of Indian Iconography : Hinduism-Buddhism-Jainism*, Satguru, 2003.

S.P. Chavan: *Jainism in Southern Karnataka (Up to AD 1565)*, D.K. Printworld, 2005.

S.R. Bakshi and Sangh Mittra: *Lord Mahavira : Saints of India*, Criterion Pub, 2002.

Sadhu, Santideva: *Mysticism in Jainism and Buddhism*, Cosmo, 2000.

Samsookha, Puranchand: *Lord Mahavira*, Calcutta, 1957.

Sangave, Vilas Adinath: *Facets of Jainology: Selected Research Papers on Jain Society, Religion and Culture*, Popular Prakashan, Mumbai, 2001.

Sangave, Vilas Adinath: *Jaina Community: A Social Survey*, Popular Prakashan, Bombay, 1980.

Seeling, Holly: *The Jain Tradition in America*, Pluralism Project Research, 1991.

Sethia, Tara: *Ahimsa, Anekanta and Jainism*, Motilal Banarsidass, Delhi, 2004.

Shah, Natubhai: *Jainism: The World of Conquerors*, Motilal Banarsidass

Shah, Vikram V.: *Jain Heritage—Then, Now, and Forever: Pratishtha Mahotsav Souvenir*, Bartlett, Chicago, 1993.

Singh, Ramjee: *Jainism in the New Millennium*, Commonwealth, 2010.

Singhvi, L. M.: *The Jain Declaration on Nature*, Office of Jaina High Commissioner for India, London, 1990.

Sital, Prasad: *A Comparative Study of Jainism and Buddhism*, Satguru, 2003.

Sukhalaji, Pandit: *The World Pacifist Meeting and the Role of Jainism*, Publishing House, Ahmedabad, 1957.

Tara, Sethia: *Ahimsa, Anekanta and Jainism*, Motilal Banarsidass, 2004.

Tobias, Michael: *Life Force: The World of Jainism*, Asian Humanities Press, Berkeley, 1991.

Trilok, Chandra Majupuria and Rohit Kumar: *Religions in Nepal : With Reference to Religions of Tibet and India : Animism, Hinduism, Buddhism, Theravada, Mahayana, Vajrayana, Tantrism, Mantrayana, Bon, Lamaism, Jhankrism, Jainism, Sikhism, Islam and Christianity*, M. Devi, 2004.

V.K. Sharma: *History of Jainism : With Special Reference to Mathura*, D.K. Printworld, 2001.

Williams, Raymond: *Religions of Immigrants from India and Pakistan: New Threads in the American Tapestry*, Cambridge University Press, Cambridge, 1988.

Zaveri, J.S.: *Microcosmology: Atom in the Jain Philosophy and Modern Science*, Jain Vishva Bharati Institute, Ladnun, Raj, 1991.

Index

C

D

E

G

H

I

J

P

R

S

❑❑❑